English 4

Writing and Grammar

Second Edition

bju press®

Greenville, South Carolina

NOTE:

The fact that materials produced by other publishers may be referred to in this volume does not constitute an endorsement of the content or theological position of materials produced by such publishers. Any references and ancillary materials are listed as an aid to the student or the teacher and in an attempt to maintain the accepted academic standards of the publishing industry.

Project Coordinator
Tammie D. Jacobs, M.Ed.

Coordinating Writers
Peggy Davenport, M.Ed.
Tammie D. Jacobs, M.Ed.
Amy Miller, M.S.

Writers
Eileen M. Berry, M.A.
Susan Burkholder, M.Ed.
Robin Sisney Wood, M.S.

Contributing Writers
Peggy S. Alier
Nancy Jean Holmes, M.S.

Project Editor
Christa Bohannon

Design Coordinator
Duane Nichols

Cover and Title Page
Elly Kalagayan

Illustration Coordinator
John Bjerk

Illustrators
John Bjerk
Matt Bjerk
Paula Cheadle
Bruce Day
Michael Cory Godbey
Preston Gravely, Jr.
Dyke Habegger
James Hargis
Kathy Pflug
David Schuppert
Lynda Slattery

Composition
Florida Imaging
Peggy Hargis

Project Manager
Richard Ayers

Photo Acquisition
Carla Thomas

ENGLISH 4: WRITING AND GRAMMAR
Second Edition

"Hopscotch" and "Nest," from *SPRING: An Alphabet Acrostic* by Steven Schnur, illustrated by Leslie Evans. Text copyright © 1999 by Steven Schnur. Illustrations copyright © 1999 by Leslie Evans. Reprinted by permission of Clarions Books/Houghton Mifflin Company. All rights reserved.

Photo credits appear on page 369.

© 2004, 2009 BJU Press, Greenville, South Carolina 29609
First Edition © 1985 BJU Press

Printed in the United States of America
All rights reserved

ISBN 978-1-59166-916-6

15 14 13 12

Contents

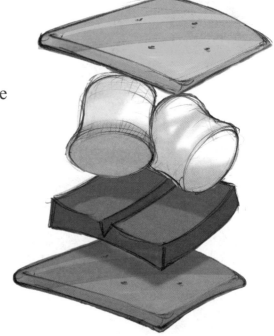

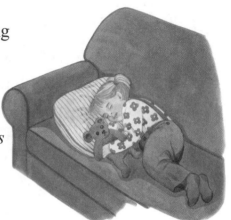

CHAPTER

15

Sentences, Phrases, & Clauses

CHAPTER

16

Writing Poetry

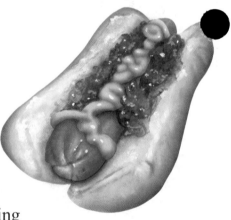

Sentences & Fragments

Name

A **sentence** is a group of words that expresses a complete thought.

> *Mrs. Carson grew vegetables in her garden.*

A **fragment** is a group of words that does not express a complete thought.

> *Picked watermelons on Friday.*
> *The tall cornstalks.*

Every sentence contains a subject and a predicate. The **subject** tells *who* or *what* the sentence is about. All the words in the subject part make up the **complete subject**.

The **predicate** tells what the subject *does* or *is*. All the words in the predicate part make up the **complete predicate**.

complete subject   complete predicate

> *The busy farmer | planted ten rows of tomatoes.*

> *God sends the rain to help plants grow.*
>
> Ps. 147:8   Zech. 8:12

▶ Guided Practice

▶Write *S* if the group of words is a sentence.
Write *F* if the group of words is a fragment.

_____   1. The farmer prepares the soil before planting seeds.

_____   2. Tills the ground to loosen the soil.

_____   3. Usually plants the seeds in rows.

_____   4. The seeds need water and sunlight.

_____   5. The young seedlings in long rows.

▶Underline the complete subject once and the complete predicate twice.

6. People grow many different plants in a vegetable garden.

7. Green beans grow on vines.

8. All potatoes grow under the ground.

9. Cornstalks are sometimes six feet tall.

10. Another word for *fruits* and *vegetables* is *produce*.

▶Write a complete predicate to finish the sentence.

11. The produce in a grocery store _____ .

▶Write a complete subject to finish the sentence.

12. _____ buy vegetables at the Farmer's Market.

Sentences & Fragments

◎ Independent Practice

▶Write *S* if the group of words is a sentence.
Write *F* if the group of words is a fragment.

_____ 1. Blue and purple potatoes from South America.

_____ 2. Most people in the United States buy Russet potatoes.

_____ 3. Grow mostly in California.

_____ 4. Restaurants serve many kinds of potatoes.

_____ 5. Frozen potato products.

▶Underline the complete subject once and the complete predicate twice.

6. Inca Indians grew the first potatoes around 200 B.C.

7. Potatoes came to Europe in the 1500s.

8. A ship brought potatoes to Jamestown in 1621.

9. President Jefferson's guests ate French fries at the White House.

10. Astronauts grew potatoes in space in 1995.

▶Write a complete predicate to finish each sentence.

11. Potato farms _____ .

12. Potatoes _____ .

▶Write a complete subject to finish each sentence.

13. _____ eat potatoes every day.

14. _____ are my favorite kind of potatoes.

15. _____ makes the best French fries.

◎ Apply and Write

▶Write a complete sentence telling why you like or dislike a particular vegetable.

Do you have a least favorite vegetable?

Do you have a favorite vegetable?

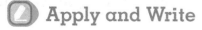

Declarative & Interrogative Sentences

Name _____

A **declarative sentence** is a sentence that gives information or tells something. It ends with a period.

Corn is my favorite vegetable.

An **interrogative sentence** asks a question. It ends with a question mark.

Where did you plant the corn?

 Guided Practice

▶ **Use the code to label each sentence.**
Add the correct ending punctuation.

```
CODE
Dec. = Declarative (Telling)
Int. = Interrogative (Question)
```

_____ 1. The first corn grew in the Americas

_____ 2. Native Americans ate corn before Columbus came

_____ 3. Did Christopher Columbus put corn on his ships

_____ 4. Ships carried corn to Europe

_____ 5. Is all corn yellow in color

_____ 6. Corn kernels may be yellow, red, white, pink, blue, or black

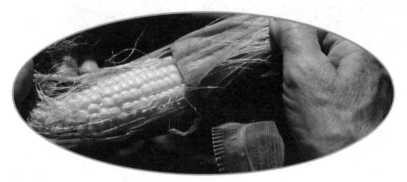

▶ **Rewrite the following sentences. Add a capital letter and ending punctuation to each sentence.**

7. corn is an important crop _____

8. what is hybrid corn _____

9. this special corn grows large and strong _____

_____

10. do you like the taste of hybrid corn _____

_____

Declarative & Interrogative Sentences

Name _____

◎ Independent Practice

▶ **Use the code to label each sentence. Add the correct ending punctuation.**

CODE

Dec. = Declarative (Telling)

Int. = Interrogative (Question)

_____ 1. Corn feeds many kinds of farm animals

_____ 2. What was the main corn product in 1900

_____ 3. Cornstarch was the most popular corn product in 1900

_____ 4. How many ways do we use corn products

_____ 5. Thousands of products contain corn

_____ 6. Some peanut butter contains corn products

A combine harvesting corn

▶ **Rewrite the following sentences. Add a capital letter and ending punctuation to each sentence.**

7. which products include corn _____

8. corn syrup makes foods sweet _____

9. cornstarch is used in lipstick _____

10. do we get corn oil from kernels or the stalk _____

_____

◁◎ Apply and Speak/Listen

▶ **A riddle is a puzzling question. Listen as your teacher reads the declarative sentence clues to an animal riddle. Use this interrogative sentence to ask about the animal after each clue is read.**

Is this animal a (an) _____ ?

Imperative & Exclamatory Sentences

Name _____

An **imperative sentence** gives a command or a request. The subject in the sentence is always understood to be *you*. The word *you* may or may not be present in the sentence. An imperative sentence ends with a period.

> *Please feed the dog.*
> *Take this medicine three times every day.*

An **exclamatory sentence** shows excitement or surprise. An exclamatory sentence ends with an exclamation point.

> *How large that elephant is!*

God wants
us to learn and keep
His commands.

Deut. 7:11   Prov. 7:1–3

 Guided Practice

▶ **Use the code to label each sentence. Add the correct ending punctuation.**

CODE

Imp. = Imperative (Command)
Exc. = Exclamatory

_____ 1. Wash the car

_____ 2. What an interesting book that was

_____ 3. How strong the wind is

_____ 4. Watch the baby, please

_____ 5. Study for your math test tonight

_____ 6. Blow out the candles on your cake

▶ **Rewrite the following sentences. Add a capital letter and ending punctuation to each sentence.**

7. lock the door behind you _____

_____

8. what a colorful painting that is _____

_____

9. please set the table _____

_____

10. how high the children swing _____

_____

Imperative & Exclamatory Sentences

◉ Independent Practice

▶ **Use the code to label each sentence. Add the correct ending punctuation.**

CODE
Imp. = Imperative (Command)
Exc. = Exclamatory

_____ 1. Oh, what a wonderful idea

_____ 2. Please help me find my keys

_____ 3. Keep your eye on the ball

_____ 4. How delicious this cake is

_____ 5. Bring your homework to class

_____ 6. Duck your head as you come into the room

▶ **Rewrite the following sentences. Add a capital letter and ending punctuation to each sentence.**

7. how beautiful you look _____

_____

8. do not walk on the grass _____

_____

9. turn off the light on your way out _____

_____

10. what a mess this room is _____

_____

◖ Apply and Speak

▶ **Commands are often used where work is being done. Work with a partner to think of commands used at a job. Be prepared to share your commands.**

Four Types of Sentences

Name _____

A **declarative sentence** is a sentence that gives information. It ends with a period.

Peanut is Samantha's dog.

An **interrogative sentence** asks a question. It ends with a question mark.

What is your dog's name?

An **imperative sentence** is a command or request. The person doing the action is always understood to be *you*. It ends with a period.

Please wash the dog.

An **exclamatory sentence** shows excitement or surprise. It ends with an exclamation point.

What a big dog he is!

 Guided Practice

▶ **Use the code to label each sentence. Add the correct ending punctuation.**

_____ 1. When does the program start

_____ 2. The orchestra warms up first

_____ 3. Where is the conductor

_____ 4. Watch the musicians tune their instruments

_____ 5. We got good tickets

_____ 6. The program was wonderful

> **CODE**
>
> Dec. = Declarative
> Int. = Interrogative
> Imp. = Imperative
> Exc. = Exclamatory

▶ **Rewrite the declarative sentence as an interrogative sentence.**

7. We are going to the campground on Friday. _____

_____

▶ **Rewrite the interrogative sentence as a declarative sentence.**

8. Have they packed the tent?

_____

Four Types of Sentences

◉ Independent Practice

▶ **Use the code to label each sentence.**
Add the correct ending punctuation.

CODE	
Dec.	= Declarative
Int.	= Interrogative
Imp.	= Imperative
Exc.	= Exclamatory

_____ 1. Hang up your clothes, please

_____ 2. How beautiful your garden is

_____ 3. The coach encouraged the team

_____ 4. The missionary left yesterday

_____ 5. Did your grandmother call last night

▶ **Rewrite the following sentences. Add a capital letter and ending punctuation to each sentence.**

6. please look for your shoes _____

7. what a scary ride that was _____

8. dad washed the car on Saturday _____

9. did the pastor shake your hand _____

▶ **Rewrite the interrogative sentence as a declarative sentence.**

10. Are you sleepy? _____

② Apply and Write

▶ **Write four sentences about playing a game. Use the four types of sentences.**

_____

_____

_____

Simple Subjects

Most sentences contain a subject and a predicate. The **complete subject** is all of the words in the subject part.

The **simple subject** is the main word in the complete subject. The simple subject may be a noun or a subject pronoun.

complete subject	complete predicate
The black *horse*	*galloped away.*
It	*ran into a young colt.*
Mr. Peterson	*will take the colt to the barn.*

Subject Pronouns

I	it
you	we
he	they
she	

Guided Practice

▶ Draw a line between the complete subject and the complete predicate. Underline the simple subject.

1. An average American eats about thirty pounds of lettuce each year.

2. California and Arizona grow most of our lettuce.

3. Many people enjoy fresh lettuce.

4. Dark green varieties have more vitamins than iceberg lettuce.

5. Romaine lettuce is a source of vitamin A and vitamin C.

6. The workers pack most lettuce as it is picked.

7. Smitty's Farmer's Market sells a large variety of lettuce.

▶ Write a complete subject to finish each sentence. Underline the simple subject.

8. _____ wrote a letter last night.

9. _____ fell into a mud puddle.

10. _____ grew in the big blue flower pot.

Simple Subjects

Name

◎ Independent Practice

▸**Draw a line between the complete subject and the complete predicate.
Underline the simple subject.**

1. Lettuce has been eaten for centuries.

2. Some lettuce leaves grow in the shape of a ball.

3. Ice keeps this "crisphead" lettuce fresh.

4. People called it "iceberg" lettuce.

5. The early Romans ate lettuce for their health.

6. Augustus Caesar had a serious disease.

7. He built a statue in honor of the healing ability of lettuce.

▸**Write a complete subject to finish each sentence.
Underline the simple subject.**

8. _____ works every day.

9. _____ ate a hamburger for lunch.

10. _____ is a fast runner.

11. _____ live in the woods.

12. _____ checked out books from the library.

13. _____ painted the room blue.

② Apply and Write

▸**Write two sentences about how your family uses lettuce.
Underline the simple subject in each sentence.**

_____

_____

Simple Predicates

Most sentences contain a subject and a predicate. The **complete predicate** in the sentence tells what the subject *does* or *is*.

The simple predicate is the main word(s) in the predicate. The simple predicate is the verb in the sentence. The simple predicate may be a linking verb or an action verb.

	complete subject	complete predicate
action verb:	Mom	bought a bag of apples.
linking verb:	The apples	are red.

Guided Practice

▶Draw a line between the complete subject and the complete predicate. Underline the simple predicate twice.

1. Mother serves broccoli for dinner.

2. Broccoli is a green vegetable.

3. It is part of the cabbage family.

4. Americans learned about broccoli in the 1920s.

5. Europeans ate broccoli hundreds of years earlier.

6. Broccoli has much nutritional value.

▶Write a complete predicate to finish each sentence. Underline the simple predicate twice.

7. The neighbor's dog _____ .

8. A large silver airplane _____ .

9. The old green chair _____ .

10. My favorite food _____ .

Simple Predicates

◎ Independent Practice

▶ **Draw a line between the complete subject and the complete predicate.**
Underline the simple predicate twice.

1. California raises the most broccoli in the United States.

2. Southern California farms grow broccoli almost all year.

3. Farmers harvest broccoli after three or four months.

4. I love broccoli!

5. Mother adds broccoli to many recipes.

6. Broccoli casserole tastes the best.

7. Broccoli protects the body against some diseases.

8. A serving of broccoli equals the vitamin C in an orange.

9. A cup of cooked broccoli contains much calcium.

▶ **Add a complete predicate to each sentence.**
Underline the simple predicate twice.

10. The little baby _____ .

11. My new blue notebook _____ .

12. The pandas at the zoo _____ .

13. A glass of cold milk _____ .

14. The grocery store _____ .

15. A night in December _____ .

◑ Apply and Write

▶ **Write a sentence about how you like to eat broccoli.**
Underline the simple predicate twice.

_____

Diagramming Subjects & Predicates

Name _____

A diagram of a sentence shows how the words in the sentence relate to each other.

simple subject	simple predicate

My grandmother's hat | is blue.

hat	is

The wind | blew her hat.

wind	blew

Aunt Liz | brought it back.

Aunt Liz	brought

▶ Guided Practice

▶ **Draw a line between the complete subject and the complete predicate. Write the simple subject and the simple predicate on the diagram.**

1. Most beets are dark red or purple.

   _____ | _____

2. Sugar beet roots look white.

   _____ | _____

3. They grow for five months.

   _____ | _____

4. These plants like rain and sunshine.

   _____ | _____

5. Farmers plant beets in the spring.

   _____ | _____

6. Harvest comes in the fall.

   _____ | _____

7. Factories process the beets into sugar.

   _____ | _____

Sugar beet field

Diagramming Subjects & Predicates

◉ Independent Practice

▶ Draw a line between the complete subject and the complete predicate.
Write the simple subject and the simple predicate on the diagram.

1. Seeds grow quickly.

_____|_____

2. Farmers fertilize the plants for better growth.

_____|_____

3. Some sugar beets weigh five pounds.

_____|_____

4. Trucks haul the harvested beets to factories.

_____|_____

5. Machines cut the beet roots into thin strips.

_____|_____

6. The strips lose their sugar in hot water.

_____|_____

7. The sugar dries into crystals.

_____|_____

8. Each beet produces nearly three teaspoons of sugar.

_____|_____

❷ Apply and Write

▶ Write a sentence about something sweet you like to eat.
Underline the simple subject once and the simple predicate twice.

Compound
Subjects & Predicates

A **compound subject** has two or more simple subjects that share the same predicate. Joining words *and* or *or* connect the subjects.

> *Snakes and iguanas* **are reptiles.**

In this sentence, *snakes* and *iguanas* are the simple subjects. They share the linking verb *are*.

Snakes
and
iguanas ⟩───── are ──────

A **compound predicate** has two or more simple predicates (verbs) that share the same subject. Joining words *and* or *or* connect the predicates.

> *The children* whistled or sang.

In this sentence, *whistled* and *sang* are the simple predicates. They will tell us what the children did.

children ───⟨ or ⟩ whistled
                    sang

A diagram of a sentence shows how the words in the sentence relate to each other.

(((Oral Practice

▶ Choose two simple subjects from the word bank to make a compound subject using *and* or *or* for each sentence. Read aloud your new sentences.

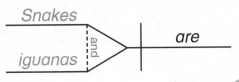

| dog | cat | mouse |
| horse | girl | cow |

1. The _____ chased each other.

2. The _____ ate in the barn.

▶ Choose two simple predicates from the word bank to make a compound predicate using *and* or *or* for each sentence. Read aloud your new sentences.

3. Jim's horse _____.

4. The striped cat _____.

| meows | jumps | gallops |
| eats | purrs | drinks |

▶ Guided Practice

▶ Draw a line between the complete subject and the complete predicate. Underline the simple subjects once and the simple predicates twice. Write the simple subjects and the simple predicates on the diagram.

1. The apples grew and ripened on the tree.

2. The boys and girls attended Bible club.

Compound Subjects & Predicates

Name _____

◎ Independent Practice

▶ Draw a line between the complete subject and the complete predicate. Underline the simple subjects once and the simple predicates twice.

1. Glue and tape hold things together.

2. Mindy and Courtney played at recess.

3. The sharks ate and swam inside the tank.

4. Funny clowns and animals performed at the circus.

5. The queen's soldiers marched and exercised on the parade grounds.

▶ Make a compound subject or a compound predicate by combining the pair of sentences using *and*.

6. Colorful leaves fell to the ground.
   Acorns fell to the ground.

   _____

7. Birds build nests.
   Mice build nests.

   _____

8. Jonathan wrote his spelling words.
   Jonathan studied his spelling words.

   _____

▶ Write the simple subjects and the simple predicates on the diagrams.

9. The crowd cheered and sang at the game.

10. The boys and girls wore costumes to the party.

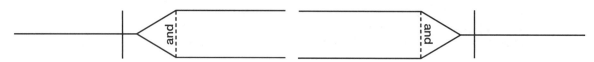

✐ Apply and Write

▶ Write a sentence with a compound predicate about two things you do on Saturdays.

Compound Sentences

Name _____

A **simple sentence** gives one complete thought. A **compound sentence** contains two simple sentences connected by a comma and a joining word. A compound sentence gives two complete thoughts. **Joining words** are *and*, *but*, and *or*.

I like cooked carrots. *My brother prefers raw carrots.*
I like cooked carrots, but *my brother prefers raw carrots.*

Joining Words

Use *and* if the second sentence gives more information similar to the first sentence.

Madison dug holes, and *Kaylee planted seeds.*

Use *but* if the second simple sentence contrasts with, or is different from, the first sentence.

Mom adds chicken to vegetable soup, but *Grandma uses beef.*

Use *or* if there is a choice between the sentences.

He waters his garden early in the morning, or *he waters it in the evening.*

Guided Practice

▶Write *S* if the sentence is a simple sentence.
 Write *C* if the sentence is a compound sentence.

_____ 1. The circus is a fun and exciting place.

_____ 2. My neighbor went with us, and my cousins met us there.

_____ 3. All the clowns tried to ride in the same car, but they didn't fit.

_____ 4. I like clowns best, but Jamie likes the tightrope walkers best.

_____ 5. The performers rode elephants or walked around the ring.

▶Make a compound sentence by combining the pair of sentences with a comma and a joining word.

6. The seals did tricks.   The trainers fed them fish.

_____

7. My cousin James was hungry.   I wasn't hungry.

_____

Compound Sentences

Independent Practice

▶Write *S* if the sentence is a simple sentence.
Write *C* if the sentence is a compound sentence.

_____ 1. My father likes to fish from the beach, and I like to swim in the water.

_____ 2. Grandma sits under the beach umbrella, but I use sunscreen.

_____ 3. I like to swim and ride my raft in the surf.

_____ 4. We bring sandwiches and chips for lunch.

_____ 5. I build sandcastles, but the tide washes them away.

_____ 6. The tide comes in during the morning, but it goes out in the afternoon.

▶Make a compound sentence by combining each pair of sentences using a comma and a joining word.

7. Canned vegetables last longer. Fresh vegetables taste better.

8. The farmer fertilizes his fields. Irrigation equipment waters his crops.

9. Horses can pull the wagon. The tractor can pull the wagon.

10. Pumpkin plants grow along the ground. Cornstalks stand tall.

Apply and Write

▶Write a compound sentence about farming.

Chapter *1* Review

**A. Write *S* if the group of words is a sentence.
Write *F* if the group of words is a fragment.**

_____ 1. An old, dusty photo album.

_____ 2. In my grandmother's attic.

_____ 3. It contains old pictures.

_____ 4. The photographs are more than fifty years old.

_____ 5. I learned a lot about Grandmother's life.

_____ 6. Took the photographs with his camera.

**B. Draw a line between the complete subject and the complete predicate.
Underline the simple subjects once and the simple predicates twice.**

7. The large, glass pitcher contains lemonade.

8. The thirsty child drank two glasses of lemonade.

9. Erica's mother made more lemonade.

**C. Use the code to label each sentence.
Add the correct ending punctuation.**

CODE	
Dec.	= Declarative
Int.	= Interrogative
Imp.	= Imperative
Exc.	= Exclamatory

_____ 10. The washing machine broke

_____ 11. Our laundry room is a mess

_____ 12. Will you call the repairman

_____ 13. Find the phone number, please

_____ 14. The repairman will come tomorrow

_____ 15. Does he know our address

_____ 16. Give him the directions

D. Combine the sentences to make a compound subject or a compound predicate.

17. Benjamin ate cereal.
    Wilson ate cereal.

_____

18. The dog ran.
    The dog hid.

_____

E. Use a comma and a joining word to make a compound sentence.

19. Mom called the office.
    It was closed.

_____

_____

20. My doctor's appointment may be on Thursday.
    It may be on Friday.

_____

_____

F. Draw a line between the complete subject and the complete predicate. Write the simple subject and the simple predicate on the diagram.

21. Grandpa sells squash at a roadside stand.

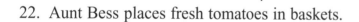

22. Aunt Bess places fresh tomatoes in baskets.

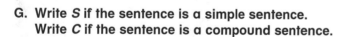

G. Write *S* if the sentence is a simple sentence. Write *C* if the sentence is a compound sentence.

_____ 23. My neighbor planted beans, but he did not plant tomatoes.

_____ 24. You may peel the carrots, or you may shell the peas.

_____ 25. The red tractor plowed a deep furrow.

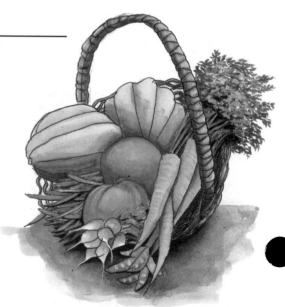

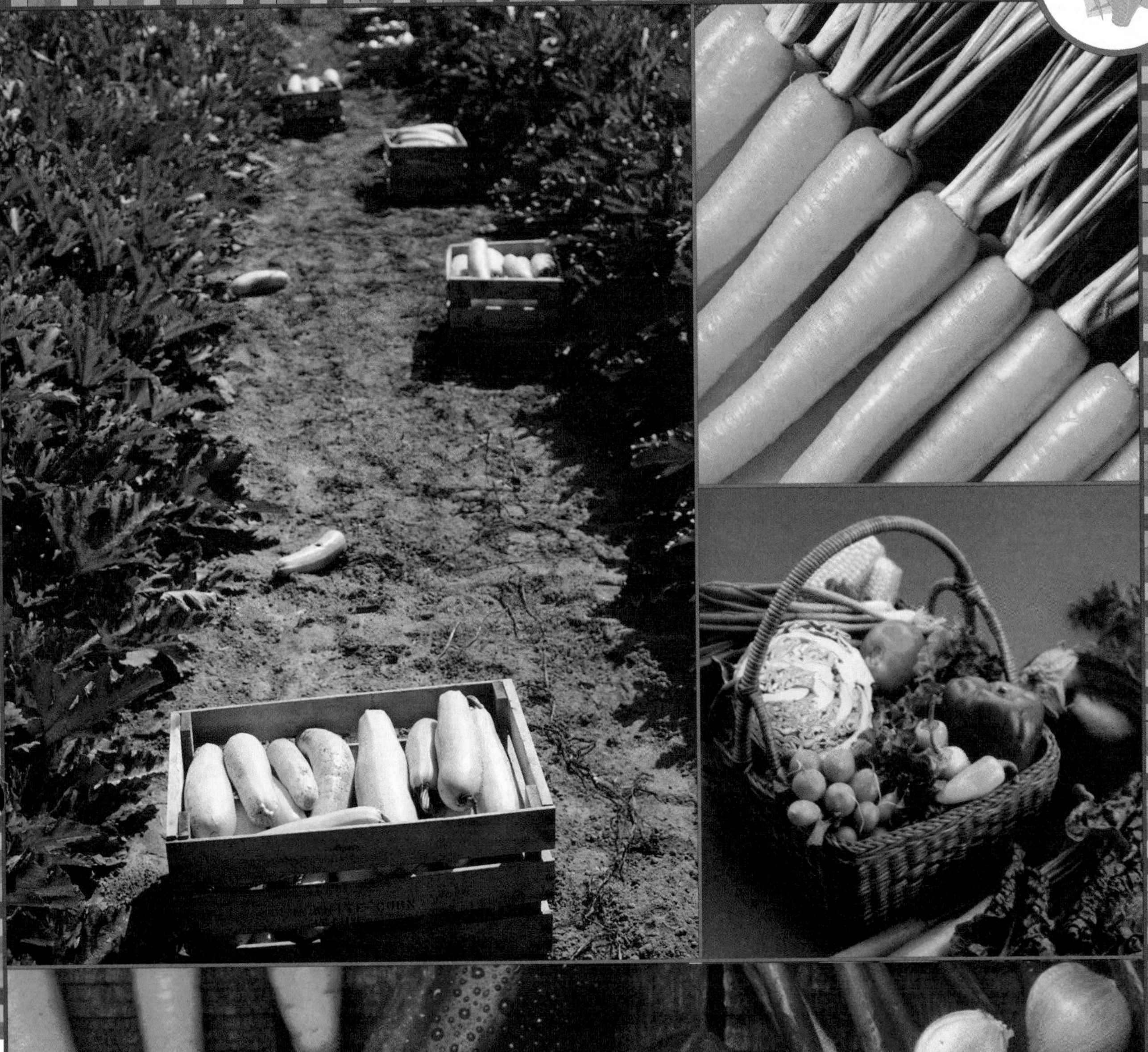

Literature Link

Excerpt from *Arby Jenkins* by Sharon Hambrick

A JourneyForth book from BJU Press

"Yikes!" I shouted. "I forgot my eyes!" I hurried upstairs and carefully rinsed and solutioned and put my lenses in. They felt cold on my eyes and made me blink. Then I ran downstairs . . . . I grabbed my stuff and ran out, slamming the door in my excitement. It is a rare day that I am so excited this early in the morning.

I could see the blades of grass at the park and the individual drops of dew. I could not only hear the birds, but I could actually see some of them. My legs were shaking as I stood up to the batter's box and pulled my bat up, just like Coach had taught me. I could see the ball clearly in my dad's hand. I realized that I had never before been able to see the ball in the pitcher's hand. This was a new and great day.

Dad threw me a perfect pitch. I swung hard. It was beautiful the way the ball sailed right over his head. My dad jumped up and hooted, really hooted. He ran to me and grabbed me in a bear hug. We jumped around and hollered, right there in the park at 6:15 in the morning!

Using the Thesaurus

When you want to describe something clearly, you need to use words that bring pictures to your reader's mind. A thesaurus can help you find the best possible words to use in your writing.

A thesaurus lists entry words and gives synonyms that go with those words.

Synonyms are words that have meanings similar to the entry word. Some thesauruses also give **antonyms**, words that have the opposite meaning of the entry word.

Here is an entry from the thesaurus in the back of your book.

big *adjective*
of great size
An elephant is a <u>big</u> animal.
enormous, gigantic, grand, great, huge, large, massive
antonym: little

When you are writing a sentence that uses the word *big*, you can check the thesaurus to find a more descriptive or a more exact word than *big*.

The girl fell asleep beneath the big tree.

This sentence can be made more descriptive by replacing *big* with a synonym. Be sure to choose a word that makes sense in the sentence.

The girl fell asleep beneath the enormous tree.
The girl fell asleep beneath the gigantic tree.
The girl fell asleep beneath the huge tree.
The girl fell asleep beneath the massive tree.

Guided Practice

▶Use the thesaurus to find a more descriptive word that could replace the underlined word in each sentence. Be sure the word makes sense in the sentence. Write the new word in the blank.

1. Be careful not to <u>break</u> that glass vase. _____

2. Do we have <u>enough</u> supplies for a cookout? _____

3. I would like to <u>give</u> some money to the missions project. _____

4. Dad had a <u>serious</u> look on his face when he came in. _____

Using the Thesaurus

Name _____

 Independent Practice

▶Read the story. Use the thesaurus to find a more descriptive word that could replace each underlined word. Be sure the word makes sense in the sentence. Write the new word in the blank.

1. _____

2. _____

3. _____

4. _____

5. _____

6. _____

7. _____

8. _____

9. _____

10. _____

▶Read the story again, replacing the underlined words with your synonyms.

Apply and Write

▶Choose one of the underlined words that has an antonym. Write a sentence using the antonym of that word.

_____

_____

Climbing St. Paul's Dome

When my family and I were in London, we toured St. Paul's Cathedral. The cathedral is big, and it is
₁
very pretty inside. It took Sir Christopher Wren a
₂
long time to make it. My dad and I decided to climb
₃
up to the top of the dome.

It was a hard climb. There are over 600 steps to
₄
the top of the dome. I felt a little afraid when we got
₅
to the Whispering Gallery partway up. The people on

the floor below looked little!
₆

When Dad and I finally reached the top, we were

tired. But the view of the city was great! I felt as if
₇ ₈
I could stand there and look at it forever. We were
₉
so glad we hadn't given up. It was an important
₁₀
day in my life.

Dome of St. Paul's Cathedral

A Personal Narrative

Name

Most of us like to read and listen to stories. **Narrative writing** is writing that tells a story. A **personal narrative** is a story about you. Have you had any unusual, exciting, happy, or scary experiences? What did you learn from your experience? You can write a personal narrative to tell about something interesting that happened to you.

Here is a personal narrative written by Shibu.

> ## My New Friend
> Last year I went with my dad to visit his grandmother at Berrydale Nursing Center. I didn't know I was going to make a new friend. I only knew I felt nervous. My great-grandmother was sitting outside the door of her room wearing a silky blue robe. Her gray hair was pulled back into a long braid. When she saw me, she smiled and said, "This must be Shibu." Her voice was soft and shaky, but her smile was full of love. I didn't feel nervous anymore.
>
> My dad wheeled her wheelchair out onto the deck. She talked to my dad in Bengali. It is the language of her people in India. I could not understand, so I just kept quiet. Then my great-grandmother turned to me and said in English, "Shibu, will you read?" She handed me the Bible in her lap, and I saw that it was open to the Twenty-third Psalm. I read it out loud. When I finished, she began to speak in Bengali. She quoted the whole psalm for me in her own language. Then she smiled again and gave my hand a squeeze. My dad prayed, and we took Great-Grandma back to her room.
>
> Now I write letters to my great-grandmother. She writes back right away. Sometimes she writes a sentence in Bengali at the end, and I ask my dad to read it for me. Great-Grandma is ninety years old, but I feel as if she is one of my best friends.

A Personal Narrative

Do you know someone who is a good storyteller? Most good storytellers think about their **audience,** or the people who will be reading or listening to the story. Then they add interesting details, dialogue, and sometimes humor to the tale for the audience to enjoy.

Stories can make us feel as if we are visiting another place or another time. We can also learn from the stories of others.

Tips for Writing a Personal Narrative

1. Think about who will read your personal narrative.

2. Write about something that you remember well.

3. Get the reader's attention with your opening sentence.

4. Tell the events of the narrative in the order that they happened.

5. Add details that will help your reader picture each event.

6. Use **dialogue** to make the people in your narrative come alive. Dialogue is spoken conversation between two people in your narrative. Remember to use quotation marks around someone's spoken words.

7. Make your ending sentence tell what you learned or how you felt about what happened.

A journal or diary is a good place to find an idea for a personal narrative.

▶ **Think about the funny, unusual, exciting, or happy things that have happened to you.**

▶ **List some as possible topics for your personal narrative.**

1. _____

2. _____

3. _____

4. _____

5. _____

▶ **Save this page for use in Lesson 13.**

Personal Narrative: Planning

Name _____

After Shibu decided to write about visiting his great-grandmother, he used this chart to plan his personal narrative.

Topic: *visiting Great-Grandma at Berrydale Nursing Center*

Opening: *I went with Dad to see her.*

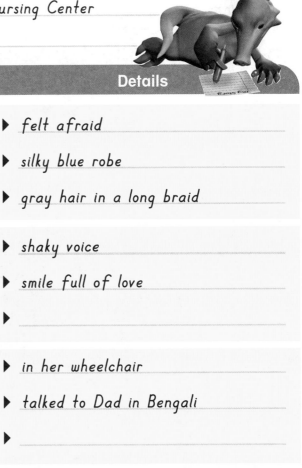

Events	Details
1. Saw Great-Grandma sitting outside her room	▸ felt afraid ▸ silky blue robe ▸ gray hair in a long braid
2. She smiled at me	▸ shaky voice ▸ smile full of love ▸
3. Took her out onto the deck	▸ in her wheelchair ▸ talked to Dad in Bengali ▸
4. Read Bible to her	▸ asked me to read ▸ read Psalm 23 ▸ quoted the psalm in Bengali
5. Ended our visit	▸ squeezed my hand ▸ Dad prayed ▸ took her back to her room

Closing: *Now we write letters. I feel like she's one of my best friends.*

Notice that Shibu included details that would help his audience see and hear what happened. He named specific places, colors, sounds, and people's movements. These details make the people and places in Shibu's narrative real to his readers. Shibu did not use complete sentences when he planned. He wrote just enough to remember his ideas.

▸**Complete the chart on page 28 to plan your personal narrative.**

Personal Narrative: Planning

Name

Topic: _____

Opening: _____

Events	Details
1. _____ _____ _____	▶ _____ ▶ _____ ▶ _____
2. _____ _____	▶ _____ ▶ _____ ▶ _____
3. _____ _____ _____	▶ _____ ▶ _____ ▶ _____
4. _____ _____ _____	▶ _____ ▶ _____
5. _____ _____ _____	▶ _____ ▶ _____ ▶ _____

Closing: _____

▶ **Save this chart for use in Lesson 14.**

Personal Narrative: Drafting

Name _____

Notice that Shibu wrote his rough draft in paragraphs. He sometimes put more than one event in a paragraph. But he changed paragraphs when the action in his narrative moved to a different place or a different time. He concentrated on following his planning chart until he had finished writing his story.

Shibu skipped lines as he wrote so that he would have space to put in changes. He knew that he would be able to make changes and fix mistakes later.

Godly friends are to be cherished.

Eccles. 4:9–10   Ps. 119:63

My New Fried

Last year I went with my dad to visit his grandmother at Berrydale Nursing Center. I felt afraid. My great-grandmother was wearing a silky blue robe. Her gray hair was pulled back into a long braid. When she saw me, she smiled and said, "This must be Shibu. Her voice was soft and shaky, but her smile was full of love.

My dad wheeled her wheelchair out onto the deck. She talked to my dad in Bengali. It is the langwich of her people in india. I also have an uncle who speaks French. I could not understand, so I just kept quiet. Then my great-grandmother turned to me and said in English, "Shibu, will you read?" She handed me the Bible in her lap, and I saw that it was open to the Twenty-third Psalm I read it out loud. When I finished, she began to speak in Bengali. She quoted the whole psalm for me in her own langwich. Then she smiled again and gave my hand a squeeze. My dad prayed, and we took Great-Grandma back to her room.

Now I write letters to my great-grandmother. She writes back right away. Sometimes she writes a sentence in Bengali at the end, and I ask my dad to read it for me. I feel as if she is one of my best friends.

Shibu used time-order words to help make the order of events clear. Time-order words tell when an action happened.

Below is a list of time-order words that you may use in your writing. You may also use any others that you know.

▶ **Underline the seven time-order words in Shibu's story as your teacher reads it aloud.**

Time-Order Words

first	later	in the meantime	two years ago
then	finally	sometimes	last year
next	when	just then	
afterward	now	after a while	

▶ **Draft your personal narrative using your planning chart as a guide. Remember to leave a blank line after each line you write.**

▶ **Save your first draft for use in Lesson 15.**

Personal Narrative: Revising

Name _____

Shibu read his rough draft to Peter. Peter liked the story, especially the part about Great-Grandma speaking in Bengali.

"Maybe you could leave out the part about your uncle who speaks French," Peter added. "That's not really what the story is about."

"Thanks. I'll take that sentence out," said Shibu. "Do you have any questions about the story?"

"Why were you afraid at the beginning?" asked Peter. "And when did you stop feeling afraid?"

Peter also wanted to know how old Shibu's great-grandmother was.

When Shibu checked his thesaurus, he found a better word than *afraid* to describe how he felt. He also thought of a better way to begin his narrative—a way that hinted at the ending. He found a good place to put in Great-Grandma's age at the end.

Here are the revisions Shibu made to his narrative. What other changes did he make?

My New Fried

Last year I went with my dad to visit his
I didn't know I was going to make a new friend. I only knew I felt nervous.
grandmother at Berrydale Nursing Center. I felt
sitting outside the door of her room
afraid. My great-grandmother was wearing a silky

blue robe. Her gray hair was pulled back into a

long braid. When she saw me, she smiled and said,

"This must be Shibu. Her voice was soft and shaky,
I didn't feel nervous anymore.
but her smile was full of love.

My dad wheeled her wheelchair out onto the

deck. She talked to my dad in Bengali. It is the

langwich of her people in india. I also have an

uncle who speaks French. I could not understand,

so I just kept quiet. Then my great-grandmother

turned to me and said in English, "Shibu, will you

read?" She handed me the Bible in her lap, and I

saw that it was open to the Twenty-third Psalm I read it out loud. When I finished, she began to speak in Bengali. She quoted the whole psalm for me in her own langwich. Then she smiled again and gave my hand a squeeze. My dad prayed, and we took Great-Grandma back to her room.

Now I write letters to my great-grandmother. She writes back right away. Sometimes she writes a sentence in Bengali at the end, and I ask my dad to read it for me. ∧ I feel as if she is one of my best friends.

Great-Grandma is ninety years old, but

▶ Use the *Revising Checklist* to revise your personal narrative. Use proofreading marks to mark your changes.

Revising Checklist

☐ 1. My opening gets the reader's attention.
☐ 2. I told about the events in order.
☐ 3. All the sentences tell about my topic.
☐ 4. I told enough details to make my experience clear.
☐ 5. I checked to see where I could use more descriptive words.
☐ 6. My ending tells what I learned or felt about what happened.

Proofreading Marks

∧∨ Add
 Delete
≡ Capital letter
/ Lowercase
↻→ Move

▶ Save your revised narrative for use in Lesson 16.

After Shibu revised his narrative, he checked it for mistakes using the *Proofreading Checklist* on the next page. He read his narrative six times, each time looking for one type of mistake on the checklist. As he finished checking for each type of mistake, he put a check beside that item on the checklist.

What mistakes did Shibu find in his narrative? What proofreading marks did he use to mark his mistakes?

My New ~~Fried~~ *Friend*

Last year I went with my dad to visit his grandmother at Berrydale Nursing Center. I didn't know I was going to make a new friend. I only knew I felt nervous. My great-grandmother was sitting outside the door of her room wearing a silky blue robe. Her gray hair was pulled back into a long braid. When she saw me, she smiled and said, "This must be Shibu. Her voice was soft and shaky, but her smile was full of love. I didn't feel nervous anymore.

My dad wheeled her wheelchair out onto the deck. She talked to my dad in Bengali. It is the ~~langwich~~ *language* of her people in india. I could not understand, so I just kept quiet. Then my great-grandmother turned to me and said in English,

Personal Narrative: Proofreading

"Shibu, will you read?" She handed me the Bible in her lap, and I saw that it was open to the Twenty-third Psalm. I read it out loud. When I finished, she began to speak in Bengali. She quoted the whole psalm for me in her own ~~langwich~~. language Then she smiled again and gave my hand a squeeze. My dad prayed, and we took Great-Grandma back to her room.

Now I write letters to my great-grandmother. She writes back right away. Sometimes she writes a sentence in Bengali at the end, and I ask my dad to read it for me. Great-Grandma is ninety years old, but I feel as if she is one of my best friends.

▶ Use the *Proofreading Checklist* as you proofread your personal narrative. Use proofreading marks to mark the mistakes.

Proofreading Checklist

☐ 1. I used complete sentences.
☐ 2. I put a capital letter at the beginning and punctuation at the end of each sentence.
☐ 3. I used capital letters correctly within the sentences.
☐ 4. I put quotation marks around any dialogue.
☐ 5. I indented each paragraph.
☐ 6. I looked for misspelled words.

Proofreading Marks

∧∨ Add
✎ Delete
≡ Capital letter
/ Lowercase
↻→ Move

▶ Save your proofread narrative to publish in Lesson 17.

Speaking: Sharing Your Narrative

Language LINK

Do you like to tell stories? Stories can be a way to entertain others, but they can also be a way to share things you have learned. A good storyteller is someone who has learned how to speak well and enjoys doing it. Being a good speaker is a skill that takes practice—but you can get off to a good start by following a few basic tips.

It is normal to be a little nervous before you speak in front of people. Nervousness can actually help you to do a better job. If you are a little nervous, you will probably have more energy and be more alert while you speak. If you feel very nervous, here are some things you can do.

God gives peace in every situation.

Isa. 26:3   Phil. 4:6–7

Before You Speak:

- Pray. Ask the Lord to calm you and give you peace.
- Take a few deep breaths without making any noise. Try to breathe as evenly as you would if you were sleeping.
- Make a fist with one hand. Press it into the palm of the other hand. Try to press back just as hard with your other hand. Stop for a while; then repeat the pressing exercise. Exercises like these help you to relax.

While You Speak:

- Smile. Sometimes smiling at your audience will make them smile back, and that will help you to relax.
- Nervousness gives you extra energy. Put that energy to work by using movement to make your story come alive. If you're talking about playing miniature golf, act out swinging the golf club. If you're talking about bird-watching, act out looking around through a pair of binoculars.
- If your voice sounds shaky, speak a little bit louder. Remember to keep breathing deeply while you speak.

The more often you speak in front of people, the less nervous you will be. Keep practicing. You might even find out that you enjoy speaking more than you thought you would!

On the next page are *Tips for Good Speaking.* Study the tips before you share your personal narrative. After you have finished speaking, think about how well you followed these tips.

Tips for Good Speaking

1. **Use expression.** You can use your voice, face, hands, and body movements to make your story come to life. If you used dialogue in your narrative, try to make each person's voice sound like his character would sound.

2. **Look at your audience.** Do not stare at one person, but try to look each person in your group in the eye at least once or twice while you speak.

3. **Speak clearly.** Pronounce your words correctly so that everyone can understand you.

4. **Speak at a good volume.** You do not need to shout, but make sure that you speak loudly enough for everyone in your group to hear you.

5. **Speak at a good pace.** Do not speak too slowly and do not rush to get through.

6. **Speak confidently.** Believe that God has given you something important to share and that your listeners will appreciate it.

▶ **Present your personal narrative to your group.**

▶ **When you finish, mark the checklist for each thing you remembered to do while speaking.**

My Speaking Self-Check

☐ 1. I used expression with my voice, face, hands, or body movements.

☐ 2. I looked at each person in my group while I spoke.

☐ 3. I spoke clearly.

☐ 4. I spoke with good volume.

☐ 5. I spoke at a good pace.

☐ 6. I spoke confidently.

A. Fill in the circle next to the sentence that uses more exact descriptive words.

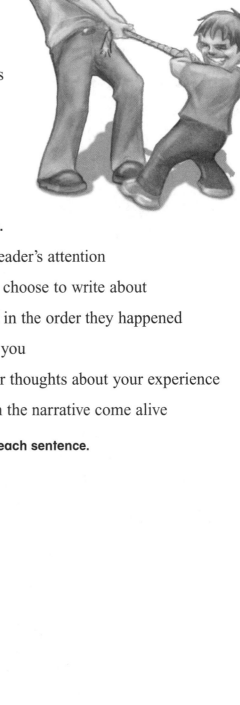

1. ○ Dad *pulled* while I *held* my end of the rope.
   ○ Dad *tugged* while I *clutched* my end of the rope.

2. ○ The rooftop was the perfect spot to *gaze* at the *luminous* stars.
   ○ The rooftop was the perfect spot to *look* at the *bright* stars.

3. ○ The party was *pleasant*, and we laughed at Kyle's *hilarious* stories.
   ○ The party was *nice*, and we laughed at Kyle's *funny* stories.

4. ○ The weather was *good*, and I felt *happy*.
   ○ The weather was *terrific*, and I felt *jubilant*.

B. Write the letter of each description next to the correct term.

_____ 5. personal narrative

_____ 6. opening

_____ 7. closing

_____ 8. dialogue

_____ 9. events

_____ 10. topic

A. should get the reader's attention

B. is the event you choose to write about

C. should be given in the order they happened

D. is a story about you

E. should give your thoughts about your experience

F. makes people in the narrative come alive

C. Fill in the circle next to the correct phrase that completes each sentence.

11. A personal narrative should always be about _____.
    ○ something funny
    ○ something you remember well
    ○ something that did not really happen

12. When you _____ you can add more details.
    ○ proofread your first draft
    ○ publish your narrative
    ○ revise your first draft

13. A personal narrative should *not* include _____.
    ○ details that do not fit with the topic
    ○ dialogue
    ○ time-order words

D. Write the letter of what is done at each stage of the Writing Process next to the correct term.

_____ 14. planning

_____ 15. drafting

_____ 16. revising

_____ 17. proofreading

_____ 18. publishing

A. adding, changing, or deleting details

B. choosing a topic and the events to include

C. writing a neat final draft

D. checking for correct spelling and punctuation

E. writing the first copy of your story

E. Fill in the circle next to the correct answer.

19. Nervousness about speaking in front of people ___.
    ○ is not normal
    ○ can be lessened or overcome
    ○ means you will not do a good job

20. Which is *not* a way to overcome nervousness?
    ○ refusing to speak when your turn comes
    ○ praying for God's help
    ○ breathing deeply before and during speaking

21. Which is the better use of your eyes while you are speaking?
    ○ looking at each person in the group
    ○ staring at your best friend the whole time

22. Which is more important to think about when you are speaking?
    ○ getting finished as soon as possible
    ○ making sure you speak clearly

F. Read the following narrative paragraph and find the four mistakes. Use proofreading marks to mark the mistakes.

> Our trip to Cedar Falls was really fun. My brother james and I took our new sleping bags. We hiked up the first part of the trail Then we stopped and set up camp. We finished our hike the next morning. The falls were beautiful! I want to come here every summer," my brother said.

Proofreading Marks

∧∨ Add

  ℓ Delete

≡ Capital letter

/ Lowercase

○→ Move

Cumulative Review

A. Write *S* if the group of words is a sentence.
Write *F* if the group of words is a fragment. *(Chapter 1)*

_____ 1. Zoomed down the bumpy hill.

_____ 2. The three go-carts.

_____ 3. Jerome's go-cart lost a wheel.

_____ 4. Slid to a stop near a bush.

_____ 5. Ava's go-cart reached the bottom safely.

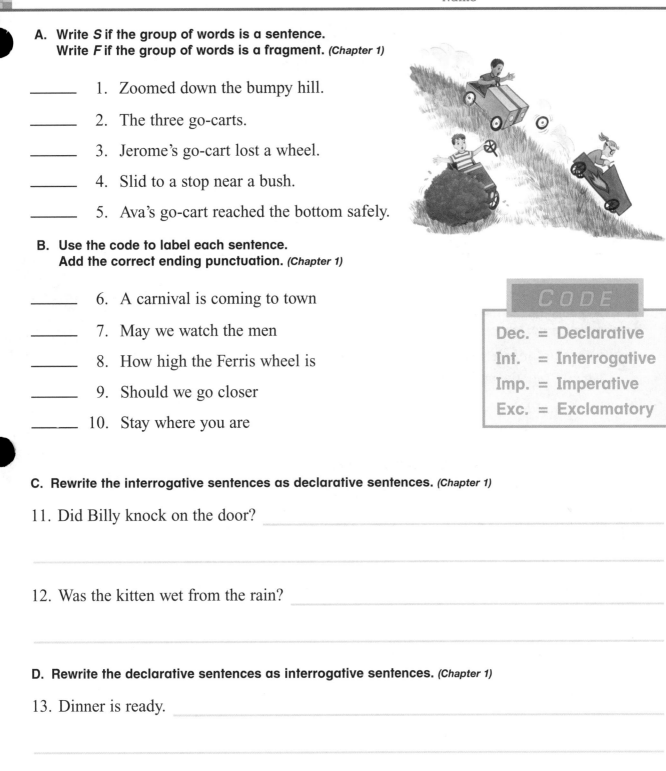

B. Use the code to label each sentence.
Add the correct ending punctuation. *(Chapter 1)*

_____ 6. A carnival is coming to town

_____ 7. May we watch the men

_____ 8. How high the Ferris wheel is

_____ 9. Should we go closer

_____ 10. Stay where you are

CODE

Dec. = Declarative
Int. = Interrogative
Imp. = Imperative
Exc. = Exclamatory

C. Rewrite the interrogative sentences as declarative sentences. *(Chapter 1)*

11. Did Billy knock on the door? _____

_____

12. Was the kitten wet from the rain? _____

_____

D. Rewrite the declarative sentences as interrogative sentences. *(Chapter 1)*

13. Dinner is ready. _____

_____

14. Luke walked the dog. _____

_____

Cumulative Review

E. Draw a line between the complete subject and the complete predicate. Write the simple subject and the simple predicate on the diagram. *(Chapter 1)*

15. The waiter gave us menus.

_____ | _____

16. We ordered dessert.

_____ | _____

17. The pie is delicious!

_____ | _____

F. Fill in the circle next to the sentence that uses more exact descriptive words. *(Chapter 2)*

18. ○ I want to *purchase* the new markers with *vivid* colors.
    ○ I want to *buy* the new markers with *bright* colors.

19. ○ The *dreadful* dragon may *demolish* the kingdom.
    ○ The *bad* dragon may *destroy* the kingdom.

20. ○ A *funny* monkey made the children *laugh*.
    ○ A *comical* monkey made the children *giggle*.

G. Write the letter of what is done at each stage of the Writing Process. *(Chapter 2)*

_____ 21. revising   A. choosing a topic and the events to include

_____ 22. publishing   B. writing the first copy of your story

_____ 23. planning   C. adding, changing, or deleting details

_____ 24. proofreading   D. correcting mistakes in punctuation and spelling

_____ 25. drafting   E. writing a neat final draft

Nouns:
Common & Proper

Name

A **noun** names a person, place, or thing.

> teacher   mall   chair

Nouns can be in the subject part or predicate part of a sentence.

> Aunt Ruth|served cookies and milk.

A **common noun** names any person, place, or thing.

> boy   church   book

A **proper noun** names a specific person, place, or thing.

> Christopher   Calvary Bible Church   Bible

> *A proper noun may be more than one word.*

▶ Guided Practice

▶ **Underline the three nouns in each sentence.**

1. Jason learned about space and the planets.

2. He attended camp at the U.S. Space & Rocket Center in Alabama.

3. His group learned how astronauts prepare for flight.

4. They saw the first rocket to carry an American astronaut into space.

5. Their activities included launching rockets and conducting experiments.

▶ **Write *C* if the underlined noun is a common noun.**
Write *P* if the underlined noun is a proper noun.

_____ 6. The U.S. Space & Rocket Center Museum is open all year.

_____ 7. Their collection of rockets is the largest on earth.

_____ 8. What does it feel like to be launched in a rocket?

_____ 9. The Space Shot is a ride that lets you find out.

_____ 10. You rise 140 feet into the air in 2.5 seconds.

_____ 11. You experience weightlessness as you free-fall to the ground.

Rocket City Legacy Exhibit

_____ 12. Visitors experience what astronaut Alan Shepard felt on the first U.S. space flight.

▶ **Write a proper noun for each common noun.**

13. woman _____

14. store _____

Nouns: Common & Proper

Name _____

○ Independent Practice

▶ Underline the three nouns in each sentence.

1. This museum tells about the history of airplanes.

2. Orville Wright flew the first plane while lying on his stomach.

3. His plane had two sets of wings.

4. William Lafayette Quick built his plane about one hundred years ago.

5. The pilot of this plane sat upright in a seat.

6. It had a single set of wings like airplanes today.

▶ Write *C* if the underlined noun is a common noun.
Write *P* if the underlined noun is a proper noun.

_____ 7. U.S. Space Camp is a popular part of the museum.

_____ 8. Children enjoy this astronaut-training program.

_____ 9. Campers live in a dormitory for five days.

_____ 10. They use real-life training simulators.

_____ 11. Kids love to ride in the Gravity Chair.

Riding the Gravity Chair

▶ Decide whether the underlined noun is a person, place, or thing.
Fill in the circle next to the correct answer.

12. Tourists can visit the Mobile Quarantine Facility (MQF) at the space museum.
○ person   ○ place   ○ thing

13. The Apollo astronauts used it at the end of each space flight.
○ person   ○ place   ○ thing

14. Scientists were afraid that germs could be brought to Earth.
○ person   ○ place   ○ thing

15. The astronauts stayed in the MQF until doctors checked them out.
○ person   ○ place   ○ thing

16. Space germs were never found.
○ person   ○ place   ○ thing

17. Shuttle astronauts are still checked today.
○ person   ○ place   ○ thing

② Apply and Write

▶ Write two sentences about what you would like to see or do if you visited
the U.S. Space & Rocket Center. Circle all the nouns in your sentences.

_____

_____

Proper Nouns: Capitalization Rules

Name _____

Each main word in a proper noun begins with a capital letter.

1. Capitalize names, initials, and titles of people.

> Eliza White   Grandma   H.T. Manning
> Reverend Johnson   Doctor Harris   Governor Stephens

2. Capitalize names and titles for God.

> Father   Holy Spirit   Son of God   Shepherd

3. Capitalize names of buildings.

> Empire State Building   Grandville Courthouse

4. Capitalize names of streets, cities, states, countries, continents, rivers, lakes, and oceans.

> Drake Drive   Phoenix, Arizona   Ghana, West Africa
> Irrawaddy River   Lake Michigan   Atlantic Ocean

5. Capitalize names of specific days of the week, months, and holidays.

> Friday   September   Fourth of July

6. Capitalize names of teams, businesses, and organizations.

> Los Angeles Lakers   Sam's Quickmart   Congress

7. Capitalize abbreviations of proper nouns. An abbreviation is a shortened form of a word written with letters missing. Abbreviations usually end with a period.
(See p. 344–45 in the Grammar Handbook for lists of abbreviations.)

> Mr.   St.   Wed.   CO

Guided Practice

▶ Mark the letters that should be capitalized using the proofreading mark ≣.

1. mrs. jacobs lives on liberty drive in thomasville, north carolina.

2. k.d. burkholder traveled to hawaii on tuesday, may 28, 2002.

3. mexico city is the capital of mexico.

> **Remember**
>
> A *proper noun* names a specific person, place, or thing.

▶ Write the correct abbreviation for each day of the week.
See page 345 for help.

4. Saturday _____   8. Tuesday _____

5. Monday _____   9. Friday _____

6. Wednesday _____   10. Thursday _____

7. Sunday _____

Proper Nouns: Capitalization Rules

Name _____

Independent Practice

▶ **Mark the letters that should be capitalized by using the proofreading mark ☰.**

1. I heard pastor taylor preach at gospel baptist church on sunday, february 2, 2004.

2. Did you know that dr. s. g. robertson has a dental office on wendover avenue?

3. reverend and mrs. rick evans are missionaries to japan.

4. On monday, miss anderson will visit her sister in st. louis, missouri.

▶ **Write the correct abbreviation. See page 345 for help.**

5. August _____   11. An adult man _____

6. President _____   12. Lane _____

7. Boulevard _____   13. A married woman _____

8. Reverend _____   14. Street _____

9. Road _____   15. November _____

10. Governor _____   16. January _____

▶ **Look for mistakes in capitalization in the sentences. Write the letter of the line that contains a mistake. Write the letter for *no mistakes* if the sentence is correct.**

_____ 17. A. Simon and Steven
        B. visited the kennedy space center
        C. in May.
        D. *no mistakes*

_____ 18. A. They learned about
        B. the marvelous planets that
        C. our heavenly father created.
        D. *no mistakes*

Inside Kennedy Space Center

Apply and Write

▶ **Write today's date using the correct abbreviation. Include the day of the week.**

_____

▶ **Write your address. Use the first line for the street address and the second line for the city and state.**

_____

Capitalizing Titles

1. Capitalize the first, last, and all important words in the titles of books, stories, and poems.

   Llamas on the Loose   "Johnny and His Mule"   "Alone over the Atlantic"

2. Book titles should be underlined when handwritten or put in italics when published.

   <u>Medallion</u>   *Iceland Adventure*   <u>Suzannah Strikes Gold</u>

3. Use quotation marks around the titles of stories and poems.

   (story) "The Rich Man and Lazarus"
   (poem) "Cherry Time"
   (story) "Pecos Bill Gets a Wife"

4. Capitalize names of the Bible, its divisions, and its books.

   God's Word   New Testament   Holy Bible   Romans 8:28

Guided Practice

▸ Fill in the circle next to the book title that is written correctly.

1. ○ <u>Carolina's Courage</u>
   ○ Carolina's Courage

2. ○ The mystery of Pelican Cove
   ○ *The Mystery of Pelican Cove*

▸ Fill in the circle next to the story title that is written correctly.

3. ○ "A Wise King and a Wise Son"
   ○ <u>A Wise King and a Wise Son</u>

4. ○ <u>"Jakko's Answer"</u>
   ○ "Jakko's Answer"

▸ Fill in the circle next to the poem title that is written correctly.

5. ○ "Over the Top"
   ○ *"Over the Top"*

6. ○ "Wind Song"
   ○ <u>Wind Song</u>

▸ Write each title correctly.

7. mountain born (book) _____

8. a narrow fellow in the grass (poem) _____

9. mort and the sour scheme (story) _____

10. courage by darkness (book) _____

11. pony penning day (story) _____

12. o say can you see? (poem) _____

Capitalizing Titles

◎ Independent Practice

▶ **Fill in the circle next to the book title that is written correctly.**

1. ○ *The Spelling Window*
   ○ The Spelling Window

2. ○ Tales from Dust River Gulch
   ○ "Tales from Dust River Gulch"

3. ○ A Place for Peter
   ○ "A Place for Peter"

4. ○ *"The Bridge"*
   ○ The Bridge

▶ **Fill in the circle next to the story title that is written correctly.**

5. ○ "The Snow-White Robin"
   ○ "The Snow-White Robin"

6. ○ Night Ride to River Station
   ○ "Night Ride to River Station"

7. ○ Sulphur Springs Challenge
   ○ "Sulphur Springs Challenge"

▶ **Fill in the circle next to the poem title that is written correctly.**

8. ○ "There was an old man from Pompeii"
   ○ "There Was an Old Man from Pompeii"

9. ○ "Rabbit Preschool"
   ○ *Rabbit Preschool*

▶ **Write each title correctly.**

10. the case of the dognapped cat (book) _____

11. cat (poem) _____

12. word of honor (story) _____

13. old testament _____

14. genesis 1:27 _____

15. holy scriptures _____

◎ Apply and Write

▶ **Write correctly the title of a favorite book and the title of a favorite story.**

Book _____

Story _____

Common Nouns: Singular & Plural

Name _____

A **singular noun** names *one* person, place, or thing. A **plural noun** names *more than one* person, place, or thing.

Add **s** to form the plural of most nouns.

> astronauts   planes   stars

Add **es** to form the plural of nouns ending in **s, sh, ch, ss, x,** or **z.**

> gases   bushes   watches   classes   foxes   buzzes

Add **s** to form the plural of nouns ending with a **vowel + y.**

> monkeys   keys   trays

Change the **y** to **i** and add **es** to form the plural of nouns ending with a **consonant + y.**

> babies   bakeries   candies

 Guided Practice

▶ Write *S* if the underlined noun is singular.
 Write *P* if the underlined noun is plural.

_____ 1. The National Air and Space Museum is in Washington, D.C.

_____ 2. The collection of aircraft and spacecraft at the museum is huge!

_____ 3. Visitors may touch some of the exhibits.

_____ 4. The museum frequently adds new exhibits.

National Air and Space Museum

▶ Write the plural of each singular noun.

5. glass _____

6. church _____

7. house _____

8. toy _____

9. puppy _____

10. box _____

11. wish _____

12. brush _____

13. party _____

14. donkey _____

Common Nouns: Singular & Plural

Name

◉ Independent Practice

▸ Write *S* if the underlined noun is singular. Write *P* if the underlined noun is plural.

_____ 1. The National Air and Space Museum opened its <u>doors</u> on July 1, 1976.

_____ 2. Less than one <u>month</u> later, over one million visitors had come.

_____ 3. It has two main floors with twenty-three exhibit <u>galleries</u>.

_____ 4. The original Wright brothers' plane hangs near the main <u>entrance</u>.

_____ 5. There are many <u>artifacts</u> about the history of space travel.

_____ 6. <u>Visitors</u> may touch a moon rock.

Moon rocks

▸ Write the plural of each singular noun.

7. radish _____	12. girl _____
8. bunch _____	13. machine _____
9. tax _____	14. carton _____
10. hobby _____	15. lady _____
11. turkey _____	16. daisy _____

▸ Fill in the circle next to the sentence that is written correctly.

17. ○ My grandmother always gives me two kisses on my forehead.
    ○ My grandmother always gives me two kiss's on my forehead.

18. ○ The girl likes to eat peachs.
    ○ The girl likes to eat peaches.

19. ○ You can see skyscrapers in some big cities.
    ○ You can see skyscrapers in some big citys.

❷ Apply and Write

▸ Write two or more sentences about a birthday party you have attended. Circle the plural nouns.

_____

_____

_____

Common Nouns:
Special Plurals

Name _____

Some plural nouns are formed by changing the spelling of the singular noun.

knife = knives	goose = geese	mouse = mice
wife = wives	tooth = teeth	woman = women
leaf = leaves	foot = feet	child = children
wolf = wolves		man = men
		ox = oxen

Some nouns use the same word for both the singular and plural forms.

deer	moose	elk	sheep	fish

Guided Practice

▶ **Fill in the circle next to the sentence that is written correctly.**

1. ○ There were four gooses in the pond.
   ○ There were four geese in the pond.

2. ○ Several women attended the missionary meeting.
   ○ Several womans attended the missionary meeting.

3. ○ Two oxes were stuck in the ditch.
   ○ Two oxen were stuck in the ditch.

▶ **Write the plural form for each noun.**

4. elk _____   7. tooth _____

5. man _____   8. sheep _____

6. mouse _____   9. wife _____

▶ **Write S if the underlined noun is singular.**
  Write P if the underlined noun is plural.

_____ 10. The <u>sheep</u> was white with a black face.

_____ 11. A blue <u>fish</u> is in the aquarium.

_____ 12. Some <u>moose</u> were at the lake.

_____ 13. We saw four baby <u>deer</u> at the zoo.

© 2004 BJU Press. Reproduction prohibited.

English 4, Chapter 3, Lesson 25

49

Common Nouns:
Special Plurals

Name

◎ Independent Practice

▶ **Fill in the circle next to the sentence that is written correctly.**

1. ○ His two front tooths are loose.
   ○ His two front teeth are loose.

2. ○ We found a nest of baby mouses.
   ○ We found a nest of baby mice.

3. ○ John raked the leaves in the yard.
   ○ John raked the leafs in the yard.

4. ○ Many children came to the circus.
   ○ Many childs came to the circus.

5. ○ Two mans rode in the taxi.
   ○ Two men rode in the taxi.

▶ **Write the plural form for each noun.**

6. deer _____ 9. foot _____

7. goose _____ 10. wolf _____

8. sheep _____ 11. ox _____

▶ **Write *S* if the underlined noun is singular.**
  Write *P* if the underlined noun is plural.

_____ 12. Three <u>deer</u> ran through the woods.

_____ 13. The mother <u>moose</u> protected her baby from danger.

_____ 14. The farmer sheared ten <u>sheep</u> yesterday.

_____ 15. Mother baked some <u>fish</u> for supper.

② Apply and Write

▶ **Write several sentences about sheep. Each time *sheep* is used as a singular noun, underline the word. When *sheep* is used as a plural noun, circle the word.**

_____

_____

_____

_____

Possessive Nouns: Singular

Name _____

A **singular noun** names one person, place, or thing.

> planetarium   star   comet

A **singular possessive noun** is a singular noun that owns or has something. Singular nouns are made possessive by adding **'s** to the end of the noun.

> the telescope of the planetarium → the planetarium's telescope
>
> the science project belonging to Tamara → Tamara's science project

▶ Guided Practice

▶ **Rewrite each phrase using a singular possessive noun.**

1. the tail of the horse _____

2. the shoe belonging to the baby _____

3. the car owned by Chad _____

4. the title of the book _____

5. the bike belonging to Ciara _____

6. the house belonging to Alexis _____

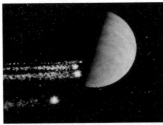

A comet's path

▶ **Write the possessive form of the singular noun in parentheses.**

7. _____ Adler Planetarium is an interesting place. (Chicago)

8. It contains the _____ first planetarium theater. (country)

9. The _____ ceiling looks like the sky at night. (planetarium)

10. You can watch a _____ path across the sky. (comet)

11. The _____ visitors can see old telescopes. (museum)

12. _____ telescopes are at the planetarium. (Galileo)

Possessive Nouns: Singular

Name _____

◎ Independent Practice

▶ **Rewrite each phrase using a singular possessive noun.**

1. the owner of the rabbit _____

2. the wing of the bird _____

3. the cap belonging to Ricardo _____

4. the computer owned by Janelle _____

5. the poster belonging to the class _____

6. the icing of the cake _____

▶ **Write the possessive form of the singular noun in parentheses.**

7. _____ dad works for the post office. (Abby)

8. _____ route is in the city. (Mr. Cantrell)

9. The _____ address helps him deliver the mail. (letter)

10. One _____ mailbox is shaped like a skyscraper. (house)

11. He explained his job at the _____ career day. (school)

12. A letter _____ job is tiring. (carrier)

◖◗ Apply and Listen

▶ Listen for singular possessive nouns as your teacher reads a short story. Write some of the possessive nouns that you hear as the story is read a second time.

Possessive Nouns: Plural

A **plural noun** names more than one person, place, or thing.

> choirs   babies   people   deer

A **plural possessive noun** is a plural noun that owns something or has something. If the plural noun ends in **s,** add just an apostrophe.

> the choirs' song   the babies' diapers

If the plural noun does not end in **s,** add **'s.**

> the people's tickets   the deer's antlers

▶ Guided Practice

▶ **Rewrite each phrase using a plural possessive noun.**

1. the lessons of the teachers _____

2. the whiskers of the lions _____

3. the beaks of the geese _____

▶ **Fill in the circle next to the correct sentence.**

4. ○ Cathy brushed the ponies' manes.
   ○ Cathy brushed the ponie's manes.

5. ○ The sheeps' wool was soft.
   ○ The sheep's wool was soft.

▶ **Write the plural possessive form of the plural noun in parentheses.**

6. The _____ meeting was long. (pastors)

7. The _____ choir sang at the meeting. (children)

8. The _____ displays were interesting. (missionaries)

9. The _____ luncheon was enjoyable. (women)

▶ **Use this phrase to write a sentence with a plural possessive noun.**

10. the books owned by the libraries _____

_____

Possessive Nouns: Plural

Name

Independent Practice

▶ **Rewrite each phrase using a plural possessive noun.**

1. the claws of the cats _____

2. the hooves of the oxen _____

3. the tires belonging to the cars _____

4. the tails of the mice _____

5. the watches owned by the men _____

6. the instruments belonging to the musicians _____

▶ **Fill in the circle next to the correct sentence.**

7. ○ The deer's antlers were beautiful.
   ○ The deers' antlers were beautiful.

8. ○ The computers's keyboards need repairs.
   ○ The computers' keyboards need repairs.

▶ **Write the plural possessive form of the plural noun in parentheses.**

9. The _____ families went on a picnic. (students)

10. The _____ skits were funny. (parents)

11. The _____ prizes were ribbons. (games)

12. The _____ colors were red, blue, and white. (ribbons)

13. The _____ favorite game was Red Rover. (children)

Apply and Write

▶ **Write several sentences telling about going on a picnic or eating a special meal. Include plural possessive nouns in your sentences.**

_____

_____

Confusing Proper Nouns

Common nouns that show family relationship become **proper nouns** when used as a name or part of a name.

> Dad   Mom   Grandmother   Grandfather   Aunt
>
> Uncle   Cousin   Father   Mother

> *My aunt brought my grandmother for a visit.*
> *Aunt Suzie brought Grandmother for a visit.*

Common nouns that describe a geographic feature become proper nouns when used as a name or part of a name.

> *(mountains) Ural Mountains*   *(plains) Great Plains*
> *(valley) Death Valley*   *(coast) Pacific Coast*
> *(ocean) Pacific Ocean*   *(lowlands) the Lowlands*
> *(highlands) Scottish Highlands*

> *The mountains are not near the ocean.*
> *The Rocky Mountains are not near the Atlantic Ocean.*

Compass words become proper nouns when used to refer to a region.

> North   South   East   West
> *I live north of the old church.*
> *There are many large cities in the North.*

▶ Guided Practice

Fill in the circle next to the correct sentence.

Basket of rice

1. ○ "Is supper ready, mom?"
   ○ "Is supper ready, Mom?"

2. ○ My cousin is in the third grade.
   ○ My Cousin is in the third grade.

3. ○ Nebraska is located in the Great Plains region of the United States.
   ○ Nebraska is located in the great plains region of the United States.

4. ○ Rice is often grown in the lowlands, a region in South Carolina.
   ○ Rice is often grown in the Lowlands, a region in South Carolina.

▶ **Write one sentence with *grandfather* used as a common noun and another sentence with *grandfather* used as a proper noun.**

5. _____

6. _____

Confusing Proper Nouns

Name

◉ Independent Practice

▶ **Fill in the circle next to the correct sentence.**

1. ○ Uncle Dan visited Cousin Jim in Washington, D.C.
   ○ Uncle Dan visited cousin Jim in Washington, D.C.

2. ○ The National Air and Space Museum is just a few miles to the North.
   ○ The National Air and Space Museum is just a few miles to the north.

3. ○ My Uncle lives to the South of Cousin Jim's house.
   ○ My uncle lives to the south of Cousin Jim's house.

4. ○ The Pima Air & Space Museum is in the West.
   ○ The Pima Air & Space Museum is in the west.

5. ○ Do you know of any space museums near Monument Valley?
   ○ Do you know of any space museums near Monument valley?

6. ○ The part of Florida famous for space museums is called the Space coast.
   ○ The part of Florida famous for space museums is called the Space Coast.

7. ○ The Kansas Cosmosphere and Space Center is 50 miles to the South of Wichita.
   ○ The Kansas Cosmosphere and Space Center is 50 miles to the south of Wichita.

8. ○ There are several space museums in the South.
   ○ There are several space museums in the south.

Kansas Cosmosphere

▶ **Proofread the paragraph. Use proofreading marks to mark the six mistakes.**

> **Proofreading Marks**
> ≡ Capital letter
> / Lowercase

When my Aunt came back from her vacation in the Scottish highlands, she brought gifts for us. She had a scarf for my Grandma, a model airplane for Cousin Tom, a pair of gloves for Uncle Randy, and a necklace for me. For mom and dad, she had a painting of the coast of Scotland. We thanked aunt Cindy for the gifts.

① Apply and Write

▶ **Write two sentences about a member of your family. Write one sentence with the family word used as a common noun and the other sentence with the family word used as a proper noun.**

A. Write *C* if the underlined noun is a common noun and *P* if it is a proper noun.

_____ 1. My parents went to Furniture Town last <u>Saturday</u>.

_____ 2. The store is on <u>Randolph Street</u>.

_____ 3. <u>Mr. Davis</u> showed them some furniture.

_____ 4. They bought a new <u>sofa</u> there.

_____ 5. The sofa is green with white <u>flowers</u>.

B. Fill in the circle next to the book title that is written correctly.

6. ○ *The Next Fine Day*
   ○ The Next Fine Day

7. ○ <u>Renegade in the Hills</u>
   ○ <u>Renegade In The Hills</u>

C. Fill in the circle next to the story title that is written correctly.

8. ○ <u>River's Rising</u>
   ○ "River's Rising"

9. ○ *A Pocket Full of Money*
   ○ "A Pocket Full of Money"

D. Write the plural form for each noun.

10. monkey _____

11. punch _____

12. gas _____

13. bunny _____

14. sheep _____

15. baseball _____

16. dress _____

17. foot _____

18. man _____

19. leaf _____

E. Rewrite each phrase using a singular possessive noun.

20. the skin of the snake _____

21. the bicycle belonging to Mark _____

22. the computer owned by Rachel _____

23. the wheel of the scooter _____

Name _____

F. Rewrite each phrase using a plural possessive noun.

24. the shoes of the players _____

25. the jackets of the children _____

26. the paws belonging to the lions _____

27. the eyes of the mice _____

G. Write the correct abbreviation for each noun.

28. Wednesday _____   31. President _____

29. Avenue _____   32. March _____

30. Reverend _____   33. Road _____

H. Fill in the circle next to the correct sentence.

34. ○ Can you tell which direction is north?
    ○ Can you tell which direction is North?

35. ○ The Appalachian Mountains reach as far as Alabama.
    ○ The Appalachian mountains reach as far as Alabama.

36. ○ We picked berries near Lake Lanier.
    ○ We picked berries near lake Lanier.

37. ○ We had a history lesson about the Native Americans who lived in the Desert.
    ○ We had a history lesson about the Native Americans who lived in the desert.

Appalachian Mountains

Cumulative Review

A. Draw a line between the complete subject and the complete predicate. Underline the simple subject once. Underline the simple predicate twice. *(Chapter 1)*

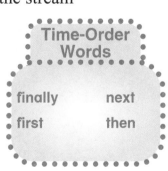

1. Last night Lindsey read a book for her book report.

2. The story tells of a missionary and his dog.

3. The missionary visits small villages.

4. The dog pulls a sled of supplies.

5. Many people hear the gospel.

B. Diagram the simple subject and simple predicate from the sentences above. *(Chapter 1)*

6. Sentence 1 _____|_____

7. Sentence 2 _____|_____

8. Sentence 3 _____|_____

9. Sentence 4 _____|_____

10. Sentence 5 _____|_____

C. Write a complete subject to finish each sentence. *(Chapter 1)*

11. _____ ran to the picnic table.

12. _____ grilled hamburgers for lunch.

13. _____ walked near the stream

D. Write time-order words to finish the instructions. The words may be used more than one time. *(Chapter 2)*

14. _____, we measured the ingredients into a bowl.

15. _____, I mixed the dough with a spoon.

16. _____, we put balls of dough on the baking sheet.

17. _____, Dina put the baking sheet into the oven.

18. _____, we tasted the warm cookies!

Time-Order Words	
finally	next
first	then

Cumulative Review

E. Write *S* if the sentence is a simple sentence.
Write *C* if the sentence is a compound sentence. *(Chapter 1)*

_____ 19. Marcus and Mindy chased butterflies.

_____ 20. They tried to catch one, but it was too fast.

_____ 21. Mindy sometimes uses a butterfly net,
or she may use her hands.

_____ 22. Some butterflies land on Mom's morning glories.

_____ 23. Morning glories open in the morning,
and they close in the evening.

F. Use proofreading marks to mark the three mistakes. *(Chapter 2)*

Joey saw the branches of the bush move as the bird flew away. Could that bird have a nest in the bush? Joey stood still and listened He heard tiny cheeping sounds. carefully he lifted the end of the branch. The inside of the bush was dark, and Joey could not hear a sound. Then he saw a messy nest of twigs. Up popped the heads of thee fuzzy gray chicks!

Proofreading Marks

∧∨ Add
⟍ℓ Delete
≡ Capital letter
/ Lowercase
⟲⟶ Move

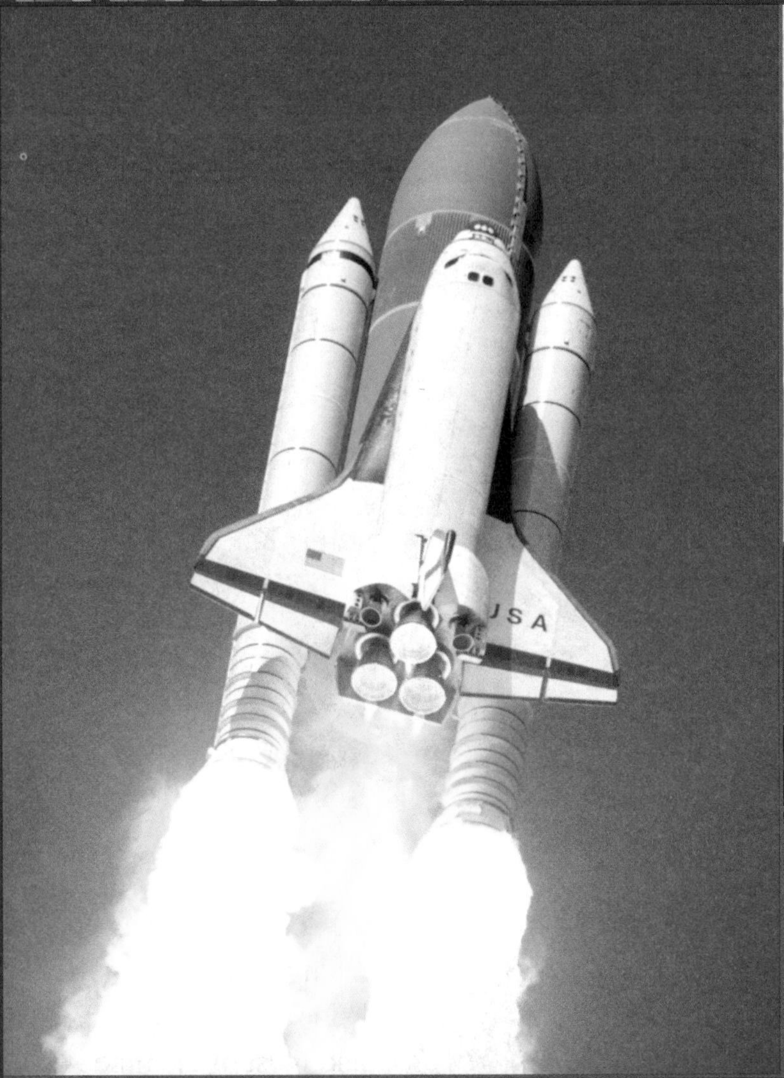
USA

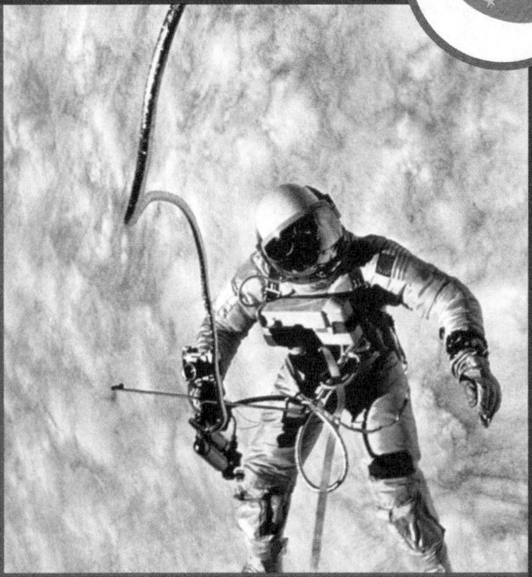

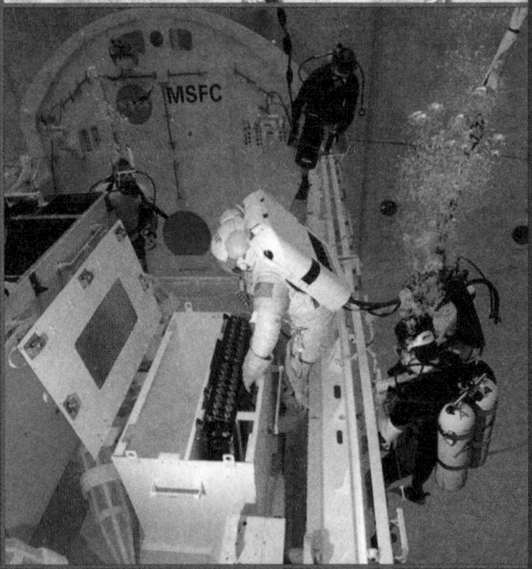
MSFC

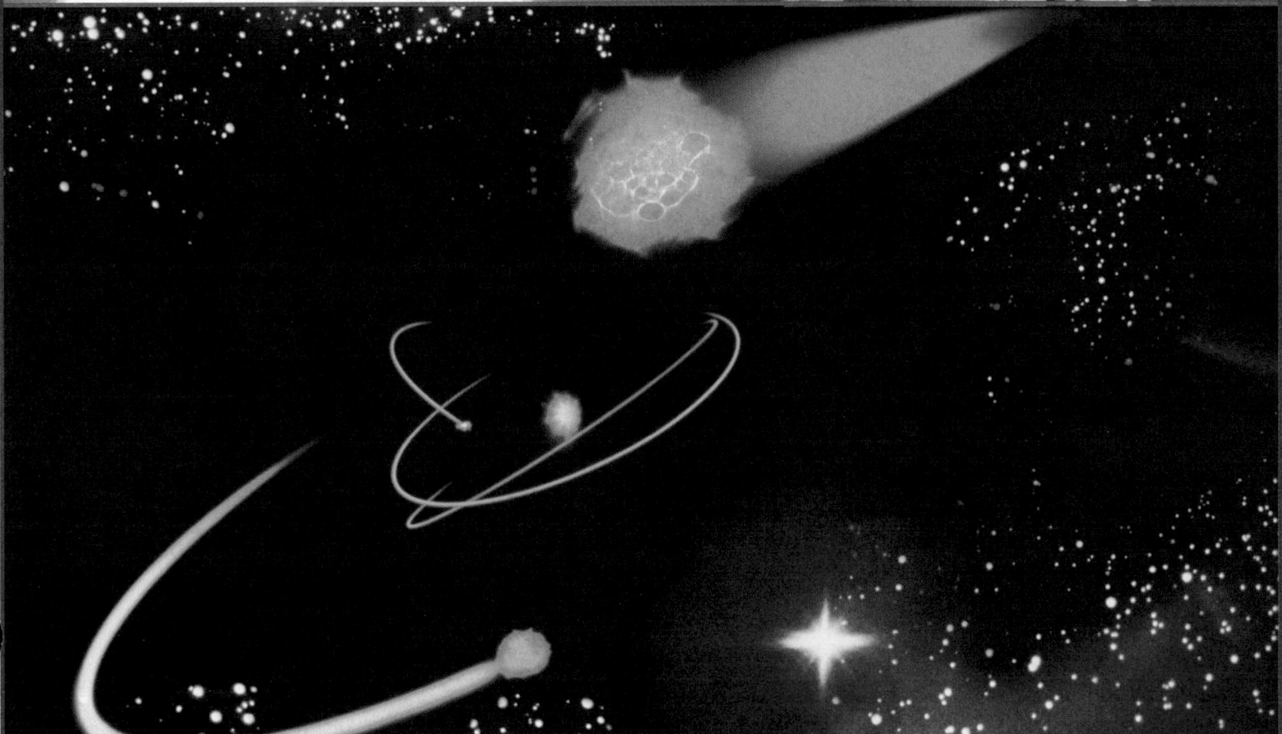

Excerpt from *Mystery of the Indian Carvings* by Gloria Repp

A JourneyForth book from BJU Press

By the time Julie had finished the dishes, Karin had disappeared down toward the beach and Aunt Myra had driven off to take Uncle Nate to the ferry.

Now she could read Melissa's letter in peace. As she ripped open the envelope, a strip of silky blue cloth fell into her lap. Absently, Julie wound it around her finger as she read. The long letter was warm and funny, just like Melissa, and it filled her with a desperate homesickness. Near the end of the letter, Melissa mentioned the bookmark she had enclosed, and Julie read her words wistfully:

The verse on the bookmark is really true, Julie. The Lord Jesus always keeps His promises. Read your Bible every day and you'll get to know Him better. You'll find out that He's the best Friend in all the world. Remember our verse in the Gospel of John? That's a good book to read. I miss you a lot these days, but I'm glad He's there with you.

Slowly Julie unwound the bookmark from her finger. The bright yellow words gleamed at her: *I will never leave thee nor forsake thee.* She stared at the verse and then read Melissa's words again: "Read your Bible every day and you'll get to know Him better."

Maybe that's what had happened. She hadn't read her Bible at all since she'd been here, and most of the time her new Friend seemed to be pretty far away. This Sunday at church, she had begun to realize that she really didn't know Him very well.

The Gospel of John? Julie dropped the bookmark into her pocket and jumped up. She'd get her Bible out of the chest and start right now.

Parts of a Friendly Letter

Name _____

A **friendly letter** is a letter to a friend or relative. Some friendly letters are written to thank someone for a gift or a special thing that person did. Some friendly letters are written to send congratulations, to give instructions, or to give advice.

Friendly letters can simply be a way to help someone catch up on the news in your life.

The **heading** includes the writer's address and the date.

The **greeting** says hello to the person getting the letter.

The **body** is the message from the writer. Notice that the writer divides his instructions into paragraphs to make them easy to read.

The **closing** says goodbye.

The **signature** is the writer's name.

1452 Lilac Circle
Denver, CO 80260
October 23, 2004

Dear Jason,

I'm glad you liked the s'mores we had at the picnic. If you'd like to try making one yourself, here's how to do it. You will need a graham cracker, part of a chocolate bar, two big marshmallows, a stick, and a bonfire.

First, break the graham cracker in half. Lay the chocolate bar on one half. Next, hold the marshmallows on a stick over the fire until they get soft and slightly brown on the outside. Then slide the marshmallows off the stick with your fingers and lay them on top of the chocolate. Finally, press the other half of the graham cracker on top to make a sandwich.

Almost everybody likes s'mores, even though they're a little sticky! Have a fun time making them.

Your friend,
Parker

Commas are used in the heading, greeting, and closing of a friendly letter.

A friend must be friendly.

Prov. 17:17

▶ Guided Practice

▶ **Use the letter to answer the questions.**

1. For what purpose was this friendly letter written? _____

   _____

2. Who lives at the address in the heading? _____

3. When was this letter written? _____

Parts of a Friendly Letter

Name _____

◎ Independent Practice

▸ **Label the parts of the letter.**

▸ **Write the letter of the correct name next to each part.**

A. body	B. closing	C. greeting	D. heading	E. signature

1. ○ ──────────────────▶

   7 Kenton Rd.
   Lawrence, KS 66049
   November 14, 2004

2. ○ ──────▶
   Dear Parker,
       Thank you for sending me the instructions
   for making s'mores. We had a cookout for
   my birthday, and my dad built a bonfire.

3. ○ ──────▶
   I invited some new friends from my church.
   They all liked the s'mores. I wish you could
   have been there too!
       I hope you're still having fun playing
   on the soccer team. Say hi to the other guys
   for me.

4. ○ ──────────────────▶
   Your friend,

5. ○ ──────────────────▶
   Jason

▸ **Read the letter and answer the questions.**

6. What information is in the greeting of the letter? _____

   _____

7. What punctuation mark is used between the city

   name and the state name? _____

8. In which part of the letter do you find the

   writer's name? _____

9. What is the purpose of Jason's letter to Parker? _____

   _____

10. Name one other reason for writing a friendly letter. _____

    _____

Writing Instructions

Instructions tell how to do something as simply and clearly as possible. Parker's letter to Jason was written to give him instructions for making s'mores.

Tips for Making Instructions Clear and Simple

1. Introduce the topic in an interesting way.

2. List all the materials needed.

3. Give the steps in order.

4. Use time-order words.

5. Use exact words and details.

6. Conclude instructions in an encouraging way.

1452 Lilac Circle
Denver, CO 80260
October 23, 2004

Dear Jason,

I'm glad you liked the s'mores we had at the picnic. If you'd like to try making one yourself, here's how to do it. You will need a graham cracker, part of a chocolate bar, two big marshmallows, a stick, and a bonfire.

First, break the graham cracker in half. Lay the chocolate bar on one half. Next, hold the marshmallows on a stick over the fire until they get soft and slightly brown on the outside. Then slide the marshmallows off the stick with your fingers and lay them on top of the chocolate. Finally, press the other half of the graham cracker on top to make a sandwich.

Almost everybody likes s'mores, even though they're a little sticky! Have a fun time making them.

Your friend,
Parker

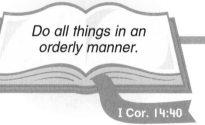

Do all things in an orderly manner.

I Cor. 14:40

Time-Order Words

first	when	after that
second	next	afterward
third	last	as soon as
then	finally	

▶**Follow these instructions for marking Parker's letter.**

1. First, underline in red the sentence that tells the materials needed to make s'mores.

2. Second, draw a green box around any details that tell what the marshmallows will feel like or look like when they are done.

3. Next, circle in blue any time-order words in the instructions.

4. Finally, underline in yellow the encouragement at the end of the instructions.

Revising Together

During the revising stage of the Writing Process, you look for ways to improve your writing.

▶ **Work together to decide how Heather's letter should be revised.**

▶ **Proofread the letter if time allows.**

1700 West Lake ave.

Cleveland, TN 37311

Dear Anna Grace,

    Would you like to know how to set up a lemonade stand? It's a lot of fun!

    First, find a good spot. You want it to be where a lot of people will see it. You also want it to be shady so you won't get too hot. Set up the cups and the lemonade on the table. Get someone to help you take the table to the spot.

    Make a sign telling the price. Decide how much you want to charge for a cup of lemonaid. You might want to have some extra cash in a box under the table so you can make change. Finally, sit at the table with a big smile and wait for your customers!

    I hope you enjoy selling lemonade. It's a nice way to make money.

              Love,

              Heather

Revising Checklist

☐ 1. The introduction gets the reader's attention.

☐ 2. All the materials are listed before the instructions begin.

☐ 3. The steps are in order.

☐ 4. Enough details are given about each step.

☐ 5. I checked to see where I could use a more exact verb to make the instructions clearer.

☐ 6. I checked to see where I could use a time-order word to make the instructions clearer.

☐ 7. The conclusion encourages the reader to follow the instructions.

Proofreading Marks

∧∨   **Add**

     Delete

≡   **Capital letter**

/   **Lowercase**

     Move

Instructions in a Letter: Planning

Name

For instructions to be clear, the steps need to be placed in a logical order.

Each step must contain all the details needed before you go on to the next step.

Planning before you write will help you keep the steps and details in order.

Here is the chart Parker used to plan his instructions for making s'mores.

Materials Needed:

graham cracker	a stick
part of a chocolate bar	a bonfire
two big marshmallows	

Time-Order Words	Steps	Details
First	Break the graham cracker in half	▶ put the chocolate bar on one ▶ ▶
Next	Hold the marshmallows over the fire	▶ on the stick ▶ till they get done ▶
Then	Take the marshmallows off the stick	▶ with your fingers ▶ lay them on top of the chocolate ▶
Finally	Smash the other half of the graham cracker on top	▶ like a sandwich ▶ ▶

What will you write instructions about? Your topic should be something you have done yourself and something you know how to do well.

You will write your instructions in a letter. Who will your audience be? Who might be interested in learning about your topic?

Instructions in a Letter: Planning

Name

▶ **Write your topic and audience.**

My instructions will tell how to _____

_____

I will write to _____

▶ **Complete the chart below to plan your instructions.**

Materials Needed:

Time-Order Words	Steps	Details
		▶ ▶ ▶
		▶ ▶ ▶
		▶ ▶ ▶
		▶ ▶ ▶

▶ **Save this chart for use in Lesson 35.**

Instructions in a Letter: Drafting

Name

Parker used his planning chart to draft the letter below. Because this letter is a rough draft, it has mistakes in it, but Parker will fix those in the revising and proofreading stages. Notice how Parker organized his letter into paragraphs.

1452 Lilac Circle

Denver, CO 80260

October 23 2004

Dear jason,

> In his first paragraph, Parker introduces the topic and lists the materials needed.

If you'd like to try making a s'more, here's how to do it. You will need a gram cracker, part of a chocolate bar, two big marshmallows, a stick, and a bonfire.

> In his second paragraph, he gives the instructions.

First, break the graham cracker in half. Put the chocolate bar on one half. Next, hold the marshmallows on a stick over the fire. Until they get done. Then take the marshmallows off the stick with your fingers and lay them on top of the chocolate finally, smash the other half of the graham cracker on top to make a sandwich.

> In his third paragraph, he concludes the instructions by giving encouragement.

Almost everybody likes s'mores, even though they're a little sticky! Have a fun time making them.

Your friend,

Parker

You may not want to write all the steps of your instructions in one paragraph. Look at the planning chart you have made. Do any of your steps have more than three details? You may want to start a new paragraph before writing those steps.

▶ **Draft your letter on your own paper.**

▶ **Save your letter for use in Lesson 36.**

Once you have a rough draft of your letter, you can make changes to improve it. Here is a checklist to help you when it is time to revise.

Revising Checklist

☐ 1. The introduction gets the reader's attention.

☐ 2. All the materials are listed before the instructions begin.

☐ 3. The steps are in order.

☐ 4. Enough details are given about each step.

☐ 5. I checked to see where I could use a more exact verb to make the instructions clearer.

☐ 6. I checked to see where I could use a time-order word to make the instructions clearer.

☐ 7. The conclusion encourages the reader to follow the instructions.

After Parker had drafted his letter, he shared it with Tonya. Tonya liked the topic Parker had chosen. She said that the letter—especially the ending—made her want to try making s'mores.

"Maybe the first sentence in the letter could be a little more interesting, though," she said. "It doesn't really sound like the way you would start a friendly letter."

Parker thought for a moment. "Maybe I could put in another sentence about the time Jason and I made s'mores," he said.

"Oh, that would be good," Tonya said. "I also had a question about cooking the marshmallows over the fire. How can you tell when they're done?"

"They get all soft and kind of brown," said Parker. "I'll add some details there."

Tonya smiled. "I'm not sure I understood the sentence that says 'Smash the other half of the graham cracker on top.' *Smash* makes me think of breaking it up into pieces."

"No . . . maybe I need a more exact verb."

"How about *press?*" suggested Tonya.

"That's perfect."

Parker found some other verbs in his instructions that needed to be more exact. He changed *take* to *slide*. He also checked his thesaurus to find a better word to replace *put*.

On the next page is Parker's letter after he marked the changes he would make. Notice the proofreading marks he used.

1452 Lilac Circle

Denver, CO 80260

October 23 2004

Dear jason,

I'm glad you liked the s'mores we had at the picnic.

∧If you'd like to try making a s'more, here's how to do it.

You will need a gram cracker, part of a chocolate bar, two

big marshmallows, a stick, and a bonfire.

    First, break the graham cracker in half. P*u*t the   *Lay*

chocolate bar on one half. Next, hold the marshmallows on

    soft and slightly brown on the outside   *slide*

a stick over the fire. Until they get done. Then take the

marshmallows off the stick with your fingers and lay them

on top of the chocolate finally, smash the other half of   *press*

the graham cracker on top to make a sandwich.

    Almost everybody likes s'mores, even though they're a

little sticky! Have a fun time making them.

                       Your friend,

                       Parker

▶ Revise your letter using the *Revising Checklist* on page 70.
   Use proofreading marks to mark your changes.

▶ Save your revised letter for use in Lesson 37.

Proofreading Marks

∧∨   **Add**

    Delete

≡   **Capital letter**

/   **Lowercase**

    Move

Instructions in a Letter: Proofreading

Name _____

After Parker revised his letter, he proofread it, using the checklist on the next page. As he finished checking for each type of mistake, he put a check beside that item on the checklist.

1452 Lilac Circle

Denver, CO 80260

October 23, 2004

Dear jason,

    I'm glad you liked the s'mores we had at the picnic. If you'd like to try making a s'more, here's how to do it. You will need a graham gram cracker, part of a chocolate bar, two big marshmallows, a stick, and a bonfire.

    First, break the graham cracker in half. Lay the chocolate bar on one half. Next, hold the marshmallows on a stick over the fire Until they get soft and slightly brown on the outside. Then slide the marshmallows off the stick with your fingers and lay them on top of the chocolate finally, press the other half of the graham cracker on top to make a sandwich.

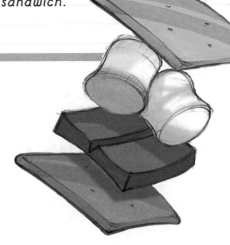

Instructions in a Letter: Proofreading

Name

▶ Use the *Proofreading Checklist* as you proofread your letter. Use proofreading marks to mark the mistakes.

Almost everybody likes s'mores, even though they're a little sticky! Have a fun time making them.

Your friend,

Parker

Proofreading Checklist

☐ 1. I used complete sentences.

☐ 2. I put a capital letter at the beginning of each sentence.

☐ 3. I put a punctuation mark at the end of each sentence.

☐ 4. I used capital letters correctly within the sentences.

☐ 5. I used commas correctly in the heading, greeting, and closing of my letter.

☐ 6. I looked for misspelled words.

Proofreading Marks

∧∨   Add

╰   Delete

≡   Capital letter

/   Lowercase

⟳➔   Move

▶ Save your proofread letter for use in Lesson 38.

Instructions in a Letter: Publishing

After Parker had copied his letter onto stationery, he addressed an envelope to Jason. He wrote his address as the **return address** in the upper left corner of the envelope. Then he wrote Jason's address as the **mailing address** in the center of the envelope. He placed a postage stamp in the upper right corner.

Return
Address →

Parker Johnson
1452 Lilac Circle
Denver, CO 80260

Remember

Remember that each address includes three parts:
1. The name of the person
2. The street address
3. The city, the state, and the ZIP Code

Mailing
Address →

Jason Vanderkellen
7 Kenton Rd.
Lawrence, KS 66049

Each address should have a comma between the city and state. The state postal abbreviations have two capital letters with no period. Names of streets can also be abbreviated. See pages 344–45 of the Grammar Handbook for state abbreviations.

▶ **Make a neat final draft of your letter on your own stationery.**
▶ **Address an envelope to the person who will receive your letter.**

A. Write the letter of the correct letter part.

_____ 1. Dear Natasha,

_____ 2. Name of the person writing the letter

_____ 3. Your friend,

_____ 4. The main part of the letter

_____ 5. The address of the person writing the letter

A. body
B. closing
C. greeting
D. heading
E. signature

B. Fill in the circle next to the correct answer.

6. In written instructions, the materials should be listed ___ the steps.
   - ○ before
   - ○ after
   - ○ in the middle of

7. Use ___ to make the order of the steps clear.
   - ○ details
   - ○ exact words
   - ○ time-order words

8. The introduction to the instructions should be ___.
   - ○ long
   - ○ interesting
   - ○ detailed

9. The conclusion to the instructions should ___.
   - ○ warn the reader not to make mistakes
   - ○ leave the reader with questions about the instructions
   - ○ encourage the reader to follow the instructions

10. Which step should come first in instructions for making a peach milkshake?
    - ○ Mix the peaches and ice cream in a blender.
    - ○ Slice the peaches.

11. Which sentence uses exact words and details?
    - ○ Use a paper cutter to cut the paper into three-inch squares.
    - ○ Cut up the paper into small pieces.

12. Which sentence belongs in the conclusion rather than among the steps?
    - ○ Next, fill the gerbil's bottle with fresh water.
    - ○ Your gerbil will be healthy and happy if cared for properly!

Chapter 4 Review

Name ____________

C. Fill in the circle next to the words that contain a mistake in punctuation.

13. ○ Dear Daniel,
    ○ Boston MA 02116
    ○ Love,

14. ○ Your cousin
    ○ Jan. 29, 2004
    ○ Dear Grandma,

D. Fill in the circle next to the words that contain a mistake in capitalization.

15. ○ 1800 Birch Ln.
    ○ Your best friend,
    ○ dear Mrs. Lewis,

16. ○ Dear Uncle Luke,
    ○ may 15, 2004
    ○ Your friend,

E. Match the correct proofreading symbol to its name.

______ 17. Add

______ 18. Capital letter

______ 19. Delete

______ 20. Lowercase

______ 21. Move

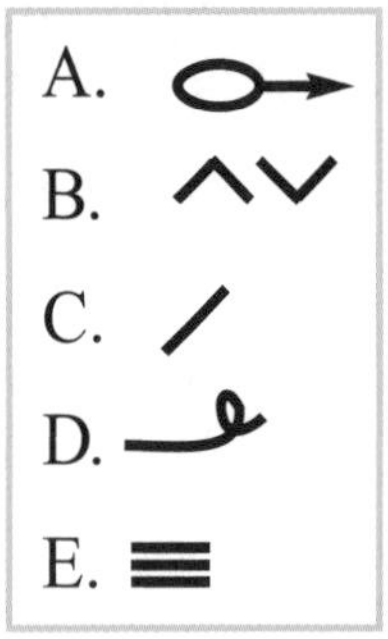
A.
B.
C.
D.
E.

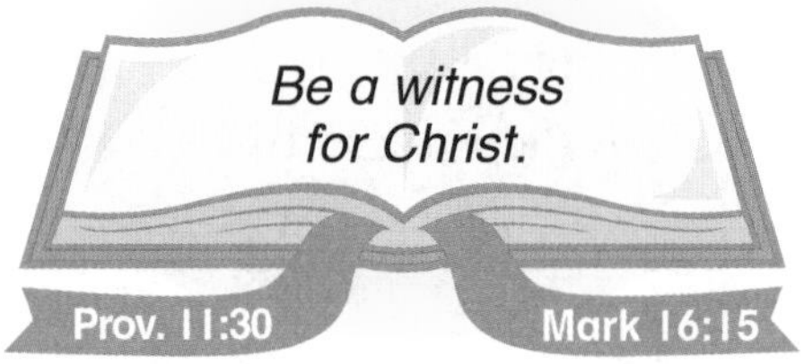
Be a witness
for Christ.
Prov. 11:30
Mark 16:15

F. Write the letter that shows the correct placement of each address. One will have two answers.

______ 22. The address of the person receiving the letter

______ 23. The address of the person writing the letter

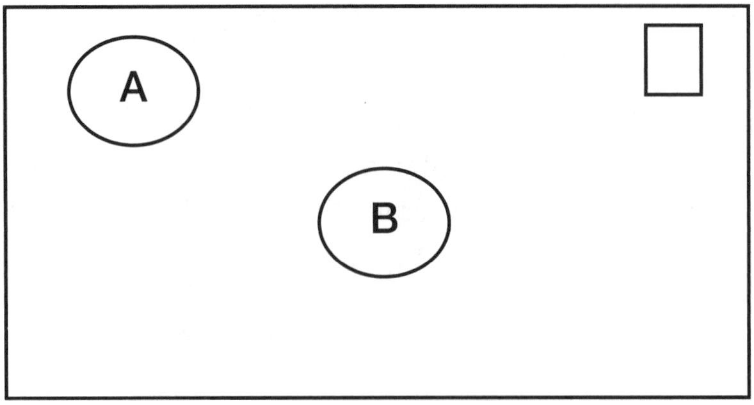
A
B

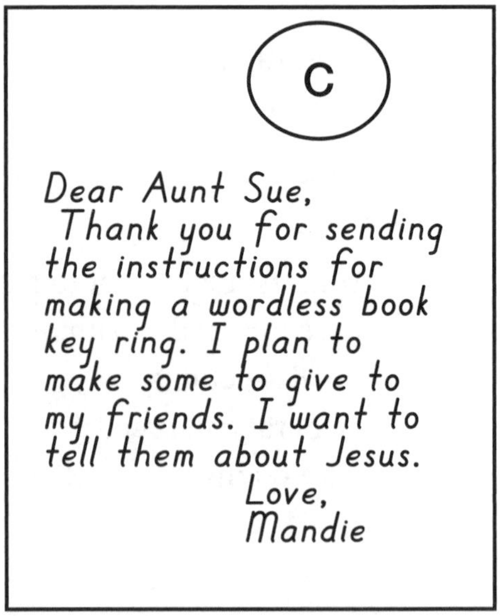
C
Dear Aunt Sue,
Thank you for sending the instructions for making a wordless book key ring. I plan to make some to give to my friends. I want to tell them about Jesus.
Love,
Mandie

Cumulative Review

Name _____

A. Draw a line between the complete subject and the complete predicate. Underline the simple subjects once and the simple predicates twice. *(Chapter 1)*

1. Melanie's dog and cat play together.

2. The cat hides and waits for the dog.

3. She pounces and chases the surprised dog.

4. They jump and run around the yard.

5. The tired cat and dog nap on the rug.

B. Diagram the compound subject and simple predicate of Sentence 1. *(Chapter 1)*

6.

C. Diagram the simple subject and compound predicate of Sentence 2. *(Chapter 1)*

7.

D. Combine the sentences to make a compound subject or a compound predicate. *(Chapter 1)*

8. Sarah plays the piano.
   Rayna plays the piano.

   _____

9. Sarah practices every day.
   Sarah studies every day.

   _____

E. Write *C* if the underlined noun is a common noun.
Write *P* if the underlined noun is a proper noun. *(Chapter 3)*

_____ 10. Mr. Johnson works at <u>Super T Hardware Store</u>.

_____ 11. Dad and I like to look at the power <u>tools</u>.

_____ 12. Last <u>Saturday</u> we took Grandpa to look for a drill.

_____ 13. Grandpa bought the <u>Deluxe Cordless Pro Drill</u>.

_____ 14. He is repairing the back porch on his <u>house</u>.

Cumulative Review

F. Write the abbreviation for the underlined word. *(Chapter 3)*

15. <u>Mister</u> Ellis teaches my Sunday school class. _____

16. Melanie lives at 1607 Butternut <u>Road</u>. _____

17. My birthday is <u>January</u> 28. _____

18. Our field trip will be next <u>Wednesday</u>. _____

19. We went skiing in Denver, <u>Colorado</u>. _____

G. Number the stages of the Writing Process in the correct sequence. *(Chapter 2)*

_____ 20. Add, delete, or change details to improve the writing.

_____ 21. Choose your topic and the events or details to include.

_____ 22. Write a final neat copy.

_____ 23. Check for correct spelling and punctuation.

_____ 24. Write the first draft.

H. Mark the letters that should be capitalized by using ☰. *(Chapter 3)*

25. nathan chose to read *sheriff at Waterstop* for his book report.

26. Pastor marcus Schmidt from New zealand spoke in the sunday services.

27. the soccer season for the centerville Wildcats begins in august.

28. The maple street Gym is open for basketball practice on thursday afternoon.

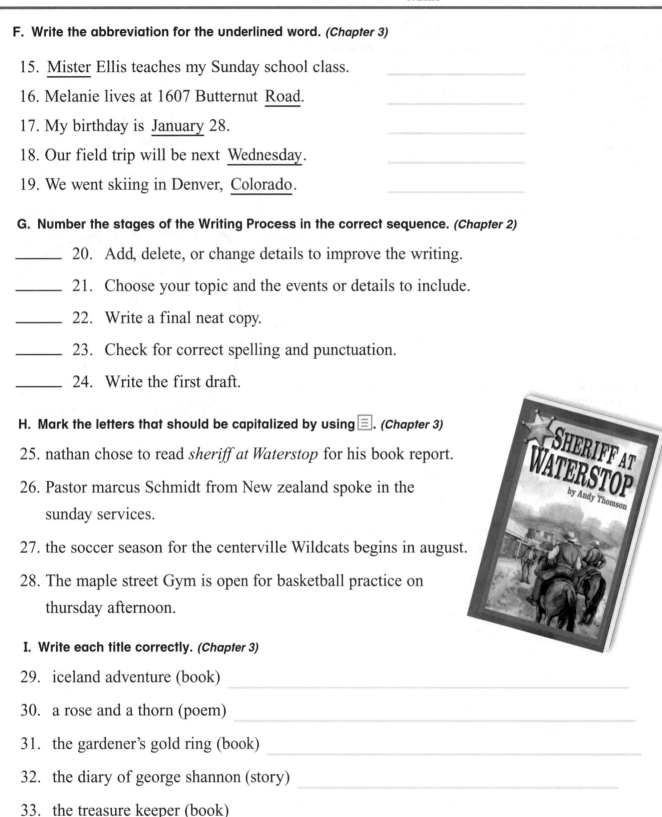

I. Write each title correctly. *(Chapter 3)*

29. iceland adventure (book) _____

30. a rose and a thorn (poem) _____

31. the gardener's gold ring (book) _____

32. the diary of george shannon (story) _____

33. the treasure keeper (book) _____

Action Verbs & Linking Verbs

Name _____

A **verb** is the main word in the predicate part of a sentence that tells what the subject does or is.

An **action verb** tells what the subject *does*.

simple subject	action verb
basketball	falls

The basketball <u>falls</u> into the basket.

A **linking verb** tells what the subject *is* by linking the subject to a *noun* or an *adjective* in the predicate part of the sentence. A **predicate noun** renames the subject. A **predicate adjective** describes the subject.

simple subject	linking verb	predicate noun
I	am	fan

I <u>am</u> a fan of basketball.

simple subject	linking verb	predicate adjective
basketball	is	orange

The basketball <u>is</u> orange.

A diagram of a sentence shows how the words in the sentence relate to each other. The vertical line crosses the base line and separates the subject part from the predicate part of the sentence. On the diagrams, notice that the slanted line points the predicate noun or predicate adjective back toward the subject.

Some verbs are **sensory words.** These include *smell, taste, look, sound,* and *feel*.

Some sensory words can be action verbs.   Some sensory words can be linking verbs.

The <u>players</u> look at the coach.   *The <u>players</u> look happy.*

Guided Practice

▶Underline the simple subject once. Underline the verb twice. If the verb is a linking verb, draw an arrow linking the subject with the predicate noun or predicate adjective.

1. The referee blew the whistle.

2. The people looked at the referee.

3. The blue team is the winner!

4. The players felt tired after the game.

Remember

Forms of the verb *be* are used as linking verbs.

is	are	am
was	were	

Action Verbs & Linking Verbs

Name

 Independent Practice

▶Underline the simple subject once. Underline the verb twice. If the verb is a linking verb, draw an arrow linking the subject with the predicate noun or predicate adjective.

1. The team's uniforms are green.

2. Tyrone is a center on our team.

3. The team ran laps around the gym.

4. Basketball players practice every day.

5. Kimi shoots baskets on her driveway.

6. She is very good at basketball.

7. Kimi was captain of her team last year.

▶Write the simple subject and the verb on each diagram. If the verb is a linking verb, draw a slanted line and write the predicate adjective or predicate noun.

8. The players' shoes smell sweaty after the game.

_____|_____

9. They cheer loudly for their favorite team.

_____|_____

10. Some fans are parents of the players.

_____|_____

 Apply and Write

▶Write two sentences about a sport. Write one sentence using an action verb. Write one sentence using a linking verb.

_____

_____

Making Subjects & Linking Verbs Agree

In a sentence, the linking verb must agree with the subject of the sentence. The most common linking verbs are forms of the verb *be*. The *be* forms tell what the subject *is* or *was*.

Correct	**Incorrect**
I am a guard on my basketball team. *My friend is a forward on the team.*	*I is a guard on my basketball team.* *My friend are a forward on the team.*

This chart shows how present-tense and past-tense linking verbs agree with singular and plural subjects.

Simple Subject	Present-Tense Linking Verb	Past-Tense Linking Verb
singular subject pronouns: he, she, it	is	was
plural subject pronouns: we, they, you	are	were
I	am	was

Guided Practice

▶ **Underline the simple subject once. Underline the correct linking verb twice.**

1. They (was, were) tired after running laps around the gym.

2. The coach (is, are) my friend's uncle.

3. My team's colors (is, are) red and white.

4. I (am, is) a devoted Bears fan.

5. Karen and Anne (be, are) cheerleaders for the Tigers.

▶ **Fill in the circle next to the sentence in which the linking verb agrees with the subject.**

God promises protection to believers.

II Chron. 16:9   Ps. 34:7

6. ○ My favorite Bible character are Daniel.
   ○ My favorite Bible character is Daniel.

7. ○ The lions were hungry.
   ○ The lions is hungry.

8. ○ Daniel was brave.
   ○ Daniel were brave.

9. ○ God were faithful.
   ○ God is faithful.

Making Subjects & Linking Verbs Agree

Name _____

○ Independent Practice

▶ Underline the simple subject once.
Underline the correct linking verb twice.

1. You (was, were) busy before the game.

2. She (is, are) sad to miss the game.

3. Dillon (be, is) good at shooting hoops.

4. I (am, be) better at dribbling the ball down the court.

5. Many people (is, are) fans of basketball.

▶ Write a correct form of *be* as a linking verb in each sentence.
Use the tense indicated in parentheses.

6. The news _____ good for the Eagles' team. (past)

7. They _____ the favorite team in the tournament. (present)

8. I _____ happy about the announcement. (present)

9. My friend _____ the Eagles' mascot. (present)

10. The Eagles _____ the victors of last year's tournament. (past)

▶ Circle the three incorrect linking verbs in the paragraph.
Write the correct form of each verb in the blanks.

Eagles Predicted to Soar over the Tigers

The Eagles are predicted to win Saturday's game against the Oakdale Tigers. The Eagles be the champions last year. They won their last five games. The Tigers was nervous about Saturday's game. They have lost their last three games. Eagles fans is confident that their team will be victorious.

11. _____

12. _____

13. _____

✐ Apply and Write

▶ Write two sentences using *am* and *are* correctly as linking verbs.

_____

_____

Main Verbs & Helping Verbs

Name _____

Sometimes a complete action verb has more than one word. The **main verb** tells the action of the subject. The **helping verb** helps the main verb. Helping verbs always come before the main verb in a sentence. The complete verb includes the helping verb and the main verb but not any extra words between the verbs.

The first basketball players would throw the ball into peach baskets.

simple subject	helping verb action verb
players	would throw

Verbs Used as Helping Verbs

am	was	have	does	would
is	were	has	do	could
are	will	had	did	should

Sometimes **adverbs** such as *usually, often, sometimes, also, even,* or *not* come between the main verb and the helping verb. These words also tell about the action of the main verb and may change the meaning of the sentence.

Geese will usually fly south in September.

They do not enjoy the cold winters in the North.

Geese	will fly
They	do enjoy

▶ Guided Practice

▶ Underline the simple subject once. Underline the complete verb twice.

1. Dr. James Naismith did invent basketball in 1891.

2. He had written thirteen rules for the new game.

3. Young men could play the game inside during the cold winter.

4. Dr. Naismith had devised the most popular indoor sport of all time.

▶ Underline the simple subject once and the complete verb twice. In the blank, write the word that is between the helping verb and the main verb.

5. Good athletes will usually practice faithfully. _____

▶ Diagram the simple subject and complete verb for Sentence 5. Remember to include the helping verb with the main verb.

_____ | _____

Main Verbs & Helping Verbs

◉ Independent Practice

▸ **Underline the simple subject once.**
Underline the complete verb twice.

1. People had nailed peach baskets to the wall.

2. Boys were playing basketball for the first time!

3. They would toss a soccer ball into their basket for points.

4. A player would push the ball out of the basket with a broom handle.

5. Nobody had thought about the bottoms of the baskets!

6. Someone did cut the bottoms from the baskets many years later.

▸ **Underline the simple subject once and the complete verb twice.**
Write the word that is between the helping verb and the main verb.

Dr. James Naismith

7. Basketball players will often practice many hours every day. _____

8. Coaches do not cancel practice sessions during the basketball season. _____

9. Reporters will sometimes write articles about the players. _____

10. Most players can also jump very high. _____

11. Some can even reach higher than the hoop! _____

▸ **Diagram the simple subject and the complete verb in these sentences.**
Remember to include the helping verb with the main verb but do not
include the adverb.

12. I am playing basketball next year.

13. Tara will sometimes join us in a practice game.

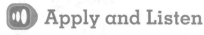

◉ Apply and Listen

▸ **Write some helping verbs that you hear.**

_____ _____ _____

Making Subjects & Helping Verbs Agree

Name _____

A helping verb must agree with the simple subject of the sentence.

A **singular subject** needs the **singular verb** form.

Kara has played basketball.
Kara does play basketball.
She is playing basketball.
She was playing basketball.

A **plural subject** needs the **plural verb** form.

Allen and Donny have played basketball.
Allen and Donny do play basketball.
They are playing basketball.
They were playing basketball.

The pronouns *I* and *you* are exceptions.

I have played basketball.
I do play basketball.
I am playing basketball.
I was playing basketball.

You have played basketball.
You do play basketball.
You are playing basketball.
You were playing basketball.

Simple Subject	Present-Tense Helping Verbs	Past-Tense Helping Verbs
singular subject pronouns: he, she, it	has is does	had was did
plural subject pronouns: we, they, you	have are do	had were did
I	have am do	had was did

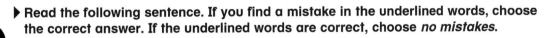 Guided Practice

▶ **Underline the simple subject once and the correct helping verb twice.**

1. Many colleges (have, has) <u>developed</u> basketball programs.

2. The National Basketball Association (did, do) <u>establish</u> official rules for the game.

3. The referees (is, are) <u>wearing</u> black and white striped uniforms.

4. One player (have, has) already <u>tripped</u> over his feet twice.

▶ **Read the following sentence. If you find a mistake in the underlined words, choose the correct answer. If the underlined words are correct, choose *no mistakes*.**

5. <u>Lyle and Al was shooting</u> baskets in the driveway.
   ○ Lyle and Al were shooting   ○ Lyle and Al is shooting   ○ *no mistakes*

Making Subjects & Helping Verbs Agree

Name _____

◯ Independent Practice

▶ **Underline the simple subject once and the correct helping verb twice.**

1. My brother's basketball (has, have) <u>lost</u> some of its air.

2. He (had, have) already <u>pumped</u> it up yesterday.

3. It (do, does) not <u>take</u> him very long.

4. We (have, has) <u>played</u> basketball on our driveway all summer.

5. Several neighborhood friends (was, were) <u>joining</u> us.

6. Jasmine (is, has) finally <u>made</u> a basket.

7. Darrell and Kirsten (have, has) <u>made</u> the most points.

8. Kirsten (do, did) not <u>play</u> on our school team this year.

9. My little sister (was, were) <u>playing</u> with us.

10. I (am, is) <u>enjoying</u> some time with my friends.

▶ **Read each sentence. If you find a mistake in the underlined words, choose the correct answer. If the underlined words are correct, choose *no mistakes*.**

11. <u>We is writing</u> about different countries.
   - ◯ We are writing
   - ◯ We have writing
   - ◯ *no mistakes*

12. <u>Cameron is looking</u> for information about Ireland.
   - ◯ Cameron have looking
   - ◯ Cameron are looking
   - ◯ *no mistakes*

13. His <u>relatives have lived</u> near Belfast for many generations.
   - ◯ relatives do lived
   - ◯ relatives has lived
   - ◯ *no mistakes*

14. <u>Cameron have found</u> a map in an encyclopedia article.
   - ◯ Cameron did found
   - ◯ Cameron has found
   - ◯ *no mistakes*

15. The <u>map do not show</u> the small village near Belfast.
   - ◯ map does not show
   - ◯ map have not show
   - ◯ *no mistakes*

◯ Apply and Write

▶ **Write two sentences about a place you have visited. Use a different helping verb in each sentence. (Make sure that each helping verb agrees with its subject.)**

_____

_____

Direct Objects

Remember that an action verb tells what the subject does. A sentence with an action verb sometimes contains a direct object.

A **direct object** is a noun in the predicate part of the sentence that receives the action of the verb. It tells *what* or *whom.*

The _boy_ <u>dribbled</u> the basketball.

The boy dribbled *what? (basketball)*

The _team_ <u>watched</u> their coach.

The team watched *whom? (coach)*

He <u>blew</u> a whistle.

He blew *what? (whistle)*

▶ Guided Practice

▶ **Underline the simple subject once and the action verb twice. Circle the direct object.**

1. The Warriors played a difficult game.

2. Michael grabbed the ball.

3. Shawn guarded the goal.

4. Jeremy caught the pass.

5. The referee called a foul.

6. Tyrone held his breath.

7. Our team scored two points!

8. The crowd chanted a cheer for the team.

▶ **Complete each sentence by writing a direct object in the blank.**

9. The clerk stacked _____ on the shelves.

10. The veterinarian examined the sick _____ .

11. Rusty and Kendal washed the _____ .

12. The children played _____ at recess.

Direct Objects

Independent Practice

▶ Underline the simple subject once and the action verb twice. Circle the direct object.

God is a
righteous judge.

Ps. 19:9–11   Rom. 1:18

1. Belshazzar gave a feast.

2. He invited his friends.

3. The people used the vessels from the temple.

4. They praised their false gods.

5. Suddenly a hand wrote a message.

6. The king called Daniel.

7. Daniel interpreted the writing on the wall.

8. God planned a judgment.

9. Enemies conquered the kingdom.

10. God controls His world.

▶ Complete each sentence by writing a direct object in the blank.

11. I ate _____ for dinner last Sunday.

12. Jason found a _____ in the flower bed at church.

Apply and Write

▶ Think of a favorite Bible character. Write two sentences telling what he or she did. Circle the direct objects that you used in your sentences.

_____

_____

_____

Diagramming Direct Objects

Name

A **direct object** is a noun in the predicate part of the sentence that receives the action of the verb. It tells *what* or *whom*.

simple subject	action verb	direct object
fans	watched	game

The fans watched the game.

Since the direct object is in the predicate, the line between the action verb and the direct object comes to the base line but does not cross it. The line between the action verb and the direct object is straight. It is not slanted like the line on the linking verb diagram that points a predicate adjective or a predicate noun back to the subject.

If a sentence has a direct object, the direct object comes *after* the action verb.

Guided Practice

▶ **Underline the simple subject once and the action verb twice. Circle the direct object. Write the subject, action verb, and the direct object on each diagram.**

1. Thomas shot a lay-up.

2. Calvin congratulated Thomas.

3. Thomas scored two points for his team.

4. His parents clapped their hands loudly for Thomas.

Diagramming Direct Objects

◉ Independent Practice

▶ Underline the simple subject once and the action verb twice. Circle the direct object. Write the subject, the action verb, and the direct object on each diagram.

God knows everything about His children.

Nah. 1:7   I Cor. 8:3

1. We played basketball during recess.

2. The two captains picked teams.

3. Nobody chose the new boy.

4. Damon hung his head sadly.

5. I invited Damon to our team.

6. I made a new friend.

🎧 Apply and Listen

▶ Listen as your teacher reads Psalm 94:11a and Psalm 116:1a. Choose one of the sentences and diagram the subject, action verb, and direct object.

English 4, Chapter 5, Lesson 46

Contractions & Double Negatives

Name _____

A **contraction** is two words that are put together and shortened to make one word. An apostrophe (') takes the place of the letter or letters that are left out of the new word. Some contractions are formed by combining pronouns and verbs.

| she | + | will | = | *she'll* |
| we | + | are | = | *we're* |

that	+	is	=	*that's*
you	+	have	=	*you've*
I	+	am	=	*I'm*

Some contractions are formed by combining verbs and the word *not*.

| are | + | not | = | *aren't* |

| does | + | not | = | *doesn't* |

Won't and *can't* are exceptions. *Won't* is formed from the words *will* and *not*. *Can't* is formed from one word, *cannot*.

A **double negative** is the use of two negative words in the same sentence. A negative word is a way of saying *no*. A contraction with *not* is a negative word.

A good writer and speaker will avoid using a double negative in a sentence. Often one of the negatives in a double negative can be deleted or can be replaced with a positive word.

Correct	I **don't** have homework.	There **is no one** at home.
	I **don't** have **any** homework.	There **isn't anyone** at home.
Incorrect	I don't have no homework.	There isn't no one at home.

Negatives	Positives
never	always, ever
no	any
nobody, no one	anyone, everyone, someone

Negatives	Positives
none	all, one, some
nothing	anything, something
nowhere	anywhere, somewhere

Guided Practice

▶ **Write the contraction for each pair of words.**

1. she is _____   2. have not _____

▶ **Underline the contraction; then write it as separate words.**

3. We're going to the mountains this weekend. _____

4. He'll run in the race tomorrow. _____

▶ **Correct the double negative by deleting or replacing one of the underlined negatives. Write your new sentence.**

5. There <u>isn't nothing</u> to do after school. _____

Independent Practice

▶ **Underline the words that can form contractions; then write the contractions.**

1. Basketballs are many colors, and they are different sizes. _____

2. Here is the NBA's official basketball size: 29.5 inches around. _____

3. The bladder that is in the center of the ball holds the basketball's air. _____

4. My brother can hardly wait for the day when he will buy a basketball. _____

5. You should not buy a basketball without trying it out first. _____

6. A basketball player cannot cross the base line when dribbling the ball. _____

▶ **Underline the contractions. Write them as separate words.**

Good Sportsmanship

   I've learned that a good sportsman is a person who can take defeat without complaining and victory without boasting. He's more concerned about pleasing God and serving others than he is about winning the game at any cost. This kind of person won't allow his emotions to control his actions. He obeys God's Word, and his attitude doesn't show selfishness. He seeks to encourage others and abides by the rules of the game. God is honored by good sportsmanship.

7. _____

8. _____

9. _____

10. _____

Kindness and humility please God.

I Pet. 3:4   I Thess. 5:14–15

▶ **Correct the double negative in each sentence by deleting or replacing one of the underlined negatives. Write your new sentence.**

11. There <u>aren't no</u> cookies left.

_____

12. The tired horse <u>wouldn't</u> go <u>nowhere</u>.

_____

Apply and Write

▶ **Do you show good sportsmanship when you play? Write a sentence using a contraction that tells what you should not be or should not do.**

_____

Prefixes

Language LINK

A **prefix** is a group of letters added to the beginning of a base word to make a new word with a different meaning or use.

Prefix	Meaning	Example	Meaning
en	in	enclose	to close in
im *in*	into	implant indoors	to plant inside inside the doors of a building
im *in* *non*	not	immature inaccurate nonessential	not mature not accurate not essential
dis *un*	not or opposite of	disagree unwrapped	to not agree or the opposite of *agree* not wrapped or the opposite of *wrapped*
mis	bad or wrong	misbehave	to behave badly
pre	before	preview	to view before
re	again or back	reread	to read again

Note: The prefix *im* is added only to words beginning with *b, m,* and *p*.

▶ Guided Practice

▶ **Make a new word by adding a prefix to the base word to fit the meaning in parentheses.**

1. Making a good grade in history seemed _____ to Leah. (not possible)

2. My goldfish are _____ today. (not active)

3. Elliot _____ peanut butter. (opposite of *likes*)

4. The flies hovered around the _____ apple pie. (not covered)

▶ **Underline the word in each sentence that has a prefix. Fill in the circle next to the correct meaning of the word you underlined.**

5. The speaker mispronounced the name of the island.
   ○ pronounced badly   ○ pronounced before

6. I am unable to go to soccer practice today.
   ○ into able   ○ not able

Prefixes

Name _____

O Independent Practice

▶ **Make a new word by adding a prefix to the base word for each meaning in parentheses.**

1. Kylie _____ her teacher. (opposite of *obeyed*)

2. Jonah _____ the revised draft of his report. (read again)

3. The water flowed _____ as the waves swelled to record heights. (into the land)

4. Our country will _____ the bank robbers. (put into prison)

5. The new soccer ball was _____ . (not expensive)

6. Mom _____ the dirty socks to get out the grass stains. (soaked before washing)

▶ **Underline the word that has a prefix in each sentence. Fill in the circle next to the correct meaning of the word you underlined.**

7. Samantha enfolded the soft kitten in her arms.
   ○ folded in   ○ folded back

8. The rabbit became entangled in the trap.
   ○ tangled in   ○ tangled again

9. Most of that paragraph is nonessential information.
   ○ essential again   ○ not essential

10. The newspaper editor misprinted the information in the advertisement.
    ○ printed wrongly   ○ printed again

11. The Bible teaches Christians that they should not be immoral.
    ○ into moral   ○ not moral

12. God promises that dishonest people will eventually be caught in their sin.
    ○ badly honest   ○ not honest

Sin cannot be hidden from God.

Num. 32:23   Luke 12:2

O Apply and Write

▶ **Write a sentence using a word with a prefix that means *not*.**

_____

 94

English 4, Chapter 5, Lesson 48

Name _____

A. Underline the simple subject once. Underline the verb twice. If the verb is a linking verb, draw an arrow linking the subject with the predicate noun or predicate adjective.

1. Both teams ran onto the court.

2. The referee blows the whistle.

3. My team looks ready!

4. The crowd is noisy.

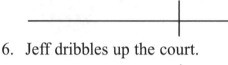

B. Write the simple subject and verb on each diagram. If the verb is a linking verb, draw a slanted line and write the predicate adjective or predicate noun.

5. The pretzels smell delicious.

_____ | _____

6. Jeff dribbles up the court.

_____ | _____

C. Underline the correct linking verb twice.

7. I (be, am) a loyal fan of basketball.

8. Nancy (is, be) tired after the game.

9. She (was, were) an active spectator in the stands.

10. You (was, were) sick during the game.

D. Underline the simple subject once. Underline the complete verb twice.

11. My family has practiced basketball at the park many times.

12. We could go tomorrow.

13. The snack stand will sometimes offer ice cream.

14. The nachos do often sell first.

15. Dad has told the man about Christ.

Salvation is by faith in Christ.

Rom. 6:23   Eph. 2:8

Name _____

E. Underline the correct form of the helping verb twice.

16. The stand (has, have) sold many hot dogs tonight.

17. I (is, am) eating two servings of nachos and cheese.

18. Austin and Jean (has, have) crunched sour pickles!

F. Underline the simple subject once and the action verb twice. Circle the direct object.

19. My sister watches the cheerleaders.

20. They sang a song about our team.

G. Diagram the simple subject, action verb, and direct object of each sentence.

21. Our team won the game.

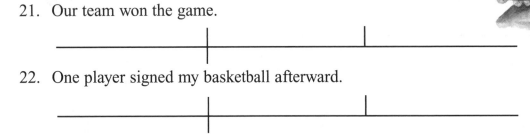

22. One player signed my basketball afterward.

H. Underline the words that can form contractions. Write the contractions.

23. The players will not stay long after the game. _____

24. We will stay after the game to clean up the trash. _____

25. Fans should not leave trash on the bleachers. _____

26. I am glad that you are a responsible fan! _____

I. Correct the double negative by deleting or replacing one of the underlined negatives. Write your new sentence.

27. Randy <u>hasn't never</u> seen a tiger.

_____

J. Underline the words that have prefixes. Fill in the circle next to the correct meaning of the word you underlined.

28. My dog misbehaved today.   ○ behaved badly   ○ behaved before

29. Some riddles are nonsense.   ○ into sense   ○ not having sense

30. The plant is too immature to have flowers.   ○ mature again   ○ not mature

Cumulative Review

Name

A. Use the code to identify each sentence. Add the correct ending punctuation. *(Chapter 1)*

_____ 1. Have you seen the sunflowers by the fence

_____ 2. Wow, how tall they have grown

_____ 3. Don't pick them yet

_____ 4. We will wait until the seeds are ripe and dry

_____ 5. Mom always toasts some for us to eat

_____ 6. Will Dad save any seeds for the birds

CODE	
Dec.	= Declarative
Int.	= Interrogative
Imp.	= Imperative
Exc.	= Exclamatory

B. Rewrite each declarative sentence as an interrogative sentence. *(Chapter 1)*

7. A robin does eat insects. _____

_____

8. Luke has filled the birdfeeder. _____

_____

C. Rewrite each interrogative sentence as a declarative sentence. *(Chapter 1)*

9. Can geese catch fish? _____

_____

10. Have they flown away? _____

_____

D. Fill in the circle next to the word that is a more descriptive word for the underlined word. Remember to keep the meaning of the sentence the same. *(Chapter 2)*

11. The <u>big</u> brown bear lumbered through the berry patch.
    ○ quiet   ○ enormous   ○ old

12. A hairy spider <u>made</u> its web in the corner.
    ○ spun   ○ put   ○ did

13. The <u>fast</u> lizard snapped at the fly.
    ○ green   ○ small   ○ quick

14. Tyler <u>held</u> the end of the rope.
    ○ grasped   ○ threw   ○ braided

15. Mr. Fisher displayed a <u>group</u> of old Bibles.
    ○ picture   ○ collection   ○ few

Name _____

E. Underline the correct plural noun. *(Chapter 3)*

16. Randall had six (piecees, pieces) of candy.

17. The (candys, candies) were cherry-flavored.

18. Did Randall share with his (friends, friendes)?

19. Randall remembered one of the (storys, stories) from the Bible.

20. A boy shared his (loaves, loafs) and fish with the crowd.

God blesses
those who give.

Acts 20:35   John 6:9–13

F. Proofread the letter. Use proofreading marks to mark the five mistakes.
(Chapter 4)

7003 forest View Ct.
Tampa, FL 33634
Nov. 10, 2004

Dear Bonnie

    Thank you for inviting us to visit during Thanksgiving break. Dad and I plan to get to your house on Friday afternoon. I think going to the museum with your family will be fun.

    We will have to start back home after dinner on sunday.

    I like visiting yor Sunday school class. Your teacher makes the Bible stories sound like they are happening now.

    I cant wait to see you in a few weeks!

        Your cousin,

        Sam

Proofreading Marks

∧∨ Add
⤸ Delete
≡ Capital letter
/ Lowercase
⌖→ Move

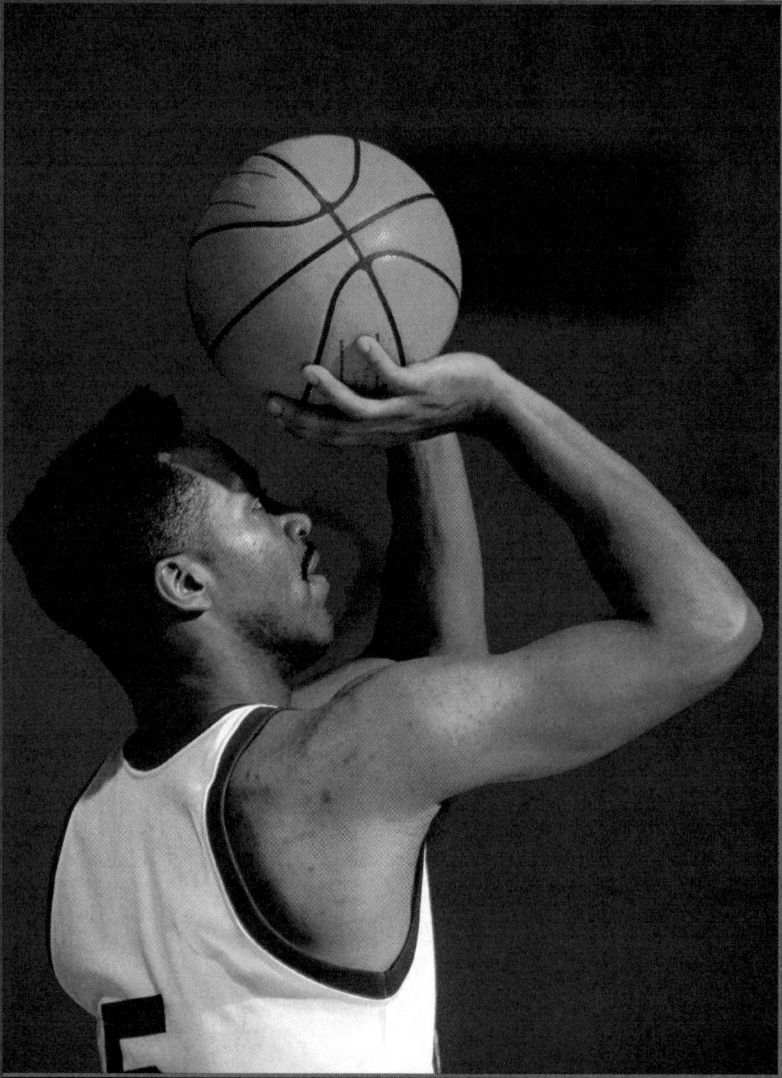

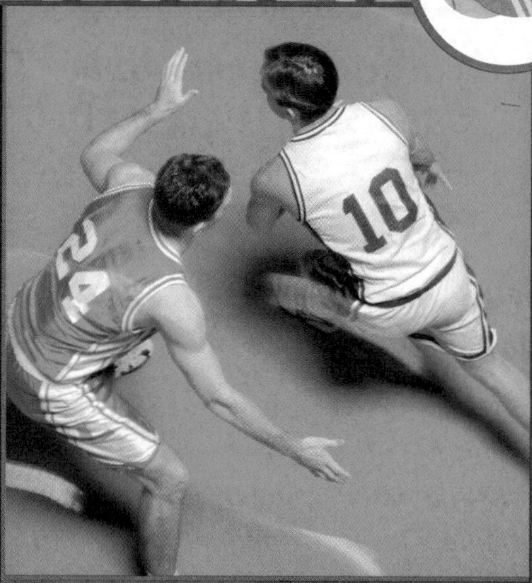
24
10

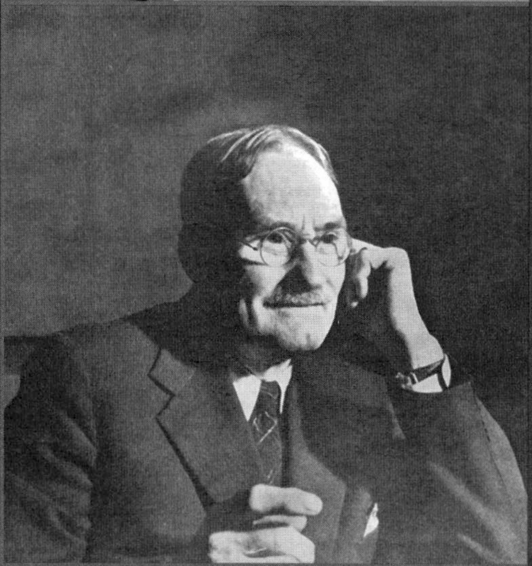

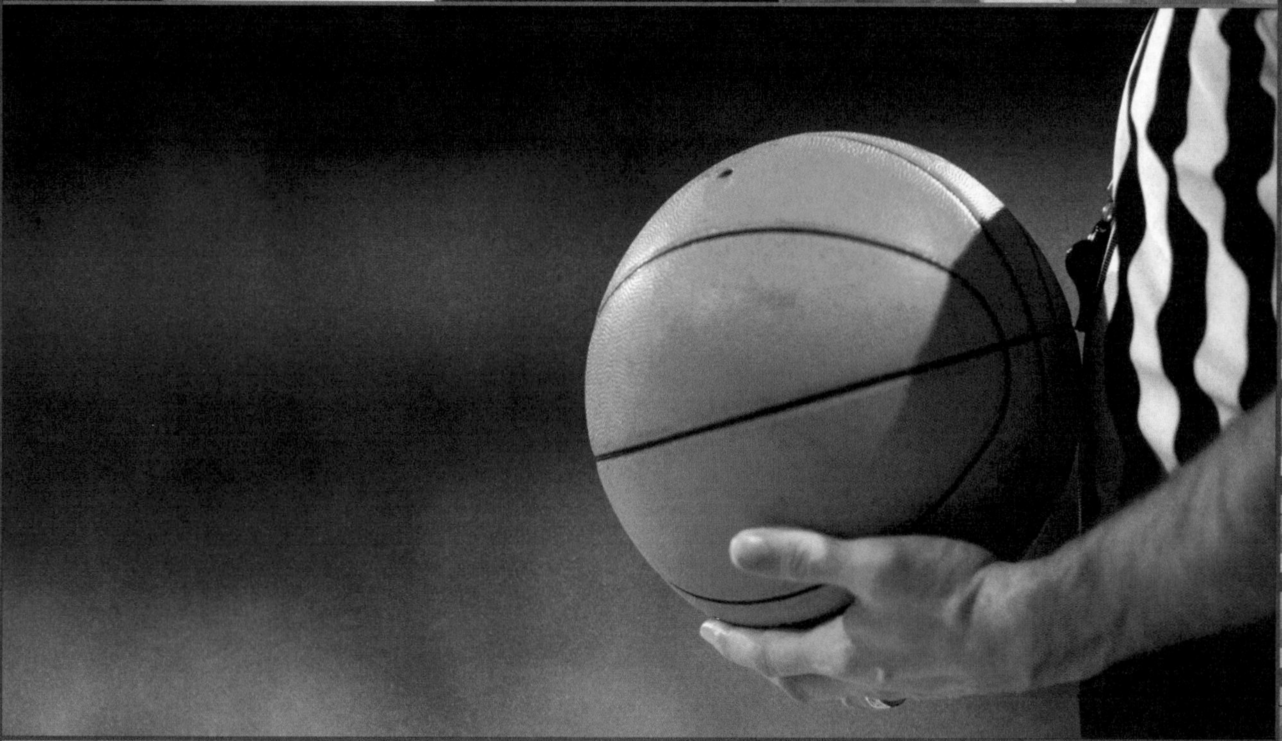

Literature Link

Excerpt from *Peanut Butter Friends in a Chop Suey World* by Deb Brammer

A JourneyForth book from BJU Press

Dear Dawn,

How are you? I miss you! I've been in Taiwan for less than two weeks, but so much has happened already.

First of all, this necklace is for you to remember me by. I bought it at the market all by myself in Chinese! I wish you could see the market. It looks like one huge garage sale. You can buy anything there. Well, not chocolate chips or peanut butter, but you can buy them at special stores. They just cost a lot more. Taiwan has all kinds of fruits that I've never even heard of. I didn't know what half of the food at the market was.

It's really different here. You know how I told you I thought Taiwan would be a lot like California? Big cities and lots of people? Well, the cities are big, but not in the same way. I can't explain it. Everything is just so different from America.

I think I'll learn a lot here. I can see how Chinese people live, and I'm going to learn to speak their language. I don't know much so far, but I'm just getting started. I've spoken to several Chinese people. You wouldn't believe how brave I've been.

Of course I don't like ALL of the differences. Some things aren't as fun here. But I keep reminding myself that I'm not here to have fun. Missionaries win souls, and there's plenty of them to win. Amy Carmichael was brave and I will be too. Really.

Don't worry about me. I already have a few friends, but you'll always be my best friend.

Next time I'll tell you about my school and the church and our neighborhood. Write soon.

Your best friend forever,

Amy Carmichael Kramer

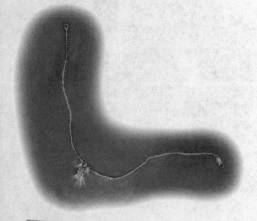

Comparing & Contrasting

Name _____

Comparing is telling how two things are *alike*.
Contrasting is telling how they are *different*.

How are a rose and a daisy alike? How are the two flowers different? An essay that compares and contrasts explains both the similarities and the differences between two people, places, or things.

Here is a paragraph from a compare-contrast essay. Does it compare or contrast?

> My twin sisters, Audrey and Amber, look very much alike. They both have curly, brown hair and blue eyes. They are also exactly the same height. They both wear glasses, and they both have braces on their teeth. Sometimes they even dress alike. Almost everyone has trouble telling them apart.

Here is the next paragraph in the essay about the twins. Does it compare or contrast?

The first paragraph **compares** the twins. It describes how they are *alike* in their looks. The second paragraph **contrasts** the twins. It describes how they are *different* in their personalities.

> Even though Audrey and Amber look alike, their personalities are very different. Audrey is daring and loves water sports. She likes people, and she is not afraid to try new things. She is always making us laugh. In contrast, Amber is more of a bookworm. She is quieter than Audrey and more serious, but she likes to laugh at Audrey's jokes. She loves babies and animals, and she is very good at tennis.

This **Venn diagram** shows the likenesses and differences between the twins. Each oval in a Venn diagram represents one of the two subjects being compared and contrasted. The two outside sections of the diagram list the differences between the two subjects. The inside section, the part where the ovals overlap, lists the likenesses.

Audrey

daring
loves water sports
likes people
tries new things
makes us laugh

blue eyes
height
curly, brown hair
braces
glasses
dress alike

Amber

bookworm
quiet, serious
loves babies and animals
good at tennis

Comparing & Contrasting

Independent Practice

This T-chart gives details about horses and donkeys.

Horses	Donkeys
short ears	long ears
carry loads	short mane
good for riding	carry loads
neighing sounds	braying sounds
live in herds	good for riding
long mane	live in herds
Bible talks about them	Bible talks about them

▶**Fill in the Venn diagram with the information from the T-chart.**

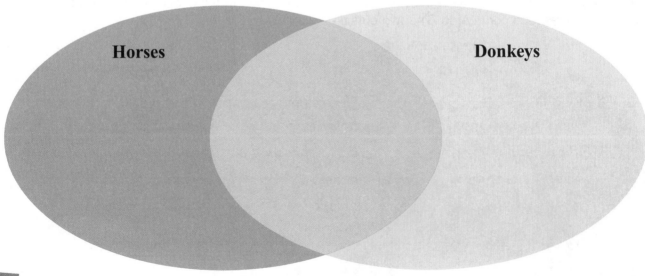

Horses

Donkeys

Parts of a Compare-Contrast Essay

Name _____

Jasmine wrote an essay that compared and contrasted two musical instruments. Jasmine's essay has four paragraphs. Here is her final draft.

The first paragraph, the **introduction,** begins the essay. It tells what the essay is going to be about and leads into the main part of the essay.

The second paragraph begins the main part of the essay. It **compares** the two instruments, telling how they are alike.

The third paragraph **contrasts** the two instruments. It tells how they are different.

The fourth paragraph, the **conclusion,** ends the essay. It sums up how the writer feels about both instruments.

The Piano and the Organ

At our house we have a piano and an organ. I can play both of them a little bit. They look similar, but they have a lot of differences.

The piano and the organ have some likenesses. They both have keyboards with black and white keys. You play them both by pressing these keys to get different notes. They both also have a pedal that changes their volume. Both the piano and the organ are often used in churches.

Pianos and organs have a lot in common, but they are very different instruments. The organ is electric, and it must be plugged in and turned on before you can play it. However, the piano does not need to be plugged in. You can just sit down and play it. Our organ has two short rows of keys, but our piano has only one long row. The organ has stops that make it sound like many different types of instruments like bells or flutes. In contrast, the piano has only one type of sound. The organ has many pedals that play different bass notes. But our piano has only three pedals, and they do not play notes.

I'm glad we have both a piano and an organ. I like the way both of them sound. Even though the piano is easier for me to play, I enjoy trying to play the organ sometimes too.

▶**Underline the topic sentence in each paragraph.**

Parts of a Compare-Contrast Essay

Guided Practice

▶ Read the essay. Label the parts of the essay.

A. comparing
B. contrasting
C. introduction
D. conclusion

1. ◯

2. ◯

3. ◯

4. ◯

Math and English

We study several different subjects each day at school. Two of the subjects we are studying are math and English. We have noticed some similarities but also some differences between these two subjects.

Math and English are similar in some ways. We have both of these subjects in the morning after recess. Both of them have a story that we listen to at the beginning of a unit. We do worktext pages for both subjects. Similarly, we do writing for both subjects. In English, we write stories, poems, and essays. In math, our teacher has us keep a journal about what we are learning every week. We also use the computer for both subjects.

But there are many differences between math and English. In math we study numbers, but in English we study words and sentences. In math we sometimes get to use calculators, but we do not need those for English. Knowing math helps us when we're counting, buying something, or slicing a pie. On the other hand, English helps us when we're reading books, writing letters, or giving oral reports in class.

We are glad God allows us to study both math and English. Some of us like one subject more than the other, but both subjects are interesting and important to learn.

© 2004 BJU Press. Reproduction prohibited.

English 4, Chapter 6, Lesson 52

Using Comparing & Contrasting Words

Name _____

In her essay, Jasmine used comparing and contrasting words to keep the points in her essay connected. Here are some examples of comparing and contrasting words.

Notice that a comma follows most of these words or phrases when they are written at the beginning of a sentence.

Comparing Words	Contrasting Words
also both like similarly in the same way	but however in contrast even though on the other hand

The paragraphs below do not include any comparing or contrasting words. The ideas seem disconnected.

www.freeimages.co.uk

▶ **Use proofreading marks to add comparing or contrasting words to make the paragraphs clearer.**

England and Scotland are alike in many ways. They are part of the United Kingdom, and they are on the same land mass. People in England and Scotland speak English, and they use the same money system. England and Scotland have big cities and beautiful countrysides.

England and Scotland have some differences. England's official church is Anglican. Scotland's official church is Presbyterian. England is famous for the sport of cricket. Scotland is known for developing the game of golf. Some of the foods that are popular in England are different from the foods that Scottish people eat.

Revising & Proofreading Together

Name

Adding more comparing and contrasting words is just one thing you may need to work on during the revising stage. Here is a checklist for you to use as you revise the class compare-contrast essay.

▶ **Revise and proofread the class essay you drafted with your teacher in Lesson 52. Use the *Revising Checklist* as you revise the class essay.**

Revising Checklist

- ☐ 1. Our essay compares two things.
- ☐ 2. Our essay contrasts two things.
- ☐ 3. Our essay has an introduction that leads into the main part of the essay.
- ☐ 4. Our essay gives just enough details in the comparing paragraph—not too many and not too few.
- ☐ 5. Our essay gives just enough details in the contrasting paragraph—not too many and not too few.
- ☐ 6. Our essay uses comparing and contrasting words.
- ☐ 7. Our essay has a conclusion that sums up the main part of the essay.

▶ **Use the *Proofreading Checklist* as you proofread the class essay. Use proofreading marks to mark the mistakes.**

Proofreading Checklist

- ☐ 1. We used correct verb forms.
- ☐ 2. We indented the first line of each paragraph.
- ☐ 3. We put a capital letter at the beginning of each sentence.
- ☐ 4. We put a punctuation mark at the end of each sentence.
- ☐ 5. We used correct punctuation within sentences.
- ☐ 6. We looked for misspelled words.

Proofreading Marks

∧∨ Add
ℓ Delete
≡ Capital letter
/ Lowercase
◯→ Move

English 4, Chapter 6, Lesson 53

Compare-Contrast Essay: Planning with a T-Chart

Name

● Jasmine began planning her essay by listing details about the piano and organ on a T-chart.

Piano	Organ
Black and white keys	Two short keyboards
Press keys to play	Black and white keys
One long keyboard	Press keys to play
Doesn't plug in	Plugs in
Three pedals	Turns on
Pedal changes volume	Many pedals
Pedals don't play notes	Pedals play notes
One type of sound	Pedal changes volume
Used in churches	Stops make it play many sounds
	Used in churches

● After marking the details that were similar on her chart, Jasmine made this Venn diagram to plan her compare-contrast essay.

Piano
Doesn't plug in
One long keyboard
One type of sound
Three pedals, do not play notes

Black and white keys
Press keys to play
Pedal changes volume
Used in churches

Organ
Plugs in and turns on
Two short keyboards
Stops make it play many sounds
Many pedals that play notes

Compare-Contrast Essay: Planning with a T-Chart

Name

What two things will you compare and contrast in your essay? Remember to choose two people, places, or things that are different but have some things in common.

Possible Ideas
- two of your aunts
- a school morning and a Saturday morning
- two of your uncles
- a bicycle and a motorcycle
- two kinds of fruit
- your watch and an alarm clock
- two kinds of storms
- your front yard and your neighbor's front yard
- two museums you have visited
- two cities you have visited
- two holidays
- two kinds of art

▶Write your two subjects as the headings on the T-chart. List details about each subject on the chart. Remember to include likenesses *and* differences.

▶Use this Venn diagram to organize the details from your T-chart.

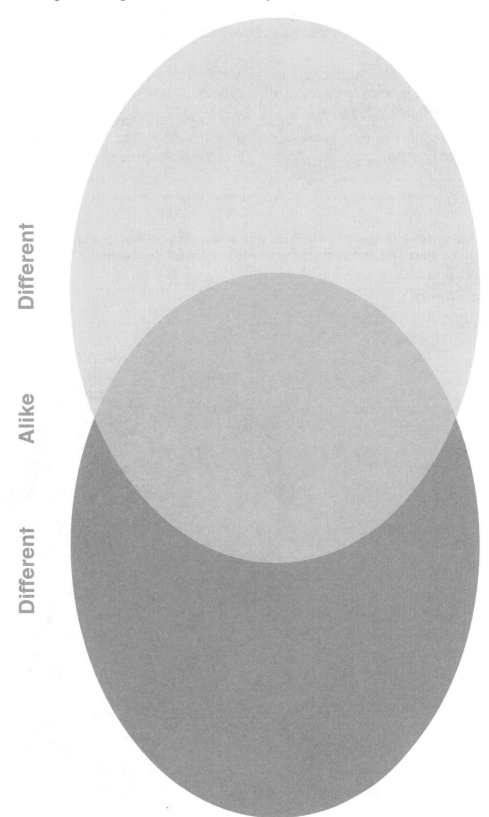

Different

Alike

Different

▶Save your Venn diagram for use in Lesson 55.

Compare-Contrast Essay: Drafting

After Jasmine completed the planning stage, she used her Venn diagram to draft her essay. The essay you write should have four paragraphs.

The first paragraph is the introduction. It tells what the essay is going to be about. It leads into the main part of the essay.

The second paragraph compares the two subjects. It tells how they are alike.

The third paragraph contrasts the two subjects. It tells how they are different.

The fourth paragraph is the conclusion. It ends the essay. The conclusion sums up how the writer feels about both subjects.

▶ **Use your Venn diagram from page 109 to draft your essay on your own paper. Remember to use comparing and contrasting words to connect your details.**

Comparing Words

also
both
like
similarly
in the same way

Contrasting Words

but
however
in contrast
even though
on the other hand

Compare-Contrast Essay: Revising

Jasmine read aloud the rough draft of her essay to Erin. Erin asked her some questions.

- "Do you think the introduction is long enough? It doesn't tell that you're going to compare and contrast the piano and the organ."

- "The contrasting paragraph didn't use very many contrasting words. Do you think you should add some more?"

- "What other kinds of instruments can the organ sound like when you use the stops?"

After talking with Erin, Jasmine revised her essay. Here is her rough draft with the revisions marked on it. What other change did she make?

Jasmine added a sentence to lead into the main part of the essay.

She deleted a detail that she had already told in the introduction.

She added contrasting words to the third paragraph.

The Piano and the Organ

At our house we have a piano and an organ. I
They look similar but they have a lot of differences.
can play both of them a little bit.

The piano and the organ have some likenesses.
~~They are both in our house.~~ They both have

keyboards with black and white keys. You play them

both by pressing these keys to get diffrent notes.

They both also have a pedal that changes the

volume. Both the piano and the organ is often used

in churches.
have a lot in common, but they
Pianos and organs are very diffrent instruments.

The organ is elektric, and it must be plugged in and
However,
turned on before you can play it. The piano does

not need to be plugged in. You can just sit down

and play it. Our organ has two short rows of keys,

Compare-Contrast Essay: Revising

Name _____

> **She added a detail about the different sounds an organ can make.**

but our piano has only one long row. The organ

has stops that make it sound like many different

like bells or flutes   In contrast,

types of instruments. The piano has only one type

of sound. The organ has many pedals that play

different bass notes. But our piano has only

three pedals, and they do not play notes.

> **She added contrasting words, and then combined two sentences.**

    I m glad we have both a piano and an organ.

Even though

I like the way both of them sound. The piano is

easier for me to play I enjoy trying to play the

organ sometimes too.

▶ **Use the *Revising Checklist* to revise your essay. Use proofreading marks to mark your changes.**

Revising Checklist

☐ 1. The essay compares two things.

☐ 2. The essay contrasts two things.

☐ 3. The essay has an introduction that leads into the main part of the essay.

☐ 4. The essay gives just enough details in the comparing paragraph—not too many and not too few.

☐ 5. The essay gives just enough details in the contrasting paragraph—not too many and not too few.

☐ 6. The essay uses comparing and contrasting words.

☐ 7. The essay has a conclusion that sums up the main part of the essay.

Proofreading Marks

∧∨ Add

Delete

≡ Capital letter

/ Lowercase

⟳→ Move

▶ **Save your revised copy for use in Lesson 57.**

Compare-Contrast
Essay: Proofreading

Name

After Jasmine finished revising her essay, she proofread it, using the checklist on the next page. She read the essay six times, looking for one type of mistake each time. After she finished each reading, she put a check beside that item on the checklist.

What mistakes did Jasmine find in her essay? What proofreading marks did she use to mark her mistakes?

The Piano and the Organ

At our house we have a piano and an organ. I can play both of them a little bit. They look similar ˄, but they have a lot of differences.

The piano and the organ have some likenesses. They both have keyboards with black and white keys. You play them both by pressing these keys to get *different* ~~diffrent~~ ˄ notes. They both also have a pedal that changes the volume. Both the piano and the organ ~~is~~ *are* ˄ often used in churches.

Pianos and organs have a lot in common, but they are very *different* ~~diffrent~~ ˄ instruments. The organ is ~~elektric~~ *electric* ˄, and it must be plugged in and turned on before you can play it. However, the piano does not need to be plugged in. You can just sit down and play it. Our organ has two short rows of keys, but our piano has only one long row.

The organ has stops that make it sound like many different types of instruments like bells or flutes. In contrast, the piano has only one type of sound. The organ has many pedals that play different bass notes. But our piano has only three pedals, and they do not play notes.

I'm glad we have both a piano and an organ. I like the way both of them sound. Even though the piano is easier for me to play, I enjoy trying to play the organ sometimes too.

▶ Use the *Proofreading Checklist* as you proofread your essay. Use proofreading marks to mark the mistakes.

Proofreading Checklist

- [ ] 1. I used correct contractions and verb forms.
- [ ] 2. I indented the first line of each paragraph.
- [ ] 3. I put a capital letter at the beginning of each sentence.
- [ ] 4. I put a punctuation mark at the end of each sentence.
- [ ] 5. I used correct punctuation within sentences.
- [ ] 6. I looked for misspelled words.

Proofreading Marks

∧∨	Add
℮	Delete
≡	Capital letter
/	Lowercase
⟲→	Move

▶ Save your proofread copy to publish in Lesson 58.

Name _____

A. Write the letter of the correct answer in the blank.

_____ 1. Telling how two things are alike

_____ 2. Telling how two things are different

_____ 3. Leads into the main part of the essay

_____ 4. *Similarly*

_____ 5. Sums up the main part of the essay

_____ 6. *However*

A. conclusion

B. comparing

C. comparing word

D. contrasting

E. contrasting word

F. introduction

**B. This T-chart gives details about sea turtles and tortoises.
Fill in the Venn diagram with the information from the chart.**

Sea Turtle	Tortoise
reptile	reptile
has webbed feet	lives on land
lives in the sea	has a hard shell
has a hard shell	feet are not webbed
streamlined shell	domed shell
fast swimmer	vertebrate
vertebrate	slow walker

Sea Turtle   **Tortoise**

C. Read the essay. Fill in the circle next to each correct answer.

Sea Turtles and Tortoises

You may have seen a sea turtle or a tortoise at the zoo. How would you tell the difference. They are very much alike, but they have some differences.

Tortoises and sea turtles have many things in common. Since they are reptiles. They are cold-blooded. They are vertebrates. They have a skeleton inside, and they have a hard outer shell.

Even though tortoises and sea turtles look similar, they are different in some ways. Sea turtles live in the sea, but tortoises live on the land. Sea turtles are fast swimmers. In contrast, tortoises walk slowly. Sea turtles have webbed feet. However, tortoises do not. They have different shells too.

There is also another kind of turtle called the terrapin.

7. Which paragraph contains no comparing or contrasting words?

   ○ the second paragraph
   ○ the third paragraph

8. The third paragraph does not include enough detail about _____.

   ○ the shells of the sea turtle and the tortoise
   ○ the feet of the sea turtle and the tortoise

9. What is the problem with the conclusion?

   ○ It does not come last.
   ○ It is too long.
   ○ It does not sum up the essay.

10. The first paragraph contains a mistake in _____.

    ○ capitalization
    ○ punctuation
    ○ spelling

11. The second paragraph contains a _____.

    ○ fragment
    ○ spelling error
    ○ capitalization mistake

diamondback
terrapin

Cumulative Review

A. Write *S* if the sentence is a simple sentence. Write *C* if the sentence is a compound sentence. Then, add any commas that are missing using ⌃.
(Chapter 1)

_____ 1. It is raining outside and the sky is gray.

_____ 2. The creek will probably overflow and flood our yard.

_____ 3. I can wear a raincoat with a hood or I can use my umbrella.

_____ 4. We want to play outside today but the ground is too wet.

_____ 5. I hope we get to play outside tomorrow morning.

_____ 6. Do you like sunny days or rainy days better?

B. Delete the fragments using —͡ . *(Chapter 1)*

7. Shone brightly all day long.

8. The rain fell gently.

9. Puddles in the street.

10. We put on our boots.

11. Mom gave us new umbrellas.

12. Walked in the rain.

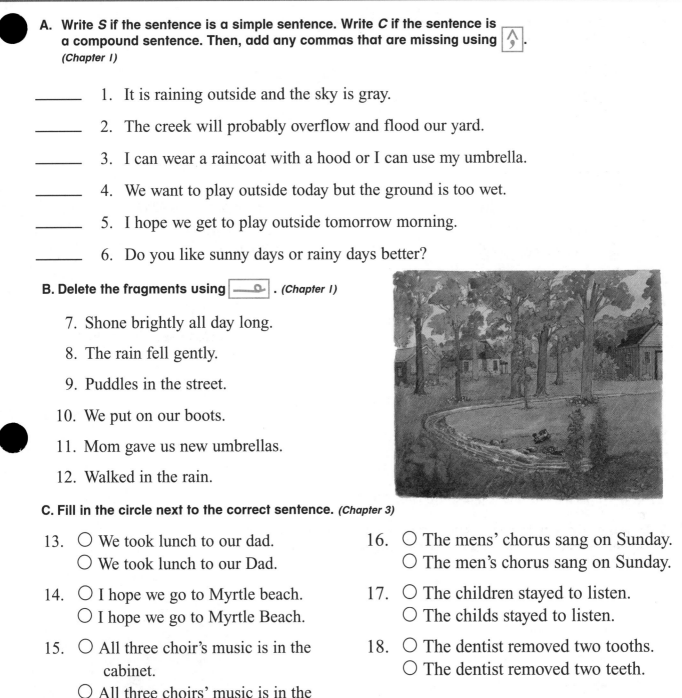

C. Fill in the circle next to the correct sentence. *(Chapter 3)*

13. ○ We took lunch to our dad.
    ○ We took lunch to our Dad.

14. ○ I hope we go to Myrtle beach.
    ○ I hope we go to Myrtle Beach.

15. ○ All three choir's music is in the cabinet.
    ○ All three choirs' music is in the cabinet.

16. ○ The mens' chorus sang on Sunday.
    ○ The men's chorus sang on Sunday.

17. ○ The children stayed to listen.
    ○ The childs stayed to listen.

18. ○ The dentist removed two tooths.
    ○ The dentist removed two teeth.

Cumulative Review

Name

D. Fill in the circle next to the words that contain a mistake in punctuation. *(Chapter 4)*

19. ○ Dear Grandma
    ○ June 15, 1785
    ○ Love,

20. ○ Your friend,
    ○ Dear Mr. Brown,
    ○ Daisytown PA 15427

E. Fill in the circle next to the words that contain a mistake in capitalization. *(Chapter 4)*

21. ○ 298 Woodland Rd.
    ○ dear Aunt Betty,
    ○ Your niece,

22. ○ Streetsboro, oh 44241
    ○ April 20, 1807
    ○ 888 Chalker St.

F. Underline twice the correct verb in each sentence. *(Chapter 5)*

23. Amy Carmichael (was, were) a missionary in India.

24. She started an orphanage for children who (was, were) rescued from the temples.

25. I (is, am) reading a book about Amy Carmichael.

26. Melissa (is, are) reading the same book.

27. We (is, are) going to write a book report about Amy Carmichael.

28. Melissa's parents (is, are) missionaries.

God uses Christians to rescue the perishing.

Luke 14:23   Matt. 4:19

G. Underline the simple subject once. Underline the complete verb twice. Do not include words that come between the helping verb and the main verb. *(Chapter 5)*

29. Naomi could not come to school.

30. She has caught the flu.

31. You could take flowers to her.

32. The sickness has kept her indoors.

33. Naomi is usually playing outside.

Parts of a Book

Books have different parts to help you find information quickly. The **title page**, the **copyright page**, and the **table of contents** are located in the front of the book.

The *title page* of a book tells
- the name of the book.
- the author of the book.
- the name of the company that published the book.
- the city or cities where the publisher is located.

The *copyright page* tells the year the book was published. This page may list several dates because the book may have been revised more than once.

TRAVELING IN BRAZIL

VLADEMIR SALAZAR

MOORE PUBLISHING
DENVER, COLORADO

Traveling in Brazil

© 2003 Moore Publishing
Denver, Colorado

Printed in the United States of America
All Rights Reserved

15 14 13 12 11 10 9 8 7 6 5 4 3 2 1

A *table of contents* usually tells
- the name and number of each chapter or division.
- the page on which each chapter or division begins.

Traveling in South America
Contents

Chapter	Page
1 Places to Visit	7
2 Where to Stay	51
3 Where to Eat	
4 Useful Portug... Words	
5 Maps and Gu...	

The **index** and **glossary** are located at the back of the book.

The *glossary*
- lists and defines words from the book in alphabetical order.
- uses guide words to help the reader locate words quickly.
- sometimes gives the pronunciation of words.

The *index*
- lists important topics in the book in alphabetical order.
- gives the page number on which each topic begins.

Equator—The imaginary line that divides the earth into the Northern and Southern Hemispheres

Rainforest—Dense forest found in tropical or temperate areas with heavy precipitation

Subsistence farming—Agriculture that supplies only the basic food and material needs of the farmer and his family

Village—A small group of dwellings in an isolated a...

Parts of a Book

Name

▶ Guided Practice

▶**Fill in the circle next to the correct answer.**

1. Where would you look to find the name of the author of a book?
   ○ index   ○ glossary   ○ title page

2. Where would you look to find the meaning of a word found in a book?
   ○ index   ○ glossary   ○ table of contents

3. Where would you look to find the year a book was published?
   ○ title page   ○ table of contents   ○ copyright page

4. Where would you look to find on which page Chapter 3 begins?
   ○ table of contents ○ index   ○ glossary

Iguaçu Falls bordering Brazil

5. Where would you look in an English grammar book to find the page number for information about using commas?
   ○ index   ○ glossary   ○ table of contents

▶**Use this table of contents and partial index to answer the questions. Fill in the circle next to the correct answer.**

6. Which chapter would probably tell you ways South Americans cook bananas?
   ○ 2   ○ 3   ○ 4

7. On which page does the chapter begin that gives advice to South American visitors?
   ○ 3   ○ 14   ○ 46

8. On which page does the chapter begin that tells a traveler how to communicate with South Americans?
   ○ 2   ○ 14   ○ 26

9. Which chapter gives a traveler ideas of beautiful sites to visit in South America?
   ○ 1   ○ 3   ○ 4

10. On which page would you find out how hot it gets in Manaus?
    ○ 1   ○ 3   ○ 5

11. On which page would you find information about the Portuguese language?
    ○ 2   ○ 14   ○ 15

12. Which chapter contains information about the Portuguese language?
    ○ 1   ○ 2   ○ 5

Traveling in South America
Contents

The Dictionary

The dictionary is a book that lists words in alphabetical order. The definitions give the meanings of the words.

Two **guide words** at the top of the page tell the first and last word found on that page. All of the other words on the page come between these two words in alphabetical order.

Each word defined in the dictionary is called an **entry word**. These words are usually printed in dark type and are divided into **syllables**.

When an entry word has more than one meaning, the definitions are numbered.

Each entry includes the **part of speech**. The part of speech is sometimes written as an initial or an abbreviation.

Sample sentences or **phrases** follow some definitions. These are provided to help the reader understand the definition and know how the entry may be used in a sentence. Sample sentences or phrases are printed in italics.

The **pronunciation** follows the entry word. Use the pronunciation key to learn how to pronounce the word.

---

mane   **man-made**

---

mane |mān| —*noun, plural* **manes** The long hair that grows from the neck and head of certain animals. *Horses and male lions have manes.*

man·ger |mān′ jər| — *noun, plural* **mangers** An open box or trough to hold food for horses or cattle.

man·go |măng′ gō| — *noun, plural* **mangoes** or **mangos** A tropical fruit with a smooth rind and sweet, juicy, yellow-orange flesh.

man·grove |măn′ grōv′| —*noun, plural* **mangroves** A tropical tree or shrub that has many roots growing above the ground.

man·hood |măn′ hŏŏd′| —*noun* 1. The time or condition of being a grown man: *He plans to do many things when he reaches manhood.* 2. The qualities that are expected of an adult man; courage and strength: *The young Indian braves had to prove their manhood by bringing home deer for food.*

man-made |măn′ mād′| —*adjective* Created or manufactured by people; artificial: *Nylon is a man-made fiber.*

A **pronunciation key** shows symbols and sample words as a guide to correctly pronounce entry words.

ă pat	ĕ pet	î fierce	oi oil	ŭ cut	ə ago, item,
ā pay	ē be	ŏ pot	ŏŏ book	û fur	pencil, atom,
â care	ĭ pit	ō go	ōō boot	*th* the	circus
ä father	ī pie	ô paw,	yōō abuse	th thin	ər butter
		for	ou out	hw which	
				zh vision	

The Dictionary

Guided Practice

preparation/prevail

prep·a·ra·tion |prĕp′ ə rā′ shən| —*noun, plural* **preparations** 1. The action of preparing or getting ready: *The preparation of dinner for six people takes time.* 2. An action necessary in getting ready for something: *They are making final preparations for the rocket launch.*

pre·pare |prĭ pâr′| —*verb* **prepared, preparing** 1. To get ready for some task or event: *Prepare the room for the party.* 2. To plan and make: *Prepare a book report.*

pre·school |prē′ skoōl′| —*adjective* Of or for a child before he or she enters elementary school.

pre·scribe |prĭ skrīb′| —*verb* **prescribed, prescribing** To order or advise the use of a drug, diet, or remedy: *The doctor prescribed rest in bed and lots of liquids for my illness.*

pre·scrip·tion |prĭ skrĭp′ shən| —*noun, plural* **prescriptions** A written instruction from a doctor telling what treatment or medicine a patient is to receive.

pres·ence |prĕz′ əns| —*noun* The fact or condition of being present: *My parents require my presence at the dinner table.*

pres·i·dent |prĕz′ ĭ dənt| —*noun, plural* **presidents** 1. **President** The chief executive of the United States. 2. The chief officer of a club, company, or university.

pre·tend |prĭ tĕnd′| —*verb* **pretended, pretending** 1. To put on a false show of: *He pretended illness.* 2. To make believe: *Pretend you are a tree.* 3. To make a claim that is not true: *He pretended to have done his homework.*

pret·zel |prĕt′ səl| —*noun, plural* **pretzels** A thin roll of dough baked in the form of a crisp knot or stick.

ă pat	ĕ pet	î fierce	oi oil	ŭ cut	ə ago, item,
ā pay	ē be	ŏ pot	oō book	û fur	pencil, atom,
â care	ĭ pit	ō go	oō boot	*th* the	circus
ä father	ī pie	ô paw, for	ou out	th thin	ər butter
				hw which	
				zh vision	

▶ **Fill in the circle next to the correct answer.**

1. Which word best completes this sentence? *The doctor will _____ medicine to treat my cold.*
   ○ prescribe   ○ pretend

2. The *e* in *prepare* sounds like the *e* in _____.
   ○ prescribe [prĭ skrīb′]
   ○ presence [prĕz′ əns]

3. What should you do to get ready for a big test?
   ○ prepare   ○ pretend

4. Which word could also be found on this dictionary page?
   ○ prestige   ○ predict

5. How would you spell the plural of *pretzel?*
   ○ pretzeles   ○ pretzels

6. Which definition of *president* is used in this sentence? *The president of the company lives nearby.*
   ○ 1   ○ 2

7. How would you spell the word that describes a child before he enters elementary school?
   ○ preskool   ○ preschool

8. How many syllables are in the word *preparation?*
   ○ 3   ○ 4

More About Dictionaries

Name _____

You can use the dictionary to help build your vocabulary. If an entry word has more than one meaning, the definitions in the entry are numbered.

Some words are spelled the same but became part of the English language from different origins. The dictionary enters each of these words separately. Notice the small raised numerals next to the two words spelled *mint*.

mint¹ |mĭnt| —*noun, plural* **mints** 1. A plant used for flavoring whose leaves have a strong, pleasant smell and taste: *Mother flavors iced tea with fresh mint.* 2. A piece of candy flavored with mint: *These mints have red and white stripes.*

mint² |mĭnt| —*noun, plural* **mints** 1. A place where coins are made by a government. 2. A large amount or supply: *Two thousand dollars is a mint of money.*
—*verb* **minted, minting** to make coins.
—*adjective* new, unused. *The old book was in mint condition.*

 ## Guided Practice

▶ **Write the number of the entry and the number of the definition for the correct meaning of *mint* in each sentence. The first one is done for you.**

Sample Sentence	Entry	Definition
1. I saw how pennies were made at the Denver <u>Mint</u>.	*2*	*1*
2. My aunt grows several varieties of <u>mint</u> in her garden.		
3. Mom gave me a <u>mint</u> to freshen my breath.		
4. That sports car must have cost a <u>mint</u>!		

▶ **Fill in the circle next to the correct part of speech for the word *mint* in each sentence.**

5. There was one pink *mint* left in the candy dish.
   ○ noun   ○ verb   ○ adjective

6. The antique car is in *mint* condition.
   ○ noun   ○ verb   ○ adjective

7. The workers *mint* pennies from copper.
   ○ noun   ○ verb   ○ adjective

The *D* underneath the year on the coin shows that it was minted in Denver.

The Denver Mint

More About Dictionaries

◉ Independent Practice

> **well**¹ |wĕl| —*noun, plural* **wells** 1. A deep hole dug or drilled into the ground to get water, oil, gas, or other materials. 2. A spring or fountain that serves as a natural source of water.

> **well**² |wĕl| —*adverb*—with skill. —*adjective* in good health, not sick. —*interjection* a word used to express surprise or sudden feelings.

▶ **Write the number of the entry and definition that match each sample sentence.**

Sample Sentence	Entry	Definition
1. Early settlers got their water from natural <u>wells</u>.		
2. He plays the French horn <u>well</u>.		
3. They drilled an oil <u>well</u> on our property.		
4. <u>Well</u>! We didn't expect this much company!		
5. We are thankful that we stayed <u>well</u> last winter.		

▶ **Fill in the circle next to the correct part of speech for the word *well* in each sentence.**

6. We must carry water from the creek because our *well* ran dry.
   ○ noun   ○ adjective   ○ adverb

7. Scott plays the violin very *well*.
   ○ noun   ○ adjective   ○ adverb

◔ Apply and Write

▶ **Read the definitions of *bill*. Write a sample sentence that could be used to help a reader better understand each definition.**

> **bill**¹ |bĭl| —*noun, plural* **bills** 1. A written statement saying how much money is to be paid for things that have been bought or work that has been done. 2. A piece of paper money worth a certain amount.

> **bill**² |bĭl| —*noun, plural* **bills** 1. The hard, projecting mouth part of a bird; a beak. 2. The projecting part of a hat that shades one's face from the sun.

bill¹ (Def. 1) _____

bill¹ (Def. 2) _____

bill² (Def. 1) _____

bill² (Def. 2) _____

Name

Periodicals and encyclopedias are two valuable sources of information.

A **periodical** is a written work that is published at regular times, or *periodically,* during a year. Some periodicals, such as newspapers, are published daily. Other periodicals, such as magazines, are published once a week or once a month.

Each new edition of a periodical is called an **issue.** The written parts are called **articles** and may be written by different authors.

Periodicals may focus on topics such as current events, news, or sports.

Similar periodicals are grouped together in a library. For example, magazines are grouped with magazines and newspapers with newspapers. Within each group, periodicals are arranged numerically by the date they were published. Your teacher or librarian can show you how to use the *Reader's Guide to Periodical Literature* to find an article on a specific topic in a magazine.

A	B	C to Ci	Ci to D	E	F	G	H to I	J	K	L	M	N to O	P	Q to R	S	T	U	V	W	X	Y to Z
1	2	3	4	5	6	7	8	9	10	11	12	13	14	15	16	17	18	19	20	21	22

The **encyclopedia** is a set of books that contain articles about important people, places, inventions, animals, and events in history. Each book is called a **volume.** Information in the encyclopedia is arranged in alphabetical order. Each volume is labeled with one or more letters. These letters tell you the beginning letter of the articles found in that volume.

To locate a subject in the encyclopedia, you must first think of a **keyword**—the subject that you want to find information about. Look for information about a person by using the person's last name as the keyword.

Guided Practice

▶ **Read the following questions. Underline the keyword you would use to find information in the encyclopedia volumes shown. Write the volume number of the encyclopedias in which you would locate the keyword(s).**

_____ 1. How many different kinds of parrots are there?

_____ 2. What do the flags of Chile and Uruguay look like?

_____ 3. What kind of money does Argentina use?

_____ 4. Which wildlife can be found in the Patanal?

▶ **Fill in the circle next to the correct answer.**

5. Which person would be listed first in an encyclopedia?
   ○ Martha Washington   ○ George Washington

Periodicals & Encyclopedias

Name _____

◉ Independent Practice

▶ **Fill in the circle next to the correct answer.**

1. Each new edition of a periodical is called a(n) _____.
   ○ article   ○ issue   ○ volume

2. In a library, periodicals are arranged _____.
   ○ alphabetically by the author's last name
   ○ numerically by the publication date

3. If you want to find information about an event that happened last week, you should look in a(n) _____.
   ○ newspaper   ○ encyclopedia   ○ biography

Rio de Janeiro, Brazil

A	B	C to Ci	Ci to D	E	F	G	H to I	J	K	L	M	N to O	P	Q to R	S	T	U	V	W	X	Y to Z
1	2	3	4	5	6	7	8	9	10	11	12	13	14	15	16	17	18	19	20	21	22

▶ **Underline the keyword(s) you would use to find information in the encyclopedia volumes shown. Write the number of the volume(s) in which you would locate the keyword(s).**

_____ 4. Where do mangoes and coconuts grow?

_____ 5. What is the climate along the Amazon River?

_____ 6. What is the population of Rio de Janeiro?

_____ 7. What is the main religion in Brazil?

_____ 8. How does a bumblebee fly?

_____ 9. Where is Suriname?

_____ 10. What is the geography like in Ecuador?

_____ 11. What is the name of the largest mountain range in Chile?

_____ 12. What are some interesting customs and holidays in Uruguay?

◉ Apply and Speak

▶ **With a partner, locate information in an encyclopedia about one of the topics in the activity above. Read one or two sentences to the class about your topic.**

The Library

Name

Libraries are a source of valuable information. Fiction, nonfiction, biographies, and reference materials are all types of information that may be found in separate sections at a library.

Sugarloaf Mountain, Brazil

Fiction books tell make-believe stories and are arranged in alphabetical order by the authors' last names.

Nonfiction books contain facts about real people, places, animals, things, and events. They are arranged by subject and are assigned *call numbers* to help locate the book on the shelf quickly.

Reference materials are used to find information quickly. A dictionary, an encyclopedia, a thesaurus, and an atlas (a book of different kinds of maps) are examples of reference materials.

Biographies contain the life stories of real people and are arranged in alphabetical order by the last name of the person about whom the book is written.

Libraries have **electronic catalogs** to help you find books. The electronic catalog is on a computer. You can search for a book by the author's last name, the book's title, or the subject of the book.

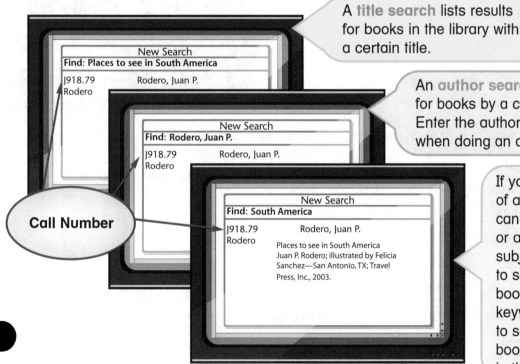

A **title search** lists results for books in the library with a certain title.

An **author search** lists results for books by a certain author. Enter the author's last name first when doing an author search.

If you don't know the title of a book or its author, you can do a **subject search** or a **keyword search**. A subject search allows you to search the library for books on a certain topic. A keyword search allows you to search the library for books with a certain word in their titles.

New Search
Find: Places to see in South America
J918.79 Rodero   Rodero, Juan P.

New Search
Find: Rodero, Juan P.
J918.79 Rodero   Rodero, Juan P.

New Search
Find: South America
J918.79 Rodero   Rodero, Juan P.
Places to see in South America Juan P. Rodero; illustrated by Felicia Sanchez—San Antonio, TX; Travel Press, Inc., 2003.

Call Number

The Library

▶ Guided Practice

▶ **Fill in the circle next to the best way to search for a particular book.**

1. You know the author's name but don't know the title of the book.
   ○ title   ○ author   ○ subject

2. You don't know the title of the book or the author's name.
   ○ title   ○ author   ○ subject

3. You know the title of the book but don't know the author's name.
   ○ title   ○ author   ○ subject

▶ **Match each description to the correct resource.**

_____ 4. Book of different kinds of maps

_____ 5. Dictionaries, encyclopedias, a thesaurus

_____ 6. Books that tell make-believe stories

_____ 7. Books that tell facts

_____ 8. Books that tell the life stories of real people

A. fiction

B. biographies

C. reference materials

D. nonfiction

E. atlas

▶ **Fill in the circle next to the subject you would search for to find a book about the following topics.**

9. How athletic shoes are made
   ○ feet   ○ shoes   ○ athletes

10. Birds in Brazil
    ○ Brazil   ○ nature   ○ toucans

11. Costumes clowns wear in a circus
    ○ parties   ○ hats   ○ clowns

▶ **Fill in the circle next to the type of search that would be best to find each book.**

12. a book by R. Labana about the way bananas grow
    ○ a subject search for "bananas"
    ○ an author search for "Labana, R."

13. a picture book called *Pedro's Little Sister*
    ○ a subject search for "little sister"
    ○ a title search for "Pedro's Little Sister"

14. several books about the history and culture of Brazil
    ○ a subject search for "Brazil history culture"
    ○ a title search for "Brazil"

The Atlas

Name

An **atlas** is a book of different kinds of maps. Some maps tell the location of countries and cities. Other maps show how many people live in a country, the kind of weather in a region, how much rain falls on a certain area of land, or the types of crops that are grown in different parts of the world.

Most maps include a **key** or **legend** that explains the meanings of special symbols used on the map. The **map scale** shows how to measure distances on a map.

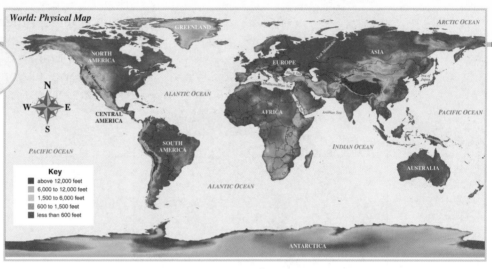

World: Physical Map

A **compass rose** tells directions.

Key
above 12,000 feet
6,000 to 12,000 feet
1,500 to 6,000 feet
600 to 1,500 feet
less than 600 feet

An **index** in the back of an atlas gives the page number on which to find cities and countries in the atlas. The locations are in alphabetical order and include the name of the country in which a city is located.

The Atlas

Name

▶ Guided Practice

South American Mining

Asunción, Paraguay 21
Bogota, Colombia 18
Brasília, Brazil 17
Buenos Aires, Argentina 15
Caracas, Venezuela 22
Cayenne, French Guiana . . . 19
Georgetown, Guyana 20
La Paz, Bolivia 16

KEY
- Gold
- Iron
- Aluminum
- Chromium
- Copper
- Manganese
- Zinc
- Petroleum

▶Use the atlas map and index to answer the questions.
Fill in the circle next to the correct answer.

1. In which country would you find gold mines?
   ○ Argentina   ○ Brazil   ○ Chile

2. In which country would you find petroleum wells?
   ○ Bolivia   ○ Peru   ○ Venezuela

3. In which country would you find copper mines?
   ○ Chile   ○ Venezuela   ○ Colombia

4. Which ocean does Brazil border?
   ○ Atlantic Ocean   ○ Indian Ocean   ○ Pacific Ocean

5. If the map scale is 1cm = 600 miles, what is the approximate distance between
   the capital cities of Chile and Uruguay?
   ○ 900 miles   ○ 1200 miles   ○ 1500 miles

6. On which page would you find La Paz, Bolivia?
   ○ 15   ○ 16   ○ 17

7. On which page would you find Brasília, Brazil?
   ○ 17   ○ 20   ○ 22

8. What continent does this index represent?
   ○ Asia   ○ Europe   ○ South America

Making an Outline

Name _____

An **outline** is a way to organize information. Outlines may be used in the planning stage of the Writing Process. Outlines may also be written to help you remember details that you hear, such as from a class or sermon.

Title

Main Idea

Supporting Details

Main Idea

Supporting Details

Main Idea

Supporting Details

Outlines Follow a Special Form

I. The main ideas
 A. Each main idea of an outline is followed by supporting details.
 B. Each main idea is labeled with a Roman numeral followed by a period.
 C. You must use at least two Roman numerals in any outline.

II. The supporting details
 A. Each supporting detail is labeled with a capital letter (beginning with *A*) followed by a period.
 B. Indent each detail to show that it belongs under the main idea.
 C. You should have at least two details under each main idea. If you have an *A,* you must have a *B*.

III. Other information
 A. The title of the outline is the topic.
 B. The main ideas and supporting details may be single words, groups of words, or sentences.
 C. The first word of each main idea or detail begins with a capital letter.

Here is an article about the Amazon River in Brazil. Notice how the main ideas and details from the article are organized in the outline.

The Great River of Brazil

The Amazon River is located in the Amazon Basin of central Brazil. It is the second longest river in the world. Only the Nile River is longer. The Amazon's muddy waters begin high in the Andes Mountains of Peru, flow across Brazil, and eventually spill into the Atlantic Ocean.

Many kinds of animals and insects live in and around the Amazon River. Flesh-eating piranhas are dangerous only when hungry. Anaconda snakes grow up to thirty feet long and dwell along the river-banks. Thousands of species of insects, including mosquitoes and water beetles, hover over the murky brown water.

The Amazon River
I. Facts about the river
 A. In Amazon Basin of Brazil
 B. Second longest river in world
 C. Begins in Peru and flows to Atlantic Ocean

II. Animals and insects around the river
 A. Dangerous piranhas
 B. Anacondas up to thirty feet long
 C. Swarming mosquitoes and water beetles

Making an Outline

Name _____

▶ Guided Practice

God's Gifts from the Land of South America

South America's rainforests provide many products used around the world. Rubber trees produce latex for making rubber and plastics. Tropical hardwood trees such as rosewood and mahogany are used for making furniture. Other trees produce dates, coconuts, bananas, and Brazil nuts for people to eat.

South America is also known for its wealth of minerals and jewels. Large mines containing valuable minerals such as copper, gold, lead, tin, and zinc are scattered across the continent. Venezuela is the continent's leading petroleum producer. Colombia is the world's leading supplier of emeralds. Peru is known for its important copper deposits.

▶ Read the article about agriculture in South America. Write the missing information for the outline.

South America's Resources

☐ Rainforests provide useful products.

A. _____

☐ Rosewood and mahogany for furniture

C. _____ for eating .

II. The land contains _____ .

A. Copper, zinc, lead, tin, and gold in mines

B. _____

☐ Emeralds in Colombia

D. _____

collecting latex from a rubber tree

▶ Fill in the circle next to the correct answer.

1. The title of the outline should be _____.
   ○ the name of the topic   ○ the main idea of the first paragraph

2. Use _____ to show the main ideas.
   ○ capital letters and periods   ○ Roman numerals and periods

Taking Notes

Taking notes when you are listening to a speaker or reading an article will help you remember the information. You may use these notes to study for a test or to write a report. Keep these guidelines in mind as you write.

Note-Taking Guidelines

1. Summarize main ideas by stating them in your own words. Do not copy sentences.

2. Write keywords to help you remember the information. Do not write complete sentences.

3. Carefully record the sources you use. Give proper credit to the authors.

4. Use quotation marks when you write the exact words of an author.

5. Take notes for only one main idea on each card.

6. Write the book's title and the page number at the bottom of the note card. (Include the volume number from an encyclopedia.)

This part of an article is from *Encyclopedia of the World,* Volume 14, page 216. The title of the article is "Peru," and it was written by Robin Williamston. Notice that each detail on the note card is about the main idea at the top of the card.

Peru's history is rich with a variety of musical traditions. Archaeologists have found drums, flutes, trumpets, and other musical artifacts in ancient tombs. The conquest by the Spanish and the arrival of missionaries affected the musical styles of Peru, making it a blending of cultures. Traditional Peruvian music includes drums, rattles, flutes, and small harps. Modern music also includes stringed instruments such as guitars, harps, violins, and mandolins as well as oboes and various kinds of flutes. Many religious ceremonies include both traditional and modern music.

Robin Williamston

Machu Picchu ruins
in Peru

Music in Peru

1. traditional music—drums, rattles, flutes, small harps
2. modern music—guitars, violins, oboes, flutes
3. religious ceremonies—modern and traditional music

Encyclopedia of the World. Vol. 14, p. 216.

Taking Notes

Name _____

 Guided Practice

▶ Read the following encyclopedia article taken from page 312 of *The Travel Encyclopedia,* Volume 17. Take notes on the card to help you remember the details. Write the information about the source.

Suriname

Suriname is a small country located on the northern coast of South America. Most Surinamese live near the coast because of the dense undergrowth of the jungles. Most of the roads in this country are also located near the coast. The jungles are only accessible by airplane or by boat. The heat and humidity are almost unbearable for most tourists.

Eli Smith

Facts About Suriname

▶ Read the following encyclopedia article taken from page 202 of *The Travel Encyclopedia,* Volume 1. Take notes on the card to help you remember the details. Write the information about the source.

Argentina

The government of Argentina maintains most communication services in the country. Its nationwide postal service is fairly dependable. About half of Argentina's residents have telephones in their homes. Most cities publish national and local newspapers. Buenos Aires, the capital, has several private publishing companies.

Yolanda Sanchez

Communicating in Argentina

How much can you remember from a sermon you heard last week? Would taking notes during the sermon help you better remember what you heard?

Name _____

A. Match each description to the correct resource.

_____ 1. Look at the ___ to find the name of the author of a book.

_____ 2. Look at the ___ to find which chapter in a math book tells about fractions.

_____ 3. Look at the ___ to find which page in a science book tells about frogs.

_____ 4. Look at the ___ to find the year a book was published.

_____ 5. Look at the book's ___ to find what a word means in a history book.

> A. glossary
> B. copyright page
> C. index
> D. title page
> E. table of contents

B. Fill in the circle next to each correct answer.

6. To find out who won the college basketball game last weekend, you should look in a(n) ____.
   ○ encyclopedia   ○ newspaper   ○ book about sports

7. To find out who the thirteenth vice-president of the United States was, you should look in a(n) ____.
   ○ dictionary   ○ magazine   ○ encyclopedia

8. To check the meanings of *membrane,* you should look in a(n) ____.
   ○ dictionary   ○ encyclopedia   ○ newspaper

9. To find the distance between two major cities, you should look in a(n) ____.
   ○ encyclopedia   ○ newspaper   ○ atlas

10. If you don't know the author or title of a book but want to find a book about tornadoes, how would you search for the book?
    ○ by subject   ○ by title   ○ by author

11. The books of an encyclopedia are called ____.
    ○ articles   ○ volumes   ○ issues

C. These definitions of *calf* need sample sentences. Write the number of the entry and definition that match each sample sentence.

calf[1] |kăf| —*noun, plural* **calves** 1. The young of cattle; a young cow or bull. 2. The young of certain other large animals, such as the whale or elephant. 3. Leather made from the skin of a calf; calfskin.

calf[2] |kăf| —*noun, plural* **calves** The fleshy back part of the leg between the knee and the ankle.

12. His new boots are made of *calf.*   Entry _____   Definition _____

13. An elephant *calf* was born at the zoo.   Entry _____   Definition _____

14. He cut his *calf* when he fell.   Entry _____   Definition _____

D. Use the table of contents and the partial index to answer the questions. Fill in each blank with the correct answer.

_____ 15. Which chapter would tell you how to say "please" and "thank you"?

_____ 16. On which page does the chapter begin that tells about the history of Bolivia?

_____ 17. On which pages would you find information about Bolivia's money called the *boliviano?*

_____ 18. On which page would you find information about the population of one of Bolivia's capital cities La Paz?

_____ 19. Which chapter would tell about the climate in La Paz?

Traveling in Bolivia
Contents

E. Read this paragraph from an article about Bolivia. Fill in the circles next to the four outline parts that are *not* correct.

Bolivia

Bolivia offers the adventuresome tourist a variety of interesting activities. Trekking through one of ten national parks is a popular excursion. Jungle tours allow the tourist to see densely forested areas from the comfort of a canoe. Many tourists enjoy hiking or skiing in the beautiful mountains. Fishing is a relaxing pastime for tourists who are less active.

Bolivia's weather is usually temperate. The temperatures vary greatly between day and night. The rainy season extends from November to March.

John Teeney

Bolivia

○ I. Activities in Bolivia
○   A. Trekking
○   B. Jungle tours
○   c. Mountains—hiking or skiing
○   D. Fishing

○ II Weather in Bolivia
○   A. Temperate climate
○   B. temperatures of night and day drastically change
○   C. Rainy season—November to March
○   D. A variety of food to eat

F. The following details are true. Which three details support the main point about animal life in South America? Fill in the circles next to each correct answer.

○ Anacondas and piranhas live in rivers.
○ Tapirs and tigers live in rain forests.

○ There is snow year-round in the Andes Mountains.
○ Toucans and parrots live in trees.

Cumulative Review

A. Draw a line between the complete subject and the complete predicate. Diagram the simple subject and the simple predicate. *(Chapter 1)*

1. The gymnast won three medals.

   _____|_____

2. Her father gave her flowers.

   _____|_____

3. The crowd cheered loudly.

   _____|_____

4. She will compete again next year.

   _____|_____

B. Write *C* if the underlined word is a common noun and *P* if it is a proper noun. *(Chapter 3)*

_____ 5. We went to Grandma's house on <u>Sunday</u>.

_____ 6. My <u>grandma</u> bakes the best biscuits in the world!

_____ 7. We go to her house every Sunday after <u>church</u>.

_____ 8. She lives next door to my teacher <u>Mrs. Gonzalez</u>.

_____ 9. They live on <u>Spring Street</u>.

C. Fill in the circle next to each correct sentence. *(Chapter 3)*

10. ○ I earned a Girl Scout badge for camping.
    ○ I earned a girl Scout badge for camping.

11. ○ My favorite team is the Chicago Bulls.
    ○ My favorite team is the Chicago bulls.

12. ○ I wrote a report about President Lincoln.
    ○ I wrote a report about president Lincoln.

13. ○ The Millers go camping in the Mountains every year.
    ○ The Millers go camping in the mountains every year.

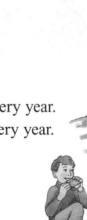

Cumulative Review

D. Write the letter of the correct stage of the Writing Process to complete each sentence. *(Chapter 2)*

A. drafting	B. planning	C. proofreading	D. publishing	E. revising

_____ 14. In the _____ stage you choose your topic and the events or details to include.

_____ 15. In the _____ stage you write the first draft.

_____ 16. In the _____ stage you may add, delete, or change details to improve the writing.

_____ 17. In the _____ stage you check for correct spelling and punctuation.

_____ 18. In the _____ stage you write a final neat copy.

E. Underline the words that can form contractions. Write the contractions in the blanks. *(Chapter 5)*

19. That is the window that we accidentally broke. _____

20. Bryan says he will go tell the man who lives there. _____

21. The man will not be happy. _____

22. I am planning to offer my allowance to pay for it. _____

23. We are going to be sure this does not happen again! _____

F. Correct the double negative by deleting or replacing one of the underlined negatives. Write your new sentence. *(Chapter 5)*

24. Clayton <u>can't</u> <u>never</u> seem to hit a home run. _____

_____

25. Jordan <u>can't</u> find his glasses <u>nowhere</u>. _____

Chapter 7 Bridge
Sightseeing in South America

Excerpt from "Fremont's Frog Farm"
by Gail Fitzgerald and Susan W. Young
(from *Not So Very Long Ago,* BJU Press)

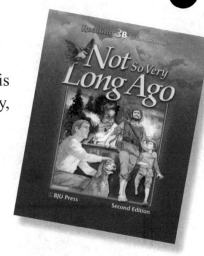

Monty paused in front of the Country Kitchen and studied his reflection in the big glass window. Balancing a large box in one hand, he tucked in his shirt with the other and then pushed open the door.

Thump, thump, thump. Monty clutched the box tightly as he wound his way among the tables of chattering people to the counter at the back. He climbed up onto a stool and waited until Mr. Murphy finished serving a stranger.

"Howdy, Mr. Murphy. I've heard that you've got the best restaurant in town."

Mr. Murphy laughed. "Thanks, Monty. I've got the only restaurant in town."

Monty was glad to see Mr. Murphy in good humor. He plunged into his speech. "Would you like to buy some frogs for your restaurant? Frog legs are delicious, delectable, and tasty. The frogs only cost twenty cents a piece. I have twenty-five with me today and can catch plenty more. If you want them, I can bring them right to your door every week. The fresher the better, you know."

Mr. Murphy shook his head. "I'm sorry, Monty, it just wouldn't work. Serving frog legs is a great idea and folks might like them, but my wife's the cook around here, and she hates frogs."

Monty looked down and kicked his toe against the counter.

"I'm sorry, kid." Mr. Murphy rubbed the counter with his cloth. "I'm sure you've got nice frogs. They sound lively enough. Maybe you could advertise in the paper. There are bound to be restaurants in other towns that would jump at a chance to sell frog legs." Mr. Murphy tipped back his head and laughed at his own joke.

"I guess I'll have to give it a try." Monty picked up his box. "Thanks anyway, Mr. Murphy."

Persuading

Name _____

Has anyone ever tried to convince you to try a new food? Has a friend ever tried to get you to like a certain sport or color of clothing as much as he does? **Persuading** is convincing someone else to do something or to agree with your opinion. In order to get someone else to agree with you, it is helpful to give good reasons for your opinion.

Emma wrote this paragraph to express an opinion. What is her opinion? What reasons does she give to support her opinion?

> I think we should all wear blue and red on the day of our spelling bee for several reasons. First, everyone would know what school we are from. We will be competing against other Christian schools in our area. Wearing our school colors would show the other students that we are from Martyn Academy. Second, we would be able to find each other easily when we all meet for lunch. But the best reason of all is that wearing blue and red would remind us to do our best. We should do our best for our school, but also for Jesus.

If you went to Emma's school, would you be convinced that you should wear blue and red to the spelling bee? Emma's opinion and reasons could be displayed like this:

Opinion: *I think we should wear blue and red to the spelling bee.*

Reason: *Everyone would know we are from Martyn Academy.*	**Reason:** *We would be able to find each other easily for lunch.*	**Reason:** *It would remind us to do our best for our school and for Jesus.*

Emma felt that her third reason was the strongest. When she wrote her paragraph, she saved her strongest reason to tell about last.

▶ Guided Practice

▶**Fill in the circle next to the stronger reason for the opinion.**

1. I think we should have class outside today.
   - ○ We could learn all about clouds, flowers, and trees.
   - ○ It is a nice day.

2. Everyone in my family should come to the play.
   - ○ It would be neat.
   - ○ They would all enjoy the funny plot.

Persuading

 Independent Practice

▶**Fill in the circle next to the stronger reason for the opinion.**

1. It is important for kids to take music lessons.
   ○ They might become famous.
   ○ They will develop skills that they can use for God.

God wants Christians to give cheerfully to others.

Eph. 4:28   II Cor. 9:7

2. Everyone should read a new book each month.
   ○ Books can teach us many things.
   ○ Books are fun to read if we don't want to do our homework.

3. I think we should take a field trip to a dairy farm.
   ○ It would be fun to ride there on the bus.
   ○ We could learn how we get our dairy products.

4. We should have more computers at our school.
   ○ They would look neat in our classroom.
   ○ More students could work on school projects at the same time.

5. Everyone should learn to play basketball.
   ○ Basketball is a fun way to get good exercise.
   ○ Basketball is the best sport.

 Apply and Write

▶**Write two strong reasons for each opinion.**

I think we should give some money to a missionary this Christmas.

1. _____

2. _____

Every family should have a pet.

1. _____

2. _____

A Book Review

A **book report** is written simply to tell someone about a book. You may give your opinion of the book in your report. However, a **book review** is written to persuade someone to feel the same way you do about a book. When you write a book review, you *always* give your opinion of the book, hoping to persuade the reader to agree with your opinion. If you liked the book, you hope that he will read it and like it too. If you didn't like the book, you hope to persuade him not to read it.

Here is a book review that Tristan wrote about the book *Summer of the Secret Cabin*.

Opinion

Reason 1

Reason 2

Recommendation

Summer of the Secret Cabin

Do you want to read a story about secrets, forgotten letters, and adventure? Then *Summer of the Secret Cabin* by Mason Hyde is a terrific book for you.

First, it is a very exciting book. Nick and Anthony find a deserted cabin in the mountains and decide to use it for a clubhouse. But soon they discover that a ring of smugglers is also using the cabin. One night the boys even get locked inside! Do you think they escape? Do the smugglers get caught? Read the book to find out.

Second, this is a book that will teach you important lessons. Nick has to learn a lesson about kindness when he meets an old man who needs his help. Anthony learns about forgiveness when his dog gets hurt in a fire in the cabin. Reading this book taught me how important it is to love others.

I would recommend this book to anyone who likes adventure. You won't have any trouble getting into the story, but you might have trouble putting it down!

Tristan included the following in his review:

- The title of the book
- The author of the book
- His opinion of the book
- Two good reasons for his opinion
- Specific examples to support his reasons
- A recommendation of the book to the reader

> **Did Tristan include any information about characters, setting, and plot in his book review? How did he work in this information?**

Planning a Book Review Together

Name

▶**Work with your teacher to complete this *Opinion Chart* for a review of a book that you read together.**

Title of the book: _____

Author of the book: _____

My Opinion of the Book

_____

_____

Reason 1	Reason 2
_____	_____
_____	_____
_____	_____

Examples from the Book	Examples from the Book
_____	_____
_____	_____
_____	_____
_____	_____
_____	_____
_____	_____

My Recommendation

_____

_____

Evaluating a Book

Name

▶**Think about the book you chose for your book review. Use these questions to help you evaluate your book. List specific reasons that support why you liked the book.**

Characters	Setting
• Did they seem like real people?	• Did you like the time period of the book?
• Was there one who seemed a lot like you?	• Did the place where the events happened interest you?
• Was there one who did something heroic?	• When you read the book, did you feel as if you were there, in that place and time?
• Was there one who made a good decision?	
• Was there one who made you laugh?	
• Was there one whom you felt sorry for?	

Plot	Lessons
• Did the plot have some exciting parts?	• Did the book teach you anything new about God?
• Did the plot have some funny parts?	• Did the book teach you anything new about yourself?
• Did the plot have some sad parts?	• Did the book remind you of an important truth from God's Word?
• Did the plot have some happy parts?	• Did the book bring to mind something you could do to please God?
• Have you ever had a problem like the one the characters had?	
• Do you think the characters solved their problem in a good way?	

Book title: _____

I like this book for the following reasons: _____

_____

_____

_____

_____

_____

_____

_____

▶**Save this page for use in Lesson 74.**

Book Review: Planning with an Opinion Chart

Name

Tristan used an *Opinion Chart* to plan his book review.

Title of the book: <u>Summer of the Secret Cabin</u>

Author of the book: Mason Hyde

My Opinion of the Book

I liked it, thought it was good

Reason 1

It was ekciting

Reason 2

It taught
important lessons

Examples from the Book

Nick and Anthony find
   cabin in the mountains
   for clubhouse
Smugglers also using cabin
Get locked inside
Fire in cabin
Thunderstorm

Examples from the Book

Kindness—Nick and old man
Forgiveness—Anthony when
   dog gets hurt in fire
Loving others

My Recommendation

Good book if you like adventure

Book Review: Planning with an Opinion Chart

Name

▶Use this *Opinion Chart* to plan your review of the book you chose. Choose two strong reasons for your opinion and use specific examples from the book.

Title of the book: _____

Author of the book: _____

My Opinion of the Book

_____

_____

Reason 1	Reason 2
_____	_____
_____	_____

Examples from the Book	Examples from the Book
_____	_____
_____	_____
_____	_____
_____	_____
_____	_____

My Recommendation

_____

_____

▶Save this chart for use in Lesson 75.

Book Review: Drafting

Name

Tristan used his *Opinion Chart* to help him draft his essay. Here is the rough draft of his second paragraph.

Tristan used a time-order word to point out his first reason.

First, it is a very ekciting book. Nick and Anthony find an empty cabin in the mountains and decide to use it for a clubhouse. But soon they discover that a ring of smugglers is also using the cabin. One night the boys even get locked inside! Do you think they ever escape? Read the book to find out.

He asked a question to raise interest in the book.

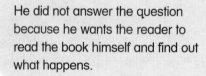

He did not answer the question because he wants the reader to read the book himself and find out what happens.

Tips for Writing a Book Review

1. Remember to tell the title and the author of the book near the beginning.
2. State your opinion close to the beginning.
3. Use time-order words to keep the order of the reasons clear.
4. Keep each reason in a separate paragraph with its examples.
5. Remember to work in details about the characters, setting, and plot in the examples.
6. Ask questions without answering them to raise interest in the book.
7. Write on every other line so that you can make changes easily later.

▶**Use your *Opinion Chart* from page 147 to draft your book review.**

Book Review: Revising

Name _____

After Tristan drafted his review, he read it to Amber. "I really like the first sentence!" said Amber. "It makes the book sound exciting. I think I would like to read it too!"

Amber suggested some changes. She pointed out some words that could be replaced with more interesting words. She also thought that Tristan should add something about what happens to the smugglers—without actually giving the ending away. She even helped Tristan find a sentence that didn't belong in a paragraph.

Tristan looked over his review after talking with Amber. He found some other changes that he wanted to make in the review. He used his

thesaurus to find interesting words to replace *good* and *empty*.

Tristan used the thesaurus to find more interesting words.

Summer of the Secret Cabin

Do you want to read a story about secrets, forgotten letters, and adventure? Then Summer of the Secret Cabin by Mason Hyde is a ~~good~~ *terrific* book for you.

First, it is a very ekciting book. Nick and Anthony find an ~~empty~~ *deserted* cabin in the mountains and decide to use it for a clubhouse. But soon they discover that a ring of smugglers is also using the cabin. One night the boys even get locked inside! Do you think they ever escape? *Do the smugglers get caught.* Read the book to find out.

Second, This is a book that will teach you important lessons. Nick has to learn a lesson about kindness. *when he meets an old man who needs his help* Anthony learns about forgiveness when his Dog gets

A time-order word shows that this is Reason 2.

Tristan added a sentence about what happens to the smugglers.

He added a detail that told more about the plot.

This sentence does not tell about the lessons in the book.

hurt in a fire in the cabin. ~~His dog doesn't die, though.~~ Reading this book taught me how important it is to love others.

I would recommend this book to anyone who like adventure. You won't have any truble getting into the story, but you might have truble putting it down!

▶ Use this *Revising Checklist* to revise your book review.

Revising Checklist

☐ 1. My book review begins in an interesting way.

☐ 2. My book review gives the opinion near the beginning.

☐ 3. My book review gives two good reasons for my opinion.

☐ 4. My book review gives examples from the book to support each reason.

☐ 5. My book review gives details about the characters, setting, and plot.

☐ 6. My book review includes time-order words and uses interesting words.

☐ 7. My book review closes with a recommendation to the reader.

Proofreading Marks

∧∨   Add

✎   Delete

≡   Capital letter

╱   Lowercase

↻→   Move

Name

After Tristan finished revising his book review, he proofread it, using the checklist on page 152. He read his book review several times, looking for each type of mistake. He placed a check mark beside each item on the checklist as he completed it.

Here is Tristan's book review with the changes he marked during the proofreading stage. What mistakes did he find? What proofreading marks did he use to correct each mistake?

<u>Summer of the Secret Cabin</u>

Do you want to read a story about secrets, forgotten letters, and adventure? Then <u>Summer of the Secret Cabin</u> by Mason Hyde is a terrific book for you.

First, it is a very ~~eksiting~~ *exciting* book. Nick and Anthony find a deserted cabin in the mountains and decide to use it for a clubhouse. But soon they discover that a ring of smugglers is also using the cabin. One night the boys even get locked inside! Do you think they ever escape? Do the smugglers get caught? Read the book to find out.

Second, this is a book that will teach you important lessons. Nick has to learn a lesson about kindness when he meets an old man who needs his help. Anthony learns about forgiveness when his ~~D~~og gets

Book Review: Proofreading

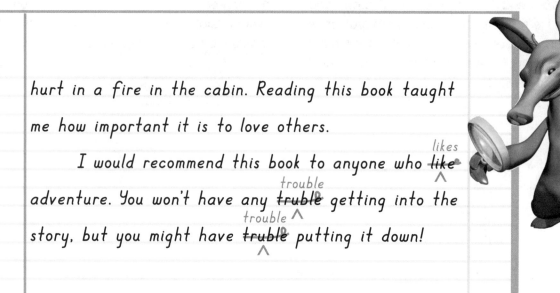

hurt in a fire in the cabin. Reading this book taught
me how important it is to love others.

I would recommend this book to anyone who ~~like~~ *likes*

adventure. You won't have any ~~truble~~ *trouble* getting into the

story, but you might have ~~truble~~ *trouble* putting it down!

▶ **Proofread your book review using the *Proofreading Checklist*.**
Use the proofreading marks to mark the mistakes.

Proofreading Checklist

☐ 1. I wrote the title of my book correctly.
☐ 2. I used correct verb forms.
☐ 3. I put a capital letter at the beginning of each sentence.
☐ 4. I put a punctuation mark at the end of each sentence.
☐ 5. I used correct punctuation within sentences.
☐ 6. I looked for misspelled words.

Proofreading Marks

∧∨	Add
ℰ	Delete
≡	Capital letter
/	Lowercase
⟳→	Move

Name

A. Write the letter of the correct answer in the blank.

A. fiction
B. examples
C. persuading
D. fact
E. opinion

_____ 1 Something you think or feel

_____ 2. Convincing someone else to agree with your opinion

_____ 3. A make-believe story

_____ 4. Specific parts of the story that support your reasons

_____ 5. Something that is true

B. Fill in the circle next to the more persuasive reason for each opinion.

6. I think everyone should learn to cook.
   ○ You will be more prepared for life as an adult.
   ○ It's a good idea.

7. Every classroom should have a pet.
   ○ You can name it.
   ○ You can learn how to take care of something.

8. Every student should learn good handwriting skills.
   ○ Good handwriting is nice.
   ○ People will be able to read what you have written.

9. I think our family should go to Florida.
   ○ We could visit the space museum.
   ○ It would just be really neat.

10. Everyone should read the book *Once upon a Safari*.
    ○ It's a good book.
    ○ The setting is unusual and interesting.

C. Circle each book title that is written correctly.

11. <u>My Dog Daisy</u>   <u>My dog Daisy</u>

12. <u>The Journeys of Israel</u>   <u>The Journeys Of Israel</u>

13. <u>Race You To The Reef</u>   <u>Race You to the Reef</u>

14. *Adventure on*   *Adventure on*
    Frozen mountain   *Frozen Mountain*

15. *A Closer Look at Bats*   *a Closer Look at Bats*

Chapter 8 Review

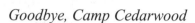

D. Read the book review. Fill in the circle next to the correct answer.

Goodbye, Camp Cedarwood

Have you ever been to camp? Even if you haven't, you will still enjoy the book *Goodbye, Camp Cedarwood*. It is a wonderful book.

First, the book has funny characters. My favorite character is Alyssa. She does funny things at camp. One time she puts a snake in the girls' cabin, and everyone screams and runs out. No one can find the snake until the next morning. Alyssa finds the snake in the sink and screams loudly enough to wake up all the girls!

Second, I think the book's setting is interesting. You would really like it too.

I would recommend this book to Anyone. Even though it is mostly about girls, I think boys would like it too.

16. The first paragraph of the book review does not include _____.
    ○ the title of the book
    ○ the author of the book
    ○ the writer's opinion of the book

17. The writer does not give enough examples to support the reason in _____.
    ○ the second paragraph
    ○ the third paragraph

18. Where would be the best place to add more details about the setting of the book?
    ○ the first paragraph
    ○ the second paragraph
    ○ the third paragraph

19. The writer of this review recommends the book to _____.
    ○ both boys and girls
    ○ just girls
    ○ just boys

20. The fourth paragraph contains a mistake in _____.
    ○ capitalization
    ○ punctuation

Cumulative Review

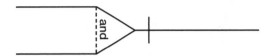
Name _____

A. Draw a line between the complete subject and the complete predicate. Underline the simple subjects once and the simple predicates twice. Diagram the sentences. *(Chapter 1)*

1. The flowers grow and bloom in the spring.

2. Stephen and Kris sang a duet.

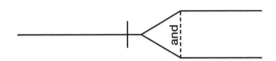

B. Write the simple subject and verb on each diagram. If the verb is a linking verb, draw a slanted line and write the predicate adjective or predicate noun. *(Chapter 5)*

3. Her shoes are tight.

4. She looks uncomfortable.

C. Underline the simple subject once and the action verb twice. Circle the direct object. Write the simple subject, the action verb, and the direct object on each diagram. *(Chapter 5)*

5. Jamie plays the flute.

6. Mrs. Barret gives her lessons.

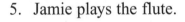

D. Underline the words that have prefixes. Fill in the circle next to the correct meaning of the word you underlined. *(Chapter 5)*

7. I have to redo my homework today.   ○ do again   ○ not do

8. Kate presorts our papers every morning.   ○ sorts back   ○ sorts before

9. The test scores are inaccurate.   ○ into accurate   ○ not accurate

Cumulative Review

E. This T-chart gives details about clarinets and saxophones. Fill in the Venn diagram with the information from the chart. *(Chapter 6)*

Clarinet	Saxophone
uses a reed	woodwind family
woodwind family	uses a reed
holes in keys	made of brass
made of wood or plastic	solid keys
black in color	gold or silver in color

Clarinet   Saxophone

F. Match each description to the correct part of a book. *(Chapter 7)*

_____ 10. Look at the ___ to find the name of the author of a book.

_____ 11. Look at the ___ to find which chapter in an English book tells about pronouns.

_____ 12. Look at the ___ to find the year a book was published.

_____ 13. Look at a science book's ___ to find which page has information about *photosynthesis*.

_____ 14. Look at a science book's ___ to find what the word *photosynthesis* means.

A. index

B. copyright page

C. glossary

D. title page

E. table of contents

Singular & Plural Pronouns

A **pronoun** takes the place of a noun (and any words that go with the noun).
A pronoun can be in the subject part or in the predicate part of a sentence.

> *He is a missionary in Africa.*   *My church sent him a new Bible.*

Singular pronouns replace singular nouns.

> *Emily has two brothers.*   *She has two brothers.*

Plural pronouns replace plural nouns or more than one noun or pronoun.

> *Mom and Dad are home now.*   *They are home now.*

The pronoun **you** can be singular or plural.

> *You need to clean your room.*   *You are my favorite cousins.*

Singular Pronouns			Plural Pronouns	
I	me	it	we	they
he	she	you	us	them
him	her		you	

▶ Guided Practice

▶**Underline the pronoun in each sentence.**

1. They are missionaries to Zimbabwe.

2. It is located on the continent of Africa.

3. Mrs. Andrews wrote us a letter from Zimbabwe.

4. She sent beautiful pictures of Victoria Falls.

5. Pastor Sherman posted them on the bulletin board.

▶**Write S if the underlined pronoun is singular.
Write P if the underlined pronoun is plural.**

_____ 6. We attended the missions conference at church last night.

_____ 7. The pastor asked me to sing during the program.

_____ 8. A missionary presented him with a gift from Africa.

_____ 9. It was a carved wooden giraffe.

▶**Circle the correct pronoun to replace the underlined words.**

10. The ushers collected an offering for the missionary.   they   he

11. My dad put a check in the offering plate.   they   he

Victoria Falls

Christians should support missionaries.

Rom. 10:15

Singular & Plural Pronouns

Independent Practice

▸**Underline the pronoun in each sentence.**

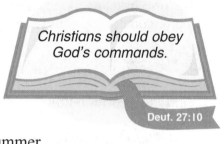

Christians should obey God's commands.

Deut. 27:10

1. Africa's geography fascinates us.

2. Most people think it is covered with desert only.

3. She wants to go on a safari in the African grasslands.

4. They are planning to hike on Mount Kilimanjaro next summer.

5. He wants to fish in Africa's large lakes.

6. Mr. Makololo will show you the animal preserves in the country.

▸**Write *S* if the underlined pronoun is singular.**
Write *P* if the underlined pronoun is plural.

_____ 7. We visited Mt. Sinai in Egypt.

_____ 8. It was an important place in the lives of Moses and the people of Israel.

_____ 9. God gave him the Ten Commandments to help the people live for God.

_____ 10. God led them across the Red Sea.

_____ 11. They disobeyed God.

_____ 12. God punished them with forty years of wandering in the wilderness.

▸**Circle the correct pronoun to replace the underlined words.**

13. Today many tourists visit the Sinai Peninsula.   us   it

14. Linda and I rode camels there.   we   he

15. Dad trekked across the desert.   he   she

Apply and Write

▸**Write two sentences about an interesting place you have visited.**
Circle the pronouns you use.

_____

_____

_____

Subject & Object Pronouns

A **subject pronoun** takes the place of a noun that is the subject of a sentence. The pronoun also replaces any words that go with the noun.

Singular	Plural
Ramon fixed the flat tire.	*The people entered the mall.*
He fixed the flat tire.	*They entered the mall.*

An **object pronoun** can replace the direct object in the predicate of a sentence, or it can be used after a word such as *for, at, of, with,* or *to.*

Singular	Plural
Mr. Donovan called Tom.	*The artist drew a picture for the girls.*
Mr. Donovan called him.	*The artist drew a picture for them.*

A *direct object* is a noun that comes after an action verb and tells *what* or *whom*.

Subject Pronouns		Object Pronouns	
Singular	**Plural**	**Singular**	**Plural**
I	we	me	us
he	they	him	them
she	you	her	you
it		it	
you		you	

▸ Guided Practice

▸Write *S* if the underlined word is a subject pronoun.
  Write *O* if the underlined word is an object pronoun.

_____ 1. <u>We</u> found the answer on page sixty-seven.

_____ 2. Jessica wrote <u>it</u> on her paper.

_____ 3. The teacher asked <u>them</u> about the answer.

_____ 4. These books from the library are for <u>you</u>.

_____ 5. <u>She</u> showed Robert how to work the math problem.

▸Circle the correct pronoun to replace the underlined word(s).
  Write *S* if the correct answer is a subject pronoun.
  Write *O* if the correct answer is an object pronoun.

_____ 6. <u>Bruce</u> builds model airplanes.   him   he

_____ 7. <u>The directions</u> help him with the construction.   they   them

_____ 8. Then Bruce paints designs on <u>the models</u>.   they   them

_____ 9. Bruce built a World War II model for <u>Grandpa</u>.   him   he

_____ 10. <u>Mom</u> took him to the craft store on Saturday.   her   she

Subject & Object Pronouns

◎ Independent Practice

▶Write *S* if the underlined word is a subject pronoun.
Write *O* if the underlined word is an object pronoun.

_____ 1. <u>I</u> want to see an African elephant.

_____ 2. <u>They</u> are found in Botswana, Africa.

_____ 3. You can find <u>them</u> in Chobe National Park.

_____ 4. This preserve also has large herds of wildebeest in <u>it</u>.

_____ 5. <u>You</u> may also see beautiful flamingoes in the park's salt pans.

▶Mark the two boxes that describe the underlined pronoun.
The first one has been done for you.

	Subject	Object	Singular	Plural
6. <u>He</u> went on a safari in Botswana, Africa.	X		X	
7. <u>They</u> have the world's largest inland river delta.				
8. <u>You</u> will see wild animals on a preserve.				
9. The desert area has few humans living in <u>it</u>.				
10. The guide told <u>us</u> about Africa's diamond mines.				

▶Circle the correct pronoun to replace each underlined word.
Write *S* if the correct answer is a subject pronoun.
Write *O* if the correct answer is an object pronoun.

_____ 11. <u>Tourists</u> need to learn about Botswana's climate.   they   us

_____ 12. <u>Botswana</u> has winter from June to August.   you   it

_____ 13. Heavy rain from December to March hides the animals   you   it
from <u>people</u>.

_____ 14. The preserve protects <u>animals</u> from injury and bad weather.   they   them

◯ Apply and Write

▶Imagine that you are able to go on an African safari. Describe what you
might see or what you would like to do on your safari. Use the subject
pronoun *I* and the object pronoun *me* in your sentences.

_____

_____

Writing with Pronouns

A **subject pronoun** replaces a noun that is the subject. An **object pronoun** replaces a direct object in the predicate or follows words such as *for, at, of, with,* or *to.*

> *Jake* **visited** *his grandparents.*   *He* **visited** *them.*

When writing with pronouns, make it clear which noun the pronoun refers to. If the sentence is not clear, a noun should be used instead of a pronoun.

> *Grandpa's red* hen **laid an** egg.   *It was very large.*

What was very large, the hen or the egg? Since the second sentence is not clear, use the noun instead of the pronoun.

> *Grandpa's red* hen **laid an** egg.   *The* egg *was very large.*

▶ Guided Practice

▶Write the correct pronoun to replace the word(s) in parentheses.

1. Mrs. Black chose _____ for the spelling bee.
    (Jim)

2. Students from each class participate in _____ .
    (the spelling bee)

3. Each student received a list from _____ .
    (Mrs. Black)

4. _____ will watch the spelling bee.
   (The fourth grade students)

5. _____ hope Jim can spell this word!
   (Lucy and I)

6. _____ and Jim tied for first place.
    (Bonnie)

7. The teacher gave prizes to _____ .
    (the winners)

Subject Pronouns	
Singular	**Plural**
I	we
he	they
she	you
it	
you	

Object Pronouns	
Singular	**Plural**
me	us
him	them
her	you
it	
you	

▶Replace the unclear pronoun to make the sentence clear. Write the new sentence.

8. The little boys play with three puppies. <u>They</u> are cute.

_____

9. Shannon gives the littlest puppy extra food. <u>She</u> needs to grow.

_____

Writing with Pronouns

◉ Independent Practice

▶ **Write the correct pronoun to replace the word(s) in parentheses.**

1. _____ are missionaries to Tanzania, Africa.
   (Rev. and Mrs. Adams)

2. The mission church has two hundred people in _____ .
   (the mission church)

Christians should be fishers of men.

Matt. 4:19

3. _____ is located near majestic Mt. Kilimanjaro.
   (The church)

4. Tanzania's beautiful lakes have many fish in _____ .
   (the lakes)

5. Rev. Adams fishes for souls in obedience to God's call
   for _____ .
   (Rev. Adams)

▶ **Read the paragraph. Replace the unclear pronouns to make the sentences clear. Write the words on the blanks.**

6. _____

7. _____

8. _____

> Natalie and Scott made tacos for dinner. <u>They</u> were delicious. Their mother thanked them for the meal and walked into the kitchen. The room was a mess! There was food on the floor. <u>It</u> needed to be mopped. Before Mrs. Tobin could call the children into the room, she noticed something furry sticking out of the pantry door. "Bitsy," she cried. "How did you get in here?"
>
> Natalie came running in and picked up Bitsy. <u>She</u> started cleaning her. "Bitsy," Natalie laughed, "You almost ended our cooking careers before they started!"

② Apply and Write

▶ **Write about something funny that has happened to you. Include pronouns in your sentences.**

_____

_____

_____

Using *I & Me, We & Us*

The pronouns *I* and *we* are **subject pronouns**.

> *I found the missing puzzle piece.*
> *We parked the car in the driveway.*

The pronouns *me* and *us* are **object pronouns**. These pronouns can replace the direct object in a sentence, or they can be used after words such as *for, at, of, with,* or *to.*

> *Hannah gave the money to me.*
> *The teacher took us on a field trip.*

The pronouns *we* and *us* can be used before a noun.

> *We girls are going to a party.*
> *The teacher helped us students.*

Name yourself last when you write or speak about another person and yourself.

> *Kevin and I worked on a science project.*
> *Mom told Shanda and me about the winning project.*

▶ Guided Practice

▶Fill in the circle next to each correct sentence.

1. ○ I made a map of Africa out of dough.
   ○ Me made a map of Africa out of dough.

2. ○ Jake helped me with the dough.
   ○ Jake helped I with the dough.

3. ○ Us students mounted the map on plywood.
   ○ We students mounted the map on plywood.

4. ○ The teacher asked Jake and me about our map.
   ○ The teacher asked Jake and I about our map.

▶Underline the correct words to complete the sentences.

5. (Jill and I, Jill and me) talked on the phone last night.

6. She bought candy bars for (we, us).

7. Will you play tag with (Chernel and I, Chernel and me)?

8. Dad scolded (we, us) boys for being outside after dark.

9. (I, Me) need to study for a math test.

10. (Me and Jon, Jon and I) asked for another piece of cake.

Using *I* & *Me*, *We* & *Us*

◉ Independent Practice

▶ **Underline the correct words to complete the sentences.**

1. (Kristina and me, Kristina and I) went to Amber's house after school.

2. Her mother gave (we, us) a snack.

3. (We, Us) thanked her and started on our homework.

4. Kristina asked (I, me) for the spelling words.

5. Amber helped (me and Kristina, Kristina and me).

6. At five o'clock it was suppertime for (we, us).

▶ **Fill in the circle next to each correct sentence.**

7. ○ My family and me visited a lighthouse.
   ○ My family and I visited a lighthouse.

8. ○ My cousin went to North Carolina with us.
   ○ My cousin went to North Carolina with we.

9. ○ Jacob and I climbed the stairs to the top of the lighthouse.
   ○ Jacob and me climbed the stairs to the top of the lighthouse.

10. ○ Dad bought souvenirs for Jacob and me.
    ○ Dad bought souvenirs for Jacob and I.

▶ **Read the paragraph. Use proofreading marks to mark and correct the five mistakes. The first one has been done for you.**

Cape Hatteras Lighthouse in North Carolina

Michael and me like to play baseball. One time the Panthers were beating we by three runs in the top of the ninth inning. When our team got up to bat, we got two men on base, but we had two outs. Me and Michael were the next two batters. The coach said the win was up to we boys. Michael got a base hit. Then it was my turn. I swung the bat and struck the ball with all my might. "Home run!" everyone yelled. Me ran the bases as fast as I could. The Cougars won the game by one run!

Proofreading Marks
- ∧∨   Add
- ⌀   Delete
- ☰   Capital letter
- /   Lowercase
- ○→   Move

◄)) Apply and Listen

▶ **Listen to your teacher read some sentences. If the correct pronoun is used, write *C*; if the pronoun is not correct, write *NC*.**

1. _____ 2. _____ 3. _____ 4. _____ 5. _____ 6. _____

Subject Pronoun/ Verb Agreement

Name

The verb form must agree with the subject of a sentence.
A **singular subject pronoun** requires the **singular form of a verb**.

> *She likes* the missionary biography.
> *It is* the story of a pioneer missionary to Africa.

A **plural subject pronoun** requires the **plural form of a verb**.

> *We support* three missionaries to Africa.
> *They are* in the countries of Niger, Zaire, and Somalia.

I and **you** are exceptions. *I* and *you* use the **plural form of a verb**.

> *I write* letters to missionary families.
> *You pray* for the missionaries every day.

▶ Guided Practice

▶**Fill in the circle next to each correct sentence.**

1. ○ She keep a missionary prayer journal.
   ○ She keeps a missionary prayer journal.

2. ○ They send photos to Carol for her journal.
   ○ They sends photos to Carol for her journal.

3. ○ I like to look at the pictures of the children.
   ○ I likes to look at the pictures of the children.

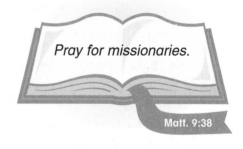

Pray for missionaries.

Matt. 9:38

▶**Underline the correct verb twice.**

4. We (mail, mails) a package to a missionary each month.

5. It (contain, contains) many things from home.

6. They (enjoys, enjoy) our care packages.

▶**Underline the correct subject pronoun once.**

7. (You, She) need to see the missionary's slides.

8. (I, He) think the slides are fascinating.

9. (She, They) passes out prayer cards after the service.

10. (We, He) have a special prayer service tonight.

Subject Pronoun/ Verb Agreement

◉ Independent Practice

▶ **Fill in the circle next to each correct sentence.**

1. ○ We work with missionaries in Africa every summer.
   ○ We works with missionaries in Africa every summer.

2. ○ I teaches the small children in children's church.
   ○ I teach the small children in children's church.

3. ○ He works on the church's buildings with the pastor.
   ○ He work on the church's buildings with the pastor.

4. ○ She cook meals for the workers.
   ○ She cooks meals for the workers.

5. ○ They have vegetables in the garden.
   ○ They has vegetables in the garden.

mission work in Africa

▶ **Underline the correct verb twice.**

6. He (witness, witnesses) to many people in northern Africa.

7. They (hear, hears) about the saving grace of Christ.

8. We (give, gives) the missionary money to help his ministry.

9. She (teach, teaches) the women's Bible study in Casablanca, Morocco.

10. Bibles (help, helps) the African Christians to grow in Christ.

▶ **Underline the correct subject pronoun once.**

11. (She, I) want to visit Morocco some day.

12. (It, They) lies on the northwest coast of Africa.

13. (He, You) reads interesting books about the Casbah, or castle, of northern Africa.

② Apply and Write

▶ **Think about a missionary family that you know or that your church supports. Write one or two sentences about something that would help the missionary. Include pronouns in your sentences.**

_____

_____

_____

Possessive Pronouns

A **possessive pronoun** shows ownership. Possessive pronouns replace possessive nouns.

> *Katie's bike is broken.*   *Her bike is broken.*

Some possessive pronouns are used before nouns.

> *My brother is six years old.*   *Their cars need repairs.*

Some possessive pronouns can stand alone.

> *That piece of pie is yours.*   *Those football tickets are ours.*

Possessive Pronouns			
With Nouns		**That Stand Alone**	
my	our	mine	ours
your	their	yours	theirs
his	its	his	
her		hers	

▶ Guided Practice

▶**Underline the possessive pronoun in each sentence.**

1. My teacher told the true story of Dr. David Livingstone.

2. His ministry was in Africa more than 160 years ago.

3. Africa was his mission field.

4. Many Africans gave their lives to Christ because of Dr. Livingstone's ministry.

> *God wants Christians to share the gospel with others.*
>
> Mark 16:15   Rom. 1:16

▶**Write the correct possessive pronoun to replace each possessive noun.**

5. Dr. Livingstone received Christ as _____ Savior at the age of twenty.
   (Dr. Livingstone's)

6. _____ early life was spent in a missionary family.
   (Mrs. Livingstone's)

7. They met at _____ missionary station in Kuruman, Africa.
   (the Moffats')

8. One of _____ six children died as a baby.
   (David's and Mary's)

▶**Underline the correct possessive pronoun.**

9. May I borrow (your, yours) book about David Livingstone?

10. The book isn't (my, mine).

11. I give (my, mine) book report on Monday.

Possessive Pronouns

◯ Independent Practice

▶Underline the possessive pronoun in each sentence.

1. David Livingstone gave his life to serve God in Africa.

2. Once, a lion with its powerful body crushed Livingstone's arm.

3. The Africans thought their friend would soon be dead.

4. God healed his arm and body at the mission station in Kuruman.

5. Mary Moffat became his wife.

6. Her father was the preacher at the wedding.

▶Write the correct possessive pronoun to replace each possessive noun.

7. _____ travels helped make true maps of Africa.
   (Dr. Livingstone's)

8. The hardships in _____ interior almost ruined Livingstone's health.
   (Africa's)

9. The harsh conditions often kept Mrs. Livingstone away from _____ husband.
   (Mrs. Livingstone's)

10. David and Mary believed that no sacrifice was too great for _____ God.
    (the Livingstones')

▶Underline the correct possessive pronoun in each sentence.

11. Dr. Livingstone's life was more exciting than (my, mine).

12. Were his sacrifices for Christ greater than (our, ours)?

13. He dedicated (his, its) life to serving God always.

14. What will you do with (your, yours)?

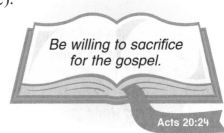

Be willing to sacrifice for the gospel.

Acts 20:24

◯ Apply and Write

▶Write two questions that you might ask Dr. Livingstone about his missionary work if he were alive today. Include a possessive pronoun in each question.

_____

_____

_____

_____

Confusing Contractions

Name _____

Some pronouns are combined with verbs to make **contractions**.

Some contractions are easily confused with similar contractions or homophones. The spelling of the word and content of the sentence will help you choose the correct word. You may want to think about the two words that form the contraction to see whether the contraction correctly fits the sentence.

> he's = he is or he has
> she's = she is or she has
>
> he'd = he had or he would
> she'd = she had or she would
>
> I'd = I had or I would
>
> its = possessive pronoun
> it's = it is or it has

> they're = they are
> there = that place; location
> their = possessive pronoun
>
> you're = you are
> your = possessive pronoun
>
> I'll = I will
>
> aisle = a passageway between
> rows of seats in a church
> or shelves in a store

▶ Guided Practice

Remember

Homophones are words that sound alike but have different meanings and usually different spellings.

▶**Underline the correct homophone in each sentence.**

1. (Their, There, They're) grandmother baked sugar cookies.

2. (I'll, Aisle) give the dog a bath this afternoon.

3. (Its, It's) exciting to ride a roller coaster at the amusement park.

4. (Their, There, They're) are twenty-two students in his class.

5. (You're, Your) homework is due on Monday morning.

6. (Their, There, They're) going to play basketball after school.

7. His seat in church is next to the (I'll, aisle).

8. The cat sharpened (its, it's) claws on the post.

9. (You're, Your) going to be late for church.

▶**Write the two words that form each underlined contraction.**

10. <u>It's</u> time to clean your room. _____

11. <u>She's</u> been invited to a slumber party this weekend. _____

12. <u>He's</u> traveling on a plane on Thursday. _____

Confusing Contractions

Name _____

⃝ Independent Practice

▶**Underline the correct homophone in each sentence.**

1. (Your, You're) supposed to practice your instrument every day.

2. Do not stand in the (I'll, aisle) when the bus is moving.

3. Jonathan left his watch over (their, there, they're).

4. (It's, Its) crowded in the parking lot at the mall.

5. (Their, There, They're) studying about reptiles of the Everglades.

6. (I'll, Aisle) pay for the ice cream sundaes.

7. Take (your, you're) little brother with you.

8. Is (their, there, they're) game being played tomorrow evening?

9. The bulldog buried (it's, its) bone in the backyard.

▶**Write the two words that form each underlined contraction.**

10. He's visited the Grand Canyon before. _____

11. They're meeting us at the bowling alley at six o'clock. _____

12. I'll study my multiplication facts. _____

13. She'd like to have another piece of cake, please. _____

14. He's coming over for dinner tomorrow. _____

15. You're going hiking with us tomorrow. _____

② Apply and Write

▶**Write three sentences using one homophone in each sentence.**

(their) _____

_____

(there) _____

_____

(they're) _____

_____

Homophones

Language LINK

Name

Homophones are words that sound alike but have different meanings and usually different spellings. Refer to pages 349–50 in the Grammar Handbook for the meanings of some common homophones.

The sky is blue.			*The wind* blew *the leaves off the trees.*	

Homophones

ate eight	heal heel	hour our	plain plane	tail tale
dear deer	here hear	new knew	right write	to too two
fair fare	him hymn	nose knows	see sea	way weigh
flower flour	hole whole	not knot	sent cent scent	week weak
hair hare	horse hoarse	pair pear pare	stair stare	wood would

▶ Guided Practice

▶**Fill in the circle next to each sentence with the correct homophone.**
Use Worktext pages 349–50 if necessary.

1. ○ I knew the answer to the question.
    ○ I new the answer to the question.

2. ○ Sailors can make many different kinds of nots.
    ○ Sailors can make many different kinds of knots.

3. ○ The sent of the flowers filled the room.
    ○ The scent of the flowers filled the room.

4. ○ How much do the bananas way?
    ○ How much do the bananas weigh?

Homophones

Independent Practice

▶ **Write the homophones correctly in each sentence.**

(would, wood)   1. _____ you please stack up the _____?

(right, write)   2. I _____ with my _____ hand.

(nose, knows)   3. Everyone _____ that a clown has a red _____.

(our, hour)   4. _____ photos will be ready in one _____.

(pear, pare)   5. I will _____ the _____ for the fruit salad.

(tail, tale)   6. We read a _____ about a donkey without a _____.

(see, sea)   7. We can _____ the _____ from our motel room.

(eight, ate)   8. They _____ dinner at _____.

(hymn, him)   9. The pastor asked _____ to play a _____.

▶ **Fill in the circle next to each sentence with the correct homophone.**

10. ○ The plain was ready to land at the airstrip.
    ○ The plane was ready to land at the airstrip.

11. ○ Hannah rode the Ferris wheel at the fair.
    ○ Hannah rode the Ferris wheel at the fare.

12. ○ The mayor's voice was horse after his long speech.
    ○ The mayor's voice was hoarse after his long speech.

13. ○ It took six weeks for Nathan's broken arm to heal.
    ○ It took six weeks for Nathan's broken arm to heel.

14. ○ I would like to eat a hamburger to.
    ○ I would like to eat a hamburger too.

15. ○ It is not polite to stair at people.
    ○ It is not polite to stare at people.

Apply and Write

▶ **Choose a pair of homophones from page 171. Write a riddle using both homophones in the question. One has been done for you.**

Riddle Question: *Why was the horse hoarse?*

Answer: *He had lost his neigh.*

Riddle Question: _____

Answer: _____

A. Mark the two boxes that describe each underlined pronoun.

	Subject	Object	Singular	Plural
1. <u>We</u> bought a new computer at the store yesterday.				
2. The salesman helped <u>us</u> put the computer in the car.				
3. Dad asked <u>me</u> to help set up the computer.				
4. <u>I</u> like to send e-mail on the new computer.				
5. <u>He</u> needs to come over to see our new computer.				

B. Write the correct pronoun to replace the word(s) in parentheses.

6. _____ is making homemade ice cream.
   (Mother)

7. _____ will be strawberry-flavored.
   (The ice cream)

8. Mom will add fresh strawberries to _____ .
   (the ice cream)

9. Dad will show _____ how to pack the ice and rock salt.
   (my sister and me)

10. _____ love homemade strawberry ice cream!
    (My sister and I)

Subject Pronouns	
Singular	**Plural**
I	we
he	they
she	you
it	
you	

Object Pronouns	
Singular	**Plural**
me	us
him	them
her	you
it	
you	

C. Fill in the circle next to each correct sentence.

11. ○ Jim and I went fishing at the lake on Saturday.
    ○ Jim and me went fishing at the lake on Saturday.

12. ○ Dad entered we in a fishing contest.
    ○ Dad entered us in a fishing contest.

13. ○ Jim beat I in the contest.
    ○ Jim beat me in the contest.

14. ○ I caught the biggest fish.
    ○ Me caught the biggest fish.

15. ○ Me and Jim had a great time!
    ○ Jim and I had a great time!

Chapter 9 Review

Name _____

◉ Independent Practice

D. Underline the correct verb twice.

16. She (like, likes) pizza with sausage and onions.

17. I (eat, eats) pepperoni on my pizza.

18. They (make, makes) homemade pizza on Friday nights.

E. Write the correct possessive pronoun to replace each possessive noun.

19. _____ mother works at the bank.
    (Candace's)

20. She helps set up _____ bank accounts.
    (the customers')

21. Mrs. Richards set up _____ account last Thursday.
    (Mr. White's)

22. _____ employees are friendly.
    (The bank's)

F. Underline the correct homophone in each sentence.

23. (I'll, aisle) wash the dishes after dinner.

24. The cat licked (its, it's) fur.

25. Were they driving (there, their, they're) car?

26. (You're, Your) shoelaces are untied.

27. It looks like (it's, its) going to rain.

28. (There, Their, They're) going to Kenya next summer.

G. Write each homophone pair correctly in the sentence.

(right, write) 29. _____ your name in the top _____ corner.

(stare, stair) 30. Why does he _____ at that _____ ?

(plane, plain) 31. Jerry ate a _____ hamburger on the _____ .

(whole, hole) 32. The _____ bag of candy fell into the _____ .

(new, knew) 33. Joel _____ where to find the _____ house.

Cumulative Review

Name _____

A. Fill in the circle next to the more descriptive word for the underlined word. Remember to keep the meaning of each sentence the same. *(Chapter 2)*

1. Can you help me <u>carry</u> these bales of hay to the barn?
   ○ return   ○ haul   ○ lift

2. Taylor <u>walked</u> home after a long, difficult day.
   ○ skipped   ○ trudged   ○ ran

3. Her <u>bright</u> diamonds sparkled under the spotlights.
   ○ brilliant   ○ dull   ○ shiny

4. There are <u>many</u> stars in the sky.
   ○ countless   ○ a lot of   ○ several

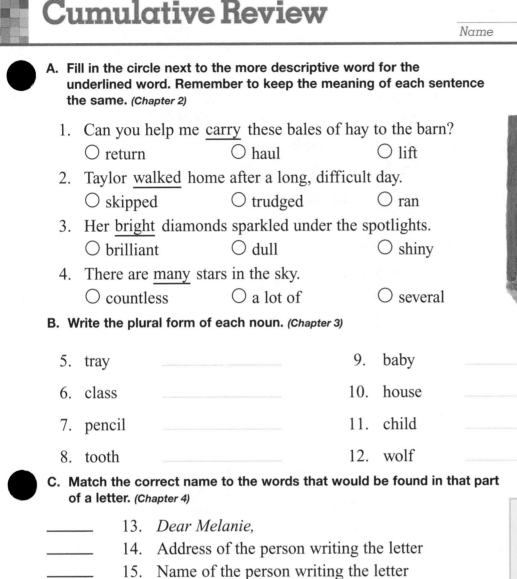

B. Write the plural form of each noun. *(Chapter 3)*

5. tray _____   9. baby _____

6. class _____   10. house _____

7. pencil _____   11. child _____

8. tooth _____   12. wolf _____

C. Match the correct name to the words that would be found in that part of a letter. *(Chapter 4)*

_____ 13. *Dear Melanie,*
_____ 14. Address of the person writing the letter
_____ 15. Name of the person writing the letter
_____ 16. Main part of the letter
_____ 17. *Your friend,*

> A. body
> B. closing
> C. greeting
> D. heading
> E. signature

D. Write the letter that shows the correct placement of each address. One will have two answers. *(Chapter 4)*

_____ 18. Address of the person writing the letter

_____ 19. Address of the person receiving the letter

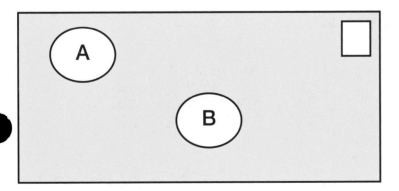

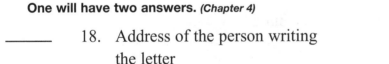

Dear Julia,

Thank you for the gospel tracts you sent. We need as many tracts in Spanish as we can get. Our family plans to pass them out in the market on Friday.

In Christ,
Mrs. Johnson

Cumulative Review

E. Fill in the circle next to each correct answer. *(Chapter 7)*

20. To find out when Mozart was born, you should look in a(n) ____.
   ○ atlas   ○ magazine   ○ encyclopedia

21. To check the meanings of *jaunty*, you should look in a(n) ____.
   ○ dictionary   ○ encyclopedia   ○ newspaper

22. To find out who won the college football game last weekend, you should look in a(n) ____.
   ○ encyclopedia   ○ newspaper   ○ book about sports

23. The books of an encyclopedia are called ____.
   ○ articles   ○ volumes   ○ issues

24. To find a map showing the mountain ranges in South America, you should look in a(n) ____.
   ○ dictionary   ○ newspaper   ○ atlas

25. If you don't know the author or title of a book but want to find a book about horses, how would you search for the book?
   ○ by subject   ○ by title   ○ by author

F. Fill in the circle next to the more persuasive reason for each opinion. *(Chapter 8)*

26. I think everyone should learn to play tennis.
   ○ You will get in shape and have better coordination.
   ○ My best friend plays tennis.

27. You should send birthday cards to your relatives.
   ○ That's what relatives do for each other.
   ○ It will show them that you care about them.

28. June is the best month of the year.
   ○ The weather is nice, and the flowers are blooming.
   ○ My birthday is in June.

29. Everyone should drink milk every day.
   ○ Chocolate milk tastes good.
   ○ It makes your bones strong.

30. Everyone should memorize a Bible verse every week.
   ○ You will know a lot of verses.
   ○ When you are tempted, God will remind you of what His Word says.

God's Word teaches us to do right.

Ps. 119:11

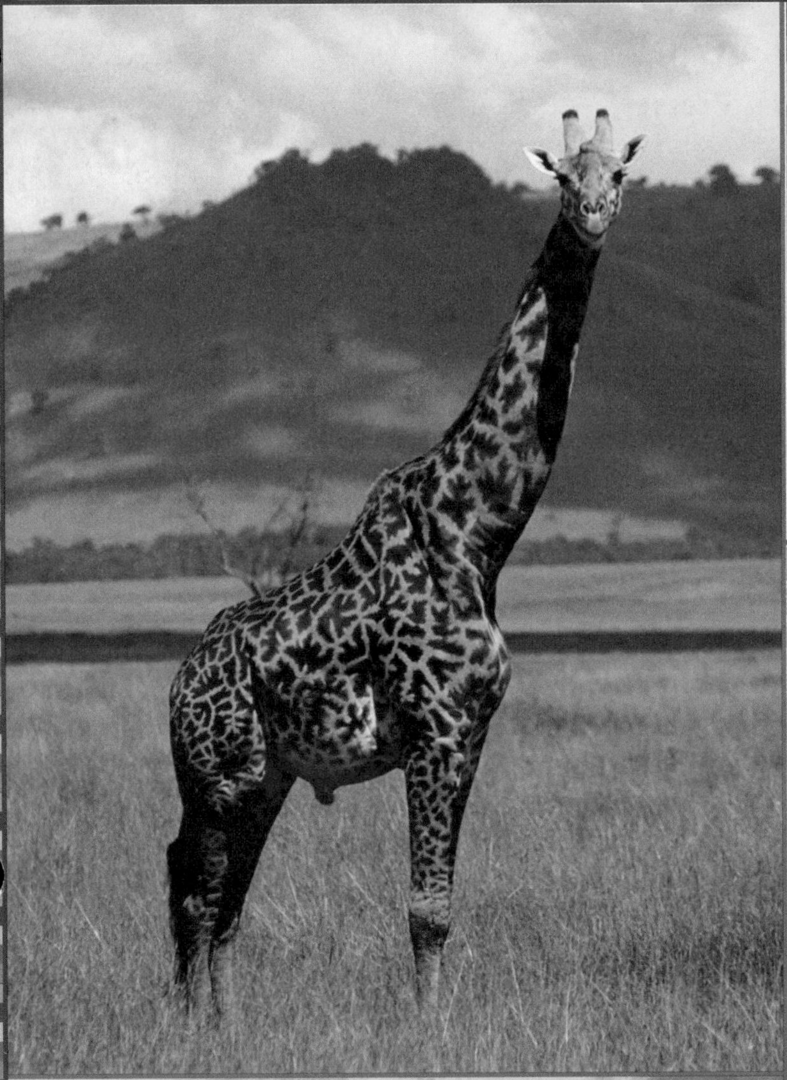

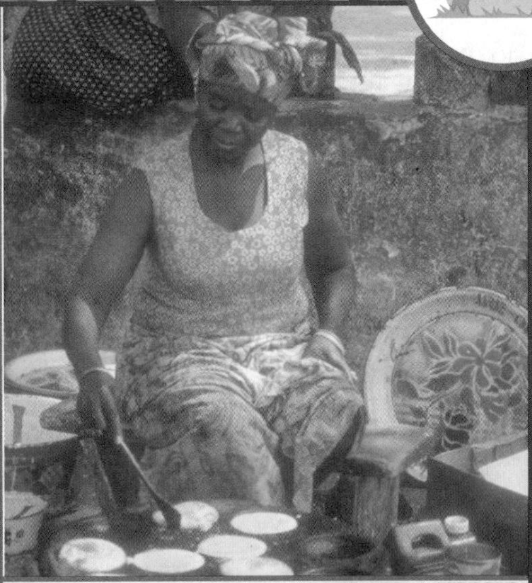

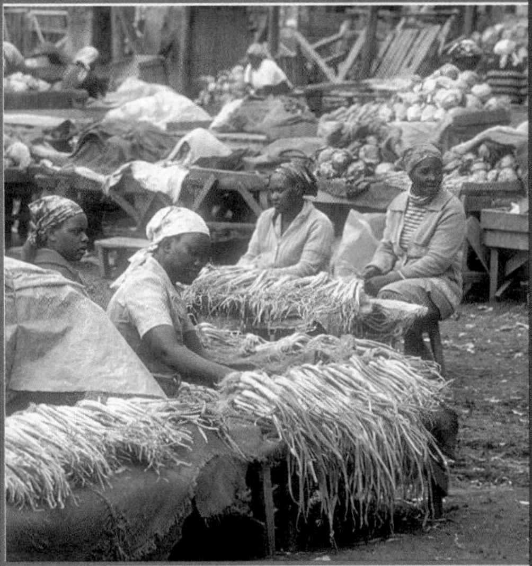

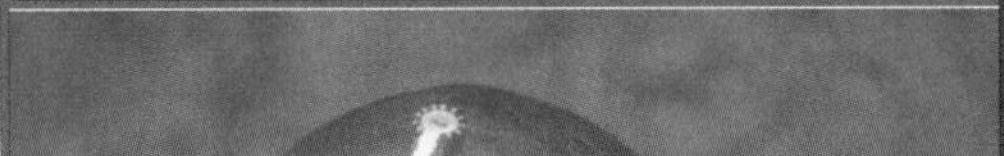

Excerpt from "Pecos Bill Gets a Wife"
(from *I Met You in a Story*, BJU Press)

Pecos Bill, that rootin' tootin' cowboy, he figured he had just about everything. Why, he had Scat the cougar. And he had Rat the python. And of course, he had Widow Maker, the biggest, brawniest horse in the West, a horse that only Pecos Bill could ride. So the cowboy was mighty content, figuring there was nothing else in the whole wide world he could ever want.

But one day Pecos Bill was moseying down the river trail on old Widow Maker's back. He was taking it kind of slow and easy, 'bout sixty miles an hour, when all of a sudden something stopped him right in his tracks.

It was a sight. A sight the likes of what Pecos Bill had never seen before in all his days. Speeding down the middle of the river on the back of a giant catfish was a cowgirl. What a cowgirl! Her hair was as red as the evening sun, all tied up in two braids, looking like two carrots sticking out of her head. Her hat flapped on the ends of its strings.

"Yippee! Yahoo!" she yelled. Her two long bony arms wrapped around the catfish's body. "Yahoo-ee! Yip-yip-yahoo!"

No doubt about it; it was love at first sight. Pecos Bill felt his heart do a double flip and the sweat stand out on his brow. He had to meet this cowgirl!

Even while he watched, the catfish took a wild leap and landed on the bank, gasping for breath. The redheaded cowgirl hopped off, and with one quick toss she flipped the catfish back into the water. Then she turned to face Pecos Bill.

"Howdy, cowboy!" She grinned wide enough to show off all six of her teeth, shining white and pearly. The freckles on her face stood out bold and orange.

Pecos Bill's heart jumped into his throat, and he couldn't speak for gazing at her beauty. So she kept right on talking.

"My name's Slewfoot Sue. I come down the river to find me new critters to ride. I done rode everything this country has to offer. I've rode grizzly bears and mountain lions and wild horses, and now I've rode a catfish too." She grinned again and poured the water out of her boot. "What have you rode, cowboy?"

All Pecos Bill could do was smile.

There was a whirlwind courtship, and Slewfoot Sue decided she loved this cowboy as much as he loved her. But as crazy as Bill was about Sue, there was one thing he wouldn't let her do.

"Sue," he told her, "I've got to warn you. Everything I have is yours, including Widow Maker. But he's a fiery horse, and he won't let anyone ride him but me. If you try, I might never see you again."

Well, those were the very words Sue needed to hear to make her want to ride Widow Maker more than anything else in the world. Sue didn't mention it again, but that's not to say it left her mind. Sue could think of hardly anything else.

Their wedding day came, and my, didn't Sue look pretty! She wore a white veil and a long white dress with a bustle the size of a bushel basket. Bustles were quite the style back then, you know, and Sue's was made from a brand new bedspring and the fanciest chicken wire around. There never was a happier man than Pecos Bill on his wedding day.

Well, no sooner had they said "I do" and the preacher pronounced his blessing than Slewfoot Sue hollered "Yahoo!" She raced outside quicker than a jackrabbit and hopped on Widow Maker's back. That was one surprised horse.

And that was one surprised bride. Widow Maker bucked hard, and Slewfoot Sue's second "Yahoo!" faded off in the distance as she disappeared from sight behind the clouds.

They all stood watching—Bill, the preacher, and all the cowboys, their mouths

hanging wide open. "We might never see her again," Pecos Bill muttered. "I warned her."

Well, rumor had it that Sue had to duck her head to keep from hitting the moon. But whatever happened, she appeared again that evening, falling right out of the sky. She would have landed with only a few bruises except for the bustle she was wearing.

Instead of landing, Sue bounced.

Sue bounced up until she was out of sight in the sky again! When she came back down, she bounced again.

This could have gone on for days or even weeks, but finally Pecos Bill decided he had had enough. He figured his new bride probably had too. So he pulled out his lariat and waited.

The next time Sue bounced, Bill lassoed her and brought her down. If it hadn't been for his strong muscles, she would have bounced again. But she stayed. She was a little dizzy and bruised, but otherwise she was fine.

From what I hear, Pecos Bill and Slewfoot Sue had a right happy life together as husband and wife. And one thing that made it happy was that never again did Slewfoot Sue ask to ride Widow Maker. She was cured of that forever.

Tall Tales

A story that is so far-fetched that nobody would ever believe it is called a **tall tale.** Writers of tall tales are not trying to make their readers believe their stories. They are trying to make their readers laugh. Humor is an important part of tall tales. This humor often comes from making the characters and their problems "bigger than life."

A tall tale is usually about a hero who is bigger, stronger, or smarter than everyone else. The hero does impossible acts, such as riding a giant catfish or lassoing a lightning bolt. Writers of tall tales use colorful descriptions to bring pictures to their readers' minds.

Here is a tall tale that Tasha wrote.

The Biggest Bee in the South

It was a hot summer morning in Georgia. Tom Toughguy was eating breakfast out on his porch. Every morning Tom ate five hundred biscuits dripping with honey. He was just about to pop the last three biscuits into his mouth when he heard a terrible sound like a chainsaw.

"Whoa!" he yelled. "That's the biggest bee I've ever seen!"

A gigantic bee was flying toward him. It was buzzing so loudly that Tom had to cover his ears. The bee was about the size of an elephant. Its stinger was as long as a telephone pole. That bee was mad because Tom had used up all the honey in its hive.

Tom tossed his glass of orange juice at the bee. That would have drowned most bees. But it just made this one madder. The bee came closer and closer.

"You won't get me!" said Tom. Then he unfolded his big red napkin. He threw it over the bee's head. Quick as a lightning flash, he tied the napkin's edges in a knot.

The bee could not see out of its blindfold! It flew around in circles. It bumped into Tom's house. It smacked into a tree.

Tom took his knife and chopped off the bee's stinger. That made the bee so upset that it just gave up and went home. Tom chopped the stinger up into small pieces and used it for firewood. People all over the South could see the smoke from that bonfire.

Tall Tales

Name

What kinds of things happen in a tall tale? Impossible things happen. Often there is some type of struggle between the hero and another powerful force. In Tasha's story, the hero, Tom Toughguy, battles the biggest bee in the South.

Remember that in a tall tale people and events are exaggerated. They are bigger and more dramatic than what they would be in real life.

▶ **Put an *X* next to events that could happen only in a tall tale.**

_____ 1. A small boy crushes an ant beneath his shoe.

_____ 2. A man stops a giant from stepping on his house.

_____ 3. A girl walks across the United States in one hour.

_____ 4. A cat leaps up on a piano.

_____ 5. A boy blows out a forest fire by himself.

_____ 6. A woman cleans a house in one day.

_____ 7. A girl wins a cookie-baking contest.

_____ 8. A boy uses a tornado as a horse.

_____ 9. A man leaves a footprint the size of a lake.

_____ 10. A bird flies to the next town.

▶ **List other events that could happen only in a tall tale.**

_____

_____

_____

_____

_____

Planning the Hero

The **hero** is the main character of a tall tale. The hero is able to do impossible things. Pecos Bill can ride a mustang that throws any other rider an impossible distance into the sky. He is able to lasso his new bride and keep her from bouncing into outer space again. In another tall tale, Paul Bunyan, a gigantic logger, takes mile-long steps, and his ox, Babe, drinks an entire river dry. The hero in Tasha's story, Tom Toughguy, is able to blindfold the biggest bee in the South and keep from being stung.

▶ **Use these questions to help you plan your hero.**

• Will your hero be a man, a woman, a girl, or a boy?

• To what could you compare your hero's size?

• To what could you compare your hero's brainpower?

• To what could you compare your hero's strength?

• What impossible acts will your hero be able to do?

▶ **Complete the information about your hero.**

My hero is a _____ named _____.

My hero is as big as _____.

My hero is as smart as _____.

My hero is as strong as _____.

My hero can _____

_____

_____

Most tall tales contain other characters besides the hero. In "Pecos Bill Gets a Wife," Pecos Bill is the hero. But Slewfoot Sue is also an important character. The story contains other minor characters: the preacher who married Bill and Sue, the other cowboys, and an animal character—Bill's horse, Widow Maker.

What other characters will be in your tall tale with the hero? Your characters may be people or animals. Remember that you don't want too many characters in a short story. Planning your characters will help you get more ideas for your story.

▶ **Plan two or three other characters for your tall tale.**
Write the name of a character in the center of a web.
In the outside ovals, write details about that character.

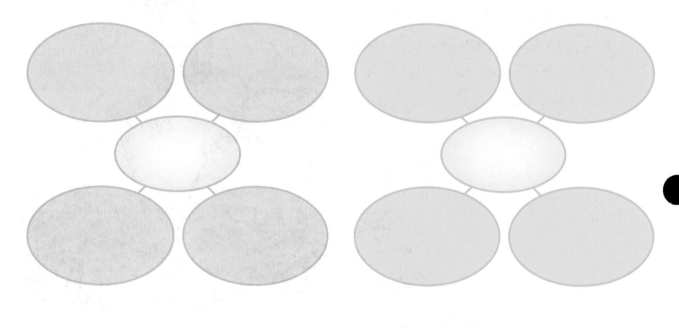

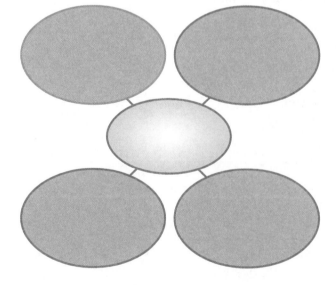

Planning the Problem

In a tall tale, the hero battles a powerful enemy. Sometimes the enemy is a force of nature, such as a tornado, a snowstorm, or a hurricane. Sometimes the enemy is an animal, such as a wild horse, a bear, or even a gigantic bee. The enemy could be another person, but it would have to be someone whose strength was equal to (or nearly equal to) the hero's strength. This struggle between the hero and an enemy is usually called the **problem** in a tall tale.

In Tasha's story, "The Biggest Bee in the South," Tom Toughguy's problem is finding a way to escape from a gigantic bee that is angry with Tom for using up all of its honey.

> Tom's problem is introduced near the beginning of the story.

. . . He was just about to pop the last three biscuits into his mouth when he heard a terrible sound like a chainsaw.

"Whoa!" he yelled. "That's the biggest bee I've ever seen!"

A gigantic bee was flying toward him. It was buzzing so loudly that Tom had to cover his ears . . .

The **solution** to the problem in a tall tale is usually an impossible act performed by the hero. In Tasha's story, Tom Toughguy blindfolds the gigantic bee with the huge red napkin he was using at breakfast. He chops off the bee's stinger so it can no longer hurt anyone.

What will the problem be in your tall tale? How will your hero solve the problem?

> Think about the things your hero can do. What type of problem would fit with your hero?

Possible Problems

- A hailstorm threatens to flatten the hero's town.
- A pack of wolves surrounds the hero's campground at night.
- A lion escapes from the zoo and ends up in the hero's backyard.
- A tidal wave puts the hero's beachside home in danger.
- A group of international thieves tries to steal some jewels in the hero's city.

Remember that the solution has to be an *impossible* act!

▶ **Plan your problem and solution. Choose from the list above or make up your own problem and solution.**

Problem: _____

_____

Solution: _____

_____

Planning the Setting

Name

The **setting** of a tall tale is the place and time in which the story happens. Many tall tales happen in particular places. The stories about Pecos Bill take place in the Old West. The tales about Paul Bunyan take place in the northern part of the United States where loggers live and work. Tasha's tall tale about Tom and the bee takes place in the southern state of Georgia.

If you set a tall tale in a particular place, make sure that the story's problem fits with that setting. What would be wrong with each of the following settings and problems being put together in a story?

> ***Problem:*** a forest fire
> ***Setting:*** the North Pole

> ***Problem:*** a whale trying to overturn a ship
> ***Setting:*** the Mexican desert

> ***Problem:*** a dust storm
> ***Setting:*** the continent of Antarctica

> ***Problem:*** a mountain rockslide
> ***Setting:*** the plains of Kansas

A tall tale's setting also includes the time at which the story happens. What would be the best time for the problem to happen? Should it happen in the middle of the night, in the morning, or at sunset? Should it happen in our time or in a long-ago time?

Times

midnight
early morning
in our time
long ago
in your grandparents' time

Places

Yellowstone National Forest
a busy city street
the desert
the Austrian Alps
the moon

What is the problem in your tall tale? In what type of setting would it fit best?

▶ **Plan your setting. Choose from the lists above or make up your own setting.**

Time: _____

Place: _____

Planning the Plot

Stories have a beginning, a middle, and an end. The events that happen in these three parts are called the **plot** of the story. A story's problem marks the point at which the story moves from the beginning to the middle. The solution marks the point at which the story moves from the middle to the end. Here is what the plot of a tall tale would include.

Plot

Beginning
- tells about the hero
- tells the setting

Problem →

Middle
- tells more about the problem
- tells how the hero tries to solve the problem

End
- tells what happens after the problem is solved

← Solution

The **plot pyramid** below shows the events that happen in each part of Tasha's tall tale.

Middle
Tom tosses orange juice at bee
Bee gets mad and comes closer

Problem
Giant bee comes after him

Solution
Tom blindfolds bee and cuts off stinger

Beginning
Tom Toughguy eats biscuits on his porch in Georgia

End
Bee leaves
Tom builds huge fire

Planning the Plot

Name

▶ Complete the plot pyramid to plan your story's plot.

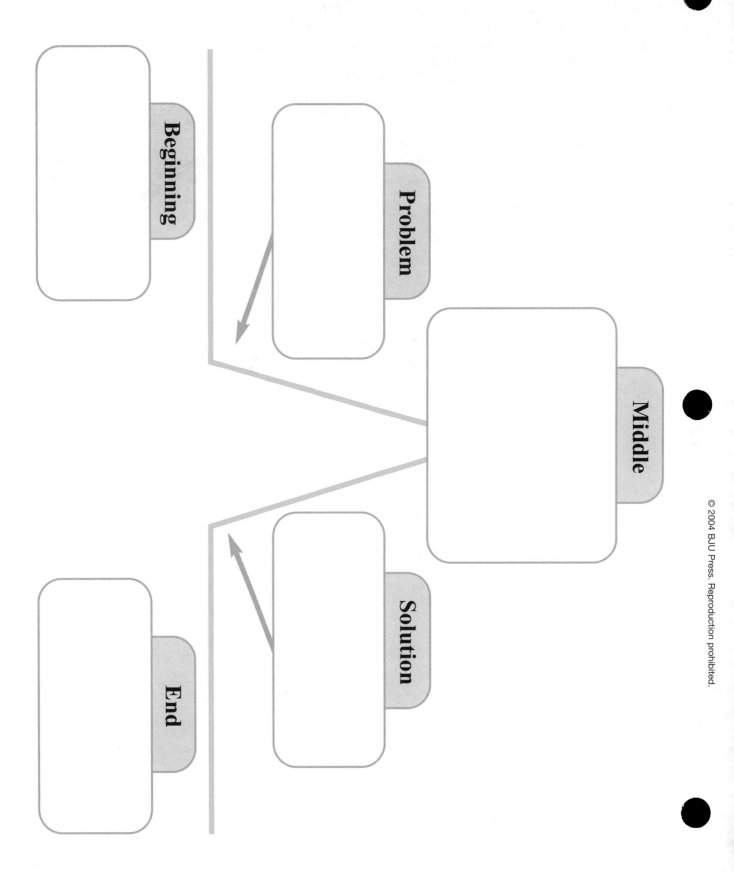

Beginning

Problem

Middle

Solution

End

English 4, Chapter 10, Lesson 94

Tall Tale: Drafting

Name

If a writer plans his story well, the drafting stage usually goes smoothly and takes less time. Using his plan as a guide, he can easily remember everything he wants to tell about in the story.

After Tasha had finished her planning, it was time to draft her tall tale. She gathered each of the pages on which she had planned her hero, the other characters in the story, the problem and solution, and the setting. She also got her plot pyramid and laid it beside her paper to use as a guide while she wrote. She included dialogue in her story.

Here is the rough draft of Tasha's tall tale.

The Biggest Bee in the South

It was a hot summer morning in georgia. Tom Toughguy was eating breakfast out on his porch. Every morning Tom ate five hundred biskits with honey on them. He was just about to pop the last three biskits into his mouth when he heard a terrible sound.

"Whoa! he yelled. "That's the biggest bee Ive ever seen!

A big bee was flying toward him. It was buzzing so loudly that Tom had to cover his ears. The bee was about the size of an elephant. Its stinger was really long. That bee was mad because Tom had used up all the honey in it's hive.

Tom tossed his glass of orange juice at the bee. That would have drowned most bees. But it just made this one madder. The bee came closer

---

and closer.

"You won't get me! said Tom. Then Tom unfolded his big red napkin. Tom threw it over the bee's head. He tied the napkin's edges in a not.

The bee could not see out of it's blindfold! Tom took his knife and chopped off the bee's stinger. That made the bee so upset that it just gave up and went home. Tom chopped the stinger up into small pieces and used it for firewood. People all over the South could see the smoke from that bonfire. People up north couldn't see it at all.

Tips for Drafting a Tall Tale

1. Write your story as if you were telling it out loud. Don't try to make it sound as if someone else has written it.

2. Tell about the hero and the setting as early as possible in the story.

3. Use the characters' spoken words to make the story come alive.

4. Use colorful words as you describe people and events in your story. Use words that will make your reader see pictures in his mind.

5. Don't worry about spelling, grammar, and punctuation mistakes as you write your first draft. You can fix those mistakes later.

6. Draft your tall tale on your own paper, skipping a line after each line you write.

7. Use your plot pyramid for help with the order of events.

▶ **Use your planning information from pages 183, 184, 185, 186, and 188 as you draft your tall tale.**

Tall Tale: Revising

After Tasha had finished drafting her tall tale, she shared it with Joseph.

"That was an exciting story!" Joseph said. "I really like your hero's name."

Joseph had some suggestions to make Tasha's tall tale even better. Tasha made the changes Joseph suggested. Then she went through the *Revising Checklist* and found some more changes that she needed to make.

> Joseph thought Tasha could add more colorful words to her tale. She chose words that would make her readers see and hear the things in her tale.

> Tasha used her thesaurus to find a more colorful word than *big*.

> Tasha described the stinger with a simile instead of an adjective.

The Biggest Bee in the South

It was a hot summer morning in georgia. Tom Toughguy was eating breakfast out on his porch. Every morning Tom ate five hundred biskits with honey ~~on them~~. *dripping* He was just about to pop the last three biskits into his mouth when he heard a terrible sound. *like a chainsaw*

"Whoa! he yelled. "That's the biggest bee Ive ever seen!

A ~~big~~ *gigantic* bee was flying toward him. It was buzzing so loudly that Tom had to cover his ears. The bee was about the size of an elephant. Its stinger was ~~really long~~. *as long as a telephone pole* That bee was mad because Tom had used up all the honey in it's hive.

Tom tossed his glass of orange juice at the bee. That would have drowned most bees. But it just made this one madder. The bee came closer

Tall Tale: Revising

Name _____

Tasha changed nouns to pronouns to avoid repeating Tom's name too often.

Tasha added exaggeration to show how fast Tom tied the knot.

Joseph wanted to see more details about how the bee acted.

Joseph felt that the ending would be stronger without the last sentence.

and closer.

"You won't get me! said Tom. Then ~~Tom~~ *he* unfolded his big red napkin. ~~Tom~~ *He* threw it over the bees head. *Quick as a lightning flash,* He tied the napkin's edges in a not.

It flew around in circles. It bumped into Tom's house. It smacked into a tree.
The bee could not see out of it's blindfold!

Tom took his knife and chopped off the bee's stinger. That made the bee so upset that it just gave up and went home. Tom chopped the stinger up into small pieces and used it for firewood. People all over the South could see the smoke from that bonfire. ~~People up north couldn't see it at all.~~

Revising Checklist

☐ 1. My tall tale has a beginning, middle, and end.

☐ 2. My tall tale has a clear problem and solution.

☐ 3. The beginning of my tall tale gives the hero and the setting.

☐ 4. The ending of my tall tale is satisfying.

☐ 5. My tall tale includes dialogue, or spoken words, of the characters.

☐ 6. My tall tale uses colorful descriptions and exaggeration.

Proofreading Marks

∧∨ Add

ℐ Delete

≡ Capital letter

/ Lowercase

↻→ Move

▶ Use the *Revising Checklist* and proofreading marks to mark changes as you revise your tall tale.

Tall Tale: Proofreading

Name _____

After Tasha finished revising her tall tale, she proofread it, using the checklist on page 194. She read her tale several times, looking for each item on the checklist. She marked the checklist as she proofread her tall tale.

Here is Tasha's tall tale with the changes she marked during the proofreading stage. What mistakes did she find? Which proofreading marks did she use to correct each mistake?

The Biggest Bee in the South

It was a hot summer morning in georgia. Tom Toughguy was eating breakfast out on his porch. Every morning Tom ate five hundred ~~biskits~~ _biscuits_ dripping with honey. He was just about to pop the last three ~~biskits~~ _biscuits_ into his mouth when he heard a terrible sound like a chainsaw.

"Whoa! he yelled. "That's the biggest bee Ive ever seen!

A gigantic bee was flying toward him. It was buzzing so loudly that Tom had to cover his ears. The bee was about the size of an elephant. Its stinger was as long as a telephone pole. That bee was mad because Tom had used up all the honey in ~~it's~~ _its_ hive.

Tom tossed his glass of orange juice at the bee. That would have drowned most bees. But it just made this one madder. The bee came closer and closer.

"You won't get me! said Tom. Then he unfolded his big red napkin. He threw it over the bee's head. Quick as a lightning flash, he tied the napkin's edges in a ~~not~~ *knot*.

The bee could not see out of ~~it's~~ *its* blindfold! It flew around in circles. It bumped into Tom's house. It smacked into a tree.

Tom took his knife and chopped off the bee's stinger. That made the bee so upset that it just gave up and went home. Tom chopped the stinger up into small pieces and used it for firewood. People all over the South could see the smoke from that bonfire.

Proofreading Checklist

1. I used contractions correctly.
2. I put each speaker's words in a new paragraph.
3. I put a capital letter at the beginning of each new sentence.
4. I put a punctuation mark at the end of each sentence.
5. I used correct punctuation within sentences.
6. I looked for misspelled words.

Proofreading Marks

∧∨   Add
ℓ   Delete
≡   Capital letter
/   Lowercase
↝   Move

▶ **Proofread your tall tale using the *Proofreading Checklist* and proofreading marks.**

English 4, Chapter 10, Lesson 97

A. Write the word that completes each sentence.

hero	plot	problem	setting	solution

1. The one who does impossible acts in a tall tale is called the _____.

2. The struggle between the hero and an enemy is called the _____.

3. The way the struggle is solved is called the _____.

4. When and where the events happen is called the _____.

5. The events that happen through a story's beginning, middle, and end are called the

_____ .

B. Fill in the circle next to the correct answer.

6. Which is the better way to tell what the character said?

   ○ Jenny said that she was thirsty.

   ○ "I'm so thirsty," Jenny moaned.

7. Which is a more colorful description of a rainstorm?

   ○ Raindrops as big as baseballs tumbled out of the sky, turning the dry ground into an ocean.

   ○ Rain fell from the sky, making the ground wet.

C. Write *TT* if the event could happen only in a tall tale. Write *R* if the event could happen in real life.

_____ 8. A boy drinks a super-size soda.

_____ 9. A woman rides a fast horse in a race.

_____ 10. A woman rides a horse that can run faster than the speed of light.

_____ 11. Lightning strikes a tree and splits a branch.

_____ 12. A cowboy lassoes a bolt of lightning and uses it to light his campfire.

_____ 13. A man drinks up a whole lake through a straw.

D. Fill in the circle next to the correct answer.

14. Which choice best describes people and events in a tall tale?
    ○ true to life
    ○ exaggerated

15. How many minor characters should you put in a tall tale?
    ○ as many as you can think of
    ○ only a few

16. In which part of a tall tale should you introduce the hero?
    ○ the beginning
    ○ the middle
    ○ the end

17. In which part of a tall tale should you introduce the setting?
    ○ the beginning
    ○ the middle
    ○ the end

18. In which part of a tall tale should you tell how the hero tries to solve the problem?
    ○ the beginning
    ○ the middle
    ○ the end

19. In which part of a tall tale should you tell what happens after the problem is solved?
    ○ the beginning
    ○ the middle
    ○ the end

E. Use proofreading marks to mark the four mistakes.

> Sam and his giant dog max raced up the mountain. Rocks were falling down the slope on either side of them? Sam grabbed a huge rock and tosed it off to the side. "We wont let a few pebbles stop us!" he said. "Keep up the good work, Max!"

Proofreading Marks

∧∨	Add
⌒	Delete
≡	Capital letter
/	Lowercase
⊶	Move

English 4, Chapter 10, Lesson 99

Cumulative Review

A. Underline twice the correct verb in each sentence. *(Chapter 5)*

1. We (be, are) tired.
2. (Is, Are) you going with us?
3. Grant (is, are) very tall.
4. Dan and Bret (is, are) shorter than Grant.

B. Fill in the circle next to the best way to search for a particular book in the library's electronic catalog. *(Chapter 7)*

5. You know the title of the book, but you don't know the author's name.
   ○ title   ○ author   ○ subject

6. You don't know the title of the book or the author's name.
   ○ title   ○ author   ○ subject

7. You know the author's name, but you don't know the title of the book.
   ○ title   ○ author   ○ subject

C. Match each description to the correct resource. *(Chapter 7)*

_____ 8. Set of books that contains articles about many subjects

_____ 9. Book of different kinds of maps

_____ 10. Book that tells definitions, pronunciations, usage in sentences, and spelling of words

_____ 11. Writing tool used to find words with similar meanings

> A. thesaurus
> B. encyclopedia
> C. dictionary
> D. atlas

D. Read this paragraph from an article about llamas. Fill in the circle next to the three outline parts that are *not* correct. *(Chapter 7)*

Lama Glama

Lama glama is the scientific name for a large plant-eating animal from South America. Its common name is llama. Llamas are mammals that graze on grass and browse on low bushes. At one time these woolly animals lived wild in herds. Today no more wild herds roam the mountains and highlands of South America. They live with, work for, and are cared for by man. They are domesticated.

Many people think that the llama looks like a camel. Its face is shaped like a camel's. It has large eyes, long eyelashes, and a split upper lip. The llama's long neck looks like a camel's too. But its body is smaller and woollier, and it does not have a camel's hump.

Lama Glama
○ I. How llamas live
○   A. Plant eaters
○   B. Once lived in wild herds
○   C. Look like camels
○   D. Domesticated
○ II. how llamas look
○   A. Eyes
○   b. Split upper lip
○   C. Neck
○   D. Body

Cumulative Review

E. Fill in the circle next to the correct definition of the word in italics to complete the sentence. *(Chapters 7 and 8)*

12. A *book review* is _____.
    ○ written to tell someone about a book and to give your opinion of the book
    ○ written to persuade someone to feel the same way you do about a book

13. *Fiction* is ____.
    ○ a make-believe story
    ○ a true story about someone's life

14. *Nonfiction* contains ____.
    ○ facts about real people, places, animals, things, and events
    ○ a story about a person

15. *Biographies* contain ____.
    ○ the life stories of real people
    ○ make-believe stories about real people

16. *Persuading* is ____.
    ○ specific parts of a story that support your reasons
    ○ convincing someone else to agree with your opinion

17. An *opinion* is ____.
    ○ something you think or feel
    ○ something that is true for everyone

18. A *fact* is ____.
    ○ something you think or feel
    ○ something that is true for everyone

←SKYWAY AIRLINES

F. Mark the two boxes that describe each underlined pronoun. *(Chapter 9)*

	Subject	Object	Singular	Plural
19. I took Emily to the airport.				
20. Emily thanked me for the ride.				
21. We carried her suitcases to the sidewalk.				
22. Emily left them there while she looked for a cart.				

Verb Tenses: Present, Past, & Future

Name _____

A **verb** tells what a subject is or does.

An **action verb** tells what the subject *does*.

> God created trees on the third day of Creation.

A **linking verb** tells what the subject *is* by linking it to a predicate noun or a predicate adjective.

> A tree is helpful to the environment.
>
> Trees are producers of oxygen.

The **tense** of a verb tells the time the subject does something.

A **present-tense verb** tells about something that is happening now or is continuing to occur.

> Jeff's company plants young pine trees.

A **past-tense verb** tells about what has already happened.

> Jeff's company planted oak trees.

A **future-tense verb** tells of a time in the future. The helping verb *will* is used to form future-tense verbs.

> Jeff's company will plant more trees.

Guided Practice

▶Underline the verb twice. Write *present, past,* or *future* to show the tense of the verb.

_____ 1. God created trees on the earth.

_____ 2. Trees are important.

_____ 3. Most trees produce oxygen.

_____ 4. Leaves collect carbon dioxide.

_____ 5. Some scientists studied a tree's use of carbon dioxide.

_____ 6. We will always thank God for designing trees for our good.

> God created plants and trees.
>
> Gen. 1:11–13

▶Write the correct verb form using the verb and tense in parentheses.

7. I _____ school at 8:00 this morning. *(past)*
   (start)

8. We _____ classes at 3:15. *(present)*
   (finish)

9. Lynn _____ to my house after school. *(future)*
   (come)

English 4, Chapter 11, Lesson 101

199

Verb Tenses: Present, Past, & Future

Name _____

◎ Independent Practice

▶ Underline the verb twice. Write *present*, *past*, or *future* to show the tense of the verb.

_____ 1. People and animals use oxygen.

_____ 2. Young trees make more oxygen than mature trees.

_____ 3. Scientists researched air pollution and trees.

_____ 4. Some trees remove pollutants from the air.

_____ 5. Healthy trees will clean the air around cities.

_____ 6. Trees are air purifiers.

_____ 7. Bare soil erodes easily.

_____ 8. Landscapers planted saplings and grass near the new highway.

_____ 9. City planners will sometimes study about trees in other cities.

_____ 10. They will usually plant more trees near new construction sites.

▶ Write the correct verb form using the verb and tense in parentheses.

11. The boys _____ piñatas at the party. *(present)*
        (break)

12. Their family _____ here from Mexico. *(past)*
        (move)

13. Their grandparents _____ to America soon. *(future)*
        (move)

14. Luis and Tony _____ this birthday custom. *(present)*
        (enjoy)

15. We _____ the twins at church tomorrow. *(future)*
        (see)

◐ Apply and Speak

▶ The sentences in this story are missing verbs. Think of a verb that will complete each sentence using the tense given. Read your story aloud to a friend.

God ____ *(past)* the world and everything in it. He ____ *(present)* people to take care of the creation. God ____ . *(future)*

Spelling
Present-Tense Verbs

Name _____

A **present-tense verb** tells about something that is happening now or is continuing to happen. The verb form must agree with the subject of the sentence.

A **singular subject** requires the **singular form of a verb**. A singular verb form ends in **s** or **es**.

> The *tree sprouts* new leaves.
> The *tree stretches* to the sky.

A **plural subject** and the pronouns *I* and *you* require the **plural form of a verb**. Most plural verb forms do not end in **s** or **es**.

> The *trees sprout* new leaves.
> The *trees stretch* to the sky.

Rules for Spelling Present-Tense Verbs with Singular Subjects

1. Add **s** to most verbs.	cut + **s** = cuts	The lumberman cuts the trees.
2. Add **es** to verbs ending in **s**, **ch**, **sh**, **x**, or **z**.	buzz + **es** = buzzes crash + **es** = crashes	The chain saw buzzes loudly. The tree crashes to the ground.
3. Change **y** to **i** and add **es** to verbs that end with a consonant and **y**.	carry – **y** + **i** + **es** = carries	The truck carries logs to the mill.

Guided Practice

▶ Underline the simple subject once. Underline the correct present-tense verb form twice.

1. Some trees (live, lives) more than two hundred years.

2. A crow (cry, cries) "Caw, caw!"

3. The sunlight (flashs, flashes) through the leaves.

4. My aunt and uncle (sell, sells) Christmas trees.

5. You (choose, chooses) the tree to be cut.

6. His helper (attachs, attaches) the tree to the top of the car.

▶ Write the correct present-tense verb form to complete each sentence.

7. The boy _____ in the lake each evening. (jump)

8. The child _____ in the water. (splash)

9. The bird _____ to its nest in the tree. (fly)

10. The man _____ the pipes under our sink. (fix)

Spelling
Present-Tense Verbs

Name _____

⦿ Independent Practice

▶ **Underline the simple subject once. Underline the correct present-tense verb form twice.**

1. Every day we (see, sees) wood in use.

2. The goalie (block, blocks) the shot with his wooden hockey stick.

3. Mark (use, uses) a wooden spoon with a long handle.

4. I (put, puts) together a wooden puzzle.

5. Companies (make, makes) paper from wood.

6. Tamara (brushs, brushes) paint on paper.

7. Soda (fizz, fizzes) in paper cups.

8. Mother and Mandy (carry, carries) the groceries in paper bags.

9. David (pass, passes) around his cardboard basketball cards.

10. Inventors (discover, discovers) new ways to use parts of trees every day.

Forester measuring a sapling

▶ **Circle the six incorrect present-tense verbs in the paragraph. Write each verb correctly.**

> Foresters manages the natural resources of forests. A wood company work with foresters. They chooses the best place to harvest trees. They plant saplings on the cleared land. A forester watch the growth of young saplings. Healthy trees replaces the old ones. A forester balance the need for wood with the needs of the environment.

11. _____

12. _____

13. _____

14. _____

15. _____

16. _____

② Apply and Write

▶ **Think of products that are made from trees. Write a sentence, using a singular subject and a present-tense verb about a tree product.**

_____

_____

▶ **Write a sentence, using a plural subject and a present-tense verb about another tree product.**

_____

_____

Spelling
Past-Tense Verbs

Name

A **past-tense verb** tells about an event that has already happened. Most past-tense verbs end in *ed*.

> *People* used *animal skins or papyrus before the invention of paper.*

Rules for Spelling Past-Tense Verbs

1. Add **ed** to most verbs.	walk + **ed** = walked	We walked through the paper factory.
2. Drop the **e** before adding **ed** to verbs ending with **e**.	move − **e** + **ed** = moved	A forklift moved large rolls of paper.
3. Double the final consonant before adding **ed** to words that end with a short vowel and a consonant.	chop + **p** + **ed** = chopped	A noisy machine chopped the wood into pulp.
4. Change **y** to **i** and add **ed** to verbs that end with a consonant and **y**.	carry − **y** + **i** + **ed** = carried	Vats on wheels carried the pulp to a large screen.
5. Add **ed** to verbs that end with a vowel and **y**.	stay + **ed** = stayed	We stayed with our groups.

Guided Practice

▶ **Write the correct past-tense verb form to complete each sentence.**

1. The Chinese _____ paper more than two thousand years ago. (invent)

2. Our art teacher _____ us his homemade paper. (show)

3. He _____ scrap paper and fabric pieces. (recycle)

▶ **Underline the correct past-tense verb form twice.**

4. Mr. Maxwell (copied, copyed) the directions for each of us.

5. Sarah Jean (stirred, stired) the paper pulp.

6. Nicholas (squished, squishd) the pulp onto a screen.

7. The sun (helped, helpped) the paper dry.

8. We (decorateed, decorated) bookmarks from our new paper.

◯ Independent Practice

▶**Write the correct past-tense verb form(s) to complete each sentence.**

1. Jesus _____ through the city of Jericho. (pass)

2. Zaccheus _____ a sycamore tree to see Jesus. (climb)

3. Jesus _____ the tree and _____

   up at him. (reach) (look)

4. He _____ Zaccheus to come down. (command)

5. Jesus _____ with Zaccheus, a sinner. (dine)

6. He _____ Zaccheus from his sin. (save)

▶**Underline the correct past-tense verb form twice.**

7. Fig trees (provided, provideed) both shade and food in Bible times.

8. People often (plantted, planted) fig trees next to wells to keep the water cool.

9. Jesus (curst, cursed) a fig tree that bore no fruit.

10. The tree (withered, witherd) immediately.

11. Jesus (conveyd, conveyed) the power of prayer through this miracle.

12. He (explaint, explained) to His disciples that they could do great things through faith.

▶**Choose the best verb to complete each sentence.**
 Write the correct past-tense form of the verb.

13. Madison _____ her brother by hiding his new tablet.

14. He _____ three guesses.

15. Madison _____ it after her brother's third guess.

| return |
| annoy |
| try |

◀ Apply and Speak

▶**The sentences in this story are missing verbs.**
 Think of past-tense action verbs that end in *ed*
 to fit each sentence. Read your story aloud to a friend.

> Taylor carefully ____ her plate out to the picnic table. Just before she ____ the table, she ____ over her shoestring and ____ her plate in a mud puddle. "Oh no!" she ____ .

Using Verb Tenses in Your Writing

Name _____

We use both the past tense and the present tense in writing. When we write about something historical, or when we write a fictional story, we usually use the past tense. When we write an essay or write about what happens in a book, we usually use the present tense. We also use the present tense to describe something in our time. When you write, keep your verbs in the same tense throughout the piece of writing. In the following paragraph, the writer switches from the **past** to the **present** tense.

> *The forest was a busy place at night. An owl hooted from its perch in an elm tree. Two rabbits hopped across the dark forest floor. Little brown mice scurry from their burrows. Two young skunks searched for night insects.*

The verb *scurry* should be changed to its past-tense form *scurried*.

▶ Guided Practice

▶ **The following story should be written in the past tense. Write the correct past-tense form of the verb to complete each sentence.**

The beaver _____ in the dirt. The beaver _____ dirty.
　　　　　　　(roll)　　　　　　　　　　　　　　　　(look)

Ants _____ into the beaver's fur. The beaver _____
　　　　(crawl)　　　　　　　　　　　　　　　　　　　　(comb)

its fur with its claws. It _____ itself carefully.
　　　　　　　　　　　　　　(groom)

▶ **The following story should be written in the present tense. Write the correct present-tense form of the verb to complete each sentence.**

The red fox _____ in the forest. It _____ very carefully.
　　　　　　　(hunt)　　　　　　　　　　　　　(move)

The crafty fox _____ toward the rabbit. It _____ close to
　　　　　　　　(creep)　　　　　　　　　　　　　　(crouch)

the ground. The fox _____ on the rabbit.
　　　　　　　　　　　(pounce)

▶ **Most of the verbs in this paragraph are past-tense. Proofread the paragraph. Use proofreading marks to delete the verbs that are not past-tense and add the correct past-tense verbs.**

Four raccoons lived in the hollow tree. They seemed curious. Father Raccoon opened some garbage cans. The baby raccoons hunt through the garbage. Mother Raccoon unlocks the chicken coop. The Raccoon family explored everything.

Proofreading Marks

∧∨　Add
⌐　Delete
≡　Capital letter
╱　Lowercase
◯→　Move

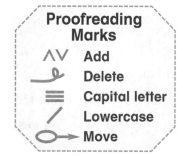

Using Verb Tenses in Your Writing

Name _____

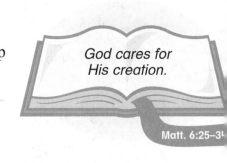

◉ Independent Practice

▶The following story should be written in the past tense. Write the correct past-tense form of the verb to complete each sentence.

The animals _____ in the forest during the winter. Deep
(stay)

snow _____ the cold ground. The snow _____
(cover)   (supply)

water for the forest animals. The animals _____ the cold
(endure)

winter months and _____ the coming of spring.
(welcome)

God cares for
His creation.

Matt. 6:25–3⁴

▶The following story should be written in the present tense. Write the correct present-tense form of the verb to complete each sentence.

Brandon _____ visiting the paper manufacturing plant. He
(enjoy)

_____ a machine mash wood fibers into pulp. Another large
(watch)

machine _____ the wood pulp and fibers from recycled paper.
(mix)

Large screens _____ water from the mixture. Heavy rollers
(filter)

_____ the mixture into thin sheets. Heaters _____
(press)   (dry)

the sheets into paper. One machine _____ the fresh paper onto
(roll)

cardboard tubes. Another machine _____ the rolled paper into
(trim)

sheets. A forklift _____ the new paper to the warehouse.
(carry)

◉ Apply and Speak

▶The sentences in this story are missing verbs. Think of past-tense action verbs to fit each sentence. Read your story aloud to a friend.

Joe ____ when the pepper got into his nose. His eyes ____ red and teary. He ____ to wash the pepper out of his eyes. He ____ to avoid pepper in the future.

Helping Verbs

Some action verbs have more than one word. The main verb tells the action of the subject. The helping verb comes before the main verb and helps it. If a helping verb is used, it must agree in number with the subject.

A **singular subject** requires the **singular form of a helping verb.**

> The *squirrel is* living in this tree.
> It *has* lived in this tree all summer.

A **plural subject** requires the **plural form of a helping verb.**

> Many *squirrels were* in this tree.
> *Squirrels have* lived there every year.

Subject	Helping Verbs	
singular subject pronouns: *he, she, it*	is, was, has, had	*Megan has gathered these leaves from a sweetgum tree.* *It is growing in Megan's yard.*
plural subject pronouns: *we, they, you*	are, were, have, had	*These birds were perching in an elm tree.* *They have joined others in their flock.*
I	am, was, have, had	*I was reading about different types of trees.* *I had brought books from the library.*

◀ Guided Practice

▶**Underline the simple subject once.**
  Underline the correct helping verb twice.

1. My grandfather (are, is) building a log cabin.

2. Several men (have, has) helped him each day.

3. They (was, were) sorting the logs yesterday.

4. Grandma (has, have) always liked log cabins.

5. Laura (have, has) visited the Sequoia National Forest twice.

6. Visitors (are, is) looking at the giant sequoia trees.

7. That tree (has, have) grown over 200 feet tall!

8. Some trees (has, have) lived for more than a thousand years.

Helping Verbs

◎ Independent Practice

▶**Underline the simple subject once. Underline the correct helping verb twice.**

1. I (am, is) <u>reading</u> about trees.

2. I (has, have) <u>read</u> a few books about trees before.

3. Sometimes the wind (have, has) <u>blown</u> the seed from far away.

4. A heavy rain (has, have) <u>helped</u> many seeds to soak into the soil.

5. Animals (have, has) <u>spread</u> seeds in several ways.

6. Squirrels (are, is) <u>burying</u> acorns to prepare for the winter.

7. Sometimes a furry animal (have, has) <u>carried</u> seeds in its fur.

8. Those trees (have, has) <u>dropped</u> their seeds into the water.

9. This kind of seed (is, are) <u>floating</u> to a new place on the shore.

10. Many seeds (are, is) <u>eaten</u> by small animals.

11. The air (have, had) <u>turned</u> colder.

12. Colorful leaves (was, were) <u>covering</u> the ground.

13. Acorns (has, had) <u>fallen</u> from the oak tree.

14. I (was, were) <u>watching</u> a gray squirrel with an acorn in its mouth.

15. The squirrel (have, had) <u>stuffed</u> its cheeks with acorns.

16. The acorns (were, was) <u>lying</u> deep in the soft soil.

17. He (was, had) <u>saved</u> the acorns for the winter.

18. Other squirrels (was, had) <u>gathered</u> nuts and seeds too.

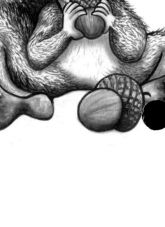

◢ Apply and Write

▶**Imagine being in or near a favorite tree. Write two sentences, using present-tense helping verbs about something that happens near the tree.**

_____

_____

_____

Irregular Verbs

Most present-tense verbs are changed to past tense by adding *ed*. These verbs are called **regular verbs.** Some verbs do not add *ed* when changed to the past tense. Because these verbs have special spellings, they are called **irregular verbs.**

Verb	Present Tense	Past Tense	Verb with *has, have,* or *had*
be	is, are	was, were	been
bring	bring, brings	brought	brought
come	come, comes	came	come
do	do, does	did	done
go	go, goes	went	gone
make	make, makes	made	made
run	run, runs	ran	run
say	say, says	said	said
sing	sing, sings	sang	sung
swim	swim, swims	swam	swum
tell	tell, tells	told	told
wear	wear, wears	wore	worn

Guided Practice

▶**Complete each sentence using the correct form of the verb in parentheses.**

1. A forest ranger _____ to our class last week. (come)

2. Ranger McNight has _____ to school for special training. (go)

3. She _____ us about a ranger's job. (tell)

4. The Forest Service _____ research at experiment stations. (do)

5. The Forest Service has _____ good use of our forests and resources. (make)

Irregular Verbs

Independent Practice

▶ **Complete each sentence using the correct form of the verb in parentheses.**

1. Allison _____ the newspaper home yesterday. (bring)

2. My family _____ in Uncle Lee's lake last summer. (swim)

3. Gabriel _____ a hymn during the church service last Sunday. (sing)

4. He has _____ in church on several occasions. (sing)

5. Caleb has _____ several carved animals with his grandfather. (make)

Sing praises to God.

Ps. 92:1   Ps. 14

▶ **Read each pair of sentences. Fill in the circle next to the correct sentence.**

6. ○ Forest firefighters wear fireproof clothing.
   ○ Forest firefighters worn fireproof clothing.

7. ○ Firefighters has runned their equipment for days.
   ○ Firefighters run their equipment for days.

8. ○ Last summer a forest fire went into three counties.
   ○ Last summer a forest fire goed into three counties.

9. ○ Some firefighters had came from other states.
   ○ Some firefighters had come from other states.

10. ○ They do an important job of saving lives and property from forest fires.
    ○ They have did an important job of saving lives and property from forest fires.

▶ **Underline the correct verb twice in each sentence.**

11. Tim (told, tell) his teacher about his family's vacation.

12. They (swum, swam) in the ocean by their uncle's house.

13. His family (worn, wore) sweaters in the cool evenings.

14. The forest fire (made, make) room for new trees to grow.

15. The wind (brought, bring) seeds from other trees.

Apply and Write

▶ **Write two sentences using the past-tense form of two irregular verbs from page 209.**

_____

_____

More Irregular Verbs

Remember that **irregular verbs** do not follow the regular rules of adding *ed* to form their past tense or when they are written with the helping verbs *has, have,* or *had.*

Verb	Present Tense	Past Tense	Verb with *has, have,* or *had*
begin	begin, begins	began	begun
drive	drive, drives	drove	driven
eat	eat, eats	ate	eaten
fall	fall, falls	fell	fallen
fly	fly, flies	flew	flown
give	give, gives	gave	given
grow	grow, grows	grew	grown
ride	ride, rides	rode	ridden
see	see, sees	saw	seen
take	take, takes	took	taken
throw	throw, throws	threw	thrown
write	write, writes	wrote	written

▶ Guided Practice

▶**Complete each sentence using the correct form of the verb in parentheses.**

1. Mr. Johnson has _____ woodworking classes at the nearby college. (take)

2. He _____ to the lumberyard yesterday to buy maple wood. (drive)

3. A scroll design always _____ at the top of each table leg. (begin)

4. The veneer _____ the table a smooth surface. (give)

5. We have _____ the table in their living room. (see)

More Irregular Verbs

◉ Independent Practice

▶Complete each sentence using the correct form of the verb in parentheses.

1. Sophia has _____ a horse at her friend's house in Texas. (ride)

2. She has never _____ from a horse. (fall)

3. Cameron _____ a report about preserving the forests. (write)

4. Some trees have _____ to over a hundred feet tall! (grow)

5. My cousins _____ to our home for their summer vacation. (fly)

6. They _____ fluffy clouds from the airplane window. (see)

7. I have _____ dinner on an airplane before. (eat)

8. Jasmine _____ the baseball to the catcher. (throw)

9. Her pitching has _____ to improve with practice. (begin)

10. Last weekend we _____ with our neighbors to the church picnic. (ride)

11. They have _____ us to church every Sunday. (drive)

▶Fill in the circle next to the correct sentence.

12. ○ The furniture making industry has growed.
    ○ The furniture making industry has grown.

13. ○ A lathe helps give shape to the spindles for the back of each chair.
    ○ A lathe helps given shape to the spindles for the back of each chair.

14. ○ Curls of wood fall to the floor as the men work.
    ○ Curls of wood fallen to the floor as the men work.

15. ○ Mr. Smythe has wrote instructions for making dovetail corners.
    ○ Mr. Smythe has written instructions for making dovetail corners.

16. ○ He taken special care to have the pieces fit together snugly.
    ○ He takes special care to have the pieces fit together snugly.

② Apply and Write

▶Write two sentences using irregular verbs from the chart on page 211. Use an irregular verb with *have, has,* or *had* in at least one of your sentences.

_____

_____

Confusing Verbs

Some action verbs in the English language may be confusing and are often used improperly.

Present Tense	Meaning	Past Tense	Verb with *had, have,* or *has*
lie, lies	to recline	lay	lain
lay, lays	to put something down	laid	laid
sit, sits	rest	sat	sat
set, sets	to put down	set	set
rise, rises	to get up	rose	risen
raise, raises	to bring up	raised	raised
learn, learns	to receive instruction	learned	learned
teach, teaches	to give instruction	taught	taught

The helping verbs *can* and *may* are also often misused.

Helping Verb	Meaning	Example
can	to be able to do something	Jose can speak loudly.
may	to be allowed or permitted to do something	You may borrow my pencil.

🔲 Guided Practice

▶ **Underline the correct verb twice.**

1. The foreman (lays, lies) a set of blueprints on the table.

2. The crew (sits, sets) in the shade during breaks.

3. They have (risen, raised) the first two stories ahead of schedule.

▶ **Write *C* if the verb used in the sentence is correct. Write *NC* if the verb used is not correct and then use** 🔄 **and** ∧ **to add the correct verb.**

_____ 4. Mr. Jordan can cut the boards accurately.

_____ 5. He has teached me about different saws.

Confusing Verbs

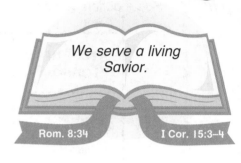

We serve a living Savior.

Rom. 8:34   I Cor. 15:3–4

◉ Independent Practice

▸**Underline the correct verb twice.**

1. Eric (may, can) use my crayons.

2. Please (set, sit) down and rest your tired feet.

3. Jesus has (risen, raised) from the dead.

4. Nicole (may, can) run faster than anyone else in the class.

5. Patrick (lies, lays) on the bed closest to the window.

6. Sophia (taught, learned) her little sister the alphabet.

7. Allison (sit, set) her books on the kitchen table.

8. She has (lain, laid) her coat on the chair.

9. Joshua (rose, raised) from his bed at 6:30 this morning.

10. Andrea has (learned, taught) a new song for her recital.

▸**Write *C* if the verb used in the sentence is correct. Write *NC* if the verb used is not correct. Use ⟨image⟩ and ⟨image⟩ to add the correct verb.**

_____ 11. Please sit your book bag on the back porch.

_____ 12. Then sit down at the table for your afternoon snack.

_____ 13. My little sister lays down for a nap every day.

_____ 14. The boys lay their coats down on the back seat of the car.

_____ 15. Mom said I can go to the party this Saturday.

◉ Apply and Speak

▸**Say two sentences using *can* and *may* correctly.**

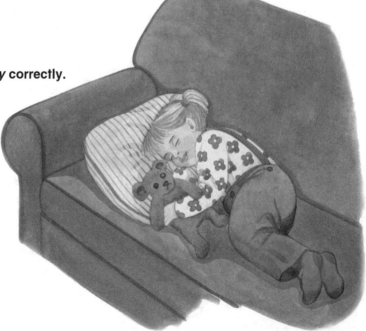

Name _____

A. Underline the verb twice. Write *present, past,* or *future* to show the tense of each verb.

_____ 1. The raindrops splatter on the windowpane.

_____ 2. The lightning flashed through the sky.

_____ 3. A rainbow will appear after the storm.

_____ 4. We watched the thunderstorm all afternoon.

_____ 5. I will write a poem about the thunder.

B. Underline the simple subject once. Underline the correct verb twice.

6. The plants (sprout, sprouts) new leaves every week.

7. A strange light (flash, flashes) in the side yard every ten minutes.

8. Emily (carry, carried) the laundry to her room.

9. She (folded, fold) her socks and put them away.

10. The bee (buzzes, buzz) through the sweet-smelling flowers.

11. I (will eat, will ate) some fresh honey on my toast tomorrow morning.

12. Garrett (live, lives) down the street from my church.

13. He (live, lived) in Baltimore for six years.

14. The swing (swayed, sway) back and forth in the summer breeze.

15. The baby (stretched, stretch) his arms to Grandpa.

C. Write the correct verb form using the verb and tense in parentheses.

16. Erin _____ an apple pie tomorrow. *(future)*
        (bake)

17. She _____ to make peach pies last summer. *(past)*
        (learn)

18. Erin _____ her own butter crust for the pie. *(present)*
        (make)

19. First, she _____ the flour and shortening together. *(present)*
        (mix)

20. Erin _____ first in her school's baking contest last week. *(past)*
        (place)

D. **Underline the simple subject once.**
   Underline the correct helping verb twice.

21. Seth (have, has) <u>written</u> a report about volcanoes.

22. I (am, has) <u>writing</u> my report about hurricanes.

23. My parents (has, have) <u>checked</u> out library books for me.

24. Marcus and Jackson (were, was) <u>planning</u> their report together.

25. Trevor (has, were) already <u>finished</u> his report.

26. I (were, was) <u>studying</u> about hurricanes last night.

E. **Read each pair of sentences. Fill in the circle next to the correct sentence.**

27. ○ Breanna and Blake singed a duet at church.
    ○ Breanna and Blake sang a duet at church.

28. ○ I have written to my grandmother three times this year.
    ○ I have wrote to my grandmother three times this year.

29. ○ You have seen giraffes at the zoo.
    ○ You have saw giraffes at the zoo.

30. ○ The birds flies to the lake for water.
    ○ The birds flew to the lake for water.

F. **Underline the correct verb twice.**

31. Mariah (sat, set) the baby down on the blanket.

32. She (lay, lie) down for a nap.

33. The sun has (risen, raised) over the sleeping forest.

34. (May, Can) I borrow your extra pencil for class?

35. My uncle (learned, taught) me a new game.

Cumulative Review

● **A. Draw a line between the complete subject and the complete predicate. Underline the simple subject once and the simple predicate twice.** *(Chapter 1)*

1. The beautiful yellow roses filled the vase.

2. The florist tied a bow around the vase.

3. My dad bought the flowers.

B. Use the code to label each sentence. Add the correct ending punctuation. *(Chapter 1)*

_____ 4. Shelby rode her bike to school

_____ 5. Shelby, watch out for that car

_____ 6. Tell her to look both ways

_____ 7. Which way will she turn

_____ 8. Her school is on the left

_____ 9. What time does school start

_____10. Hurry so you won't be late

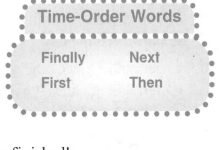

CODE

Dec. = Declarative
Int. = Interrogative
Imp. = Imperative
Exc. = Exclamatory

● **C. Write time-order words to complete the instructions.** *(Chapter 2)*

11. _____, Carlos pulled all the weeds.

12. _____, he cut the grass.

13. _____, he trimmed the bushes.

14. _____, he turned on the sprinklers and was finished!

Time-Order Words

Finally	Next
First	Then

D. Fill in the circle next to the book title that is written correctly. *(Chapter 3)*

15. ○ *A Question of Yams*
    ○ "A Question of Yams"

16. ○ The Mystery Of The Indian Carvings
    ○ The Mystery of the Indian Carvings

E. Fill in the circle next to the story title that is written correctly. *(Chapter 3)*

17. ○ The Snow-White Robin
    ○ "The Snow-White Robin"

18. ○ *Mort and the Sour Scheme*
    ○ "Mort and the Sour Scheme"

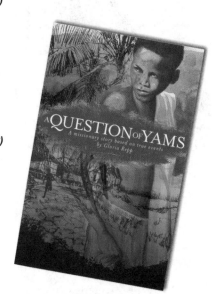

Cumulative Review

F. Rewrite each phrase using a singular possessive noun. *(Chapter 3)*

19. the feathers on the duck _____

20. the bottle belonging to the baby _____

G. Rewrite each phrase using a plural possessive noun. *(Chapter 3)*

21. the toys for the puppies _____

22. the books belonging to the women _____

H. Match the word to the correct proofreading mark. *(Chapter 4)*

_____ 23. Delete
_____ 24. Add
_____ 25. Capital letter
_____ 26. Move
_____ 27. Lowercase

A. ⟳→
B. ∧
C. /
D. ↶
E. ≡

I. Fill in the circle next to the correct sentence. *(Chapter 9)*

28. ○ Uncle Ron took we to the park.
    ○ Uncle Ron took us to the park.

29. ○ Jeff raced I down the hill.
    ○ Jeff raced me down the hill.

30. ○ Jeff and I kicked the soccer ball.
    ○ Jeff and me kicked the soccer ball.

31. ○ I made the first goal.
    ○ Me made the first goal.

32. ○ Us asked Uncle Ron to play.
    ○ We asked Uncle Ron to play.

J. Underline the correct verb twice. *(Chapter 9)*

33. She (write, writes) a letter to Grandma.

34. I (write, writes) a letter to my pen pal.

35. Mom (give, gives) us stamps for the envelopes.

36. We (take, takes) the letters to the mailbox.

37. The mailman (deliver, delivers) the letters.

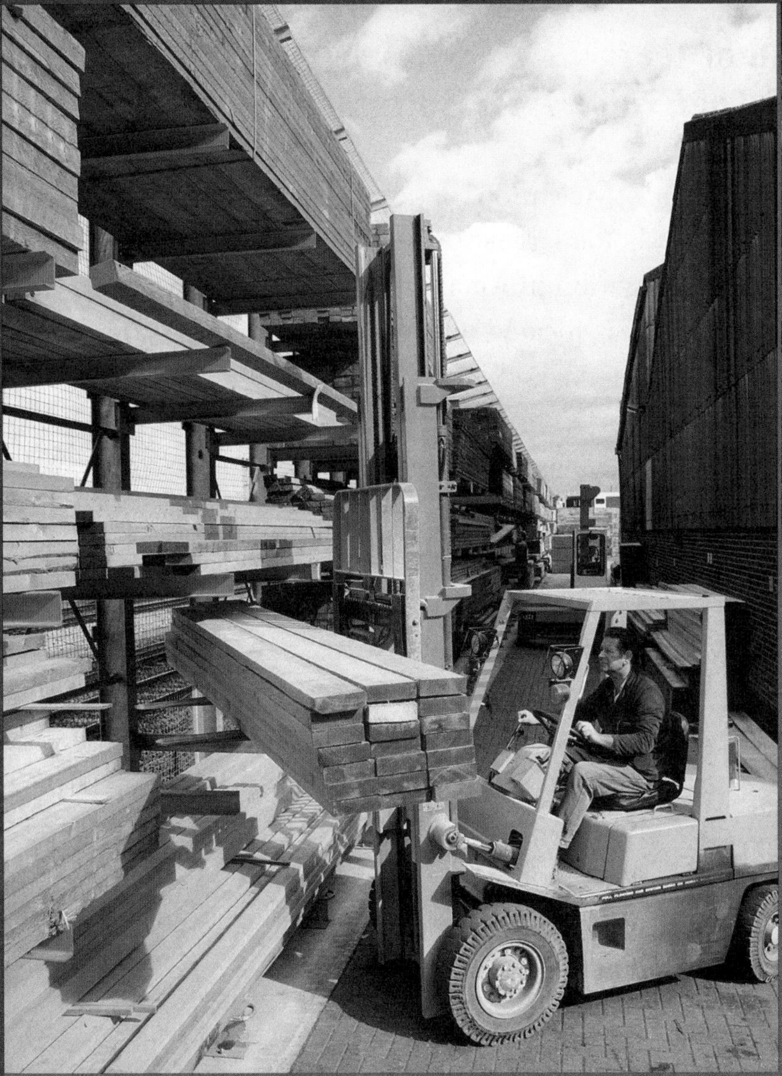

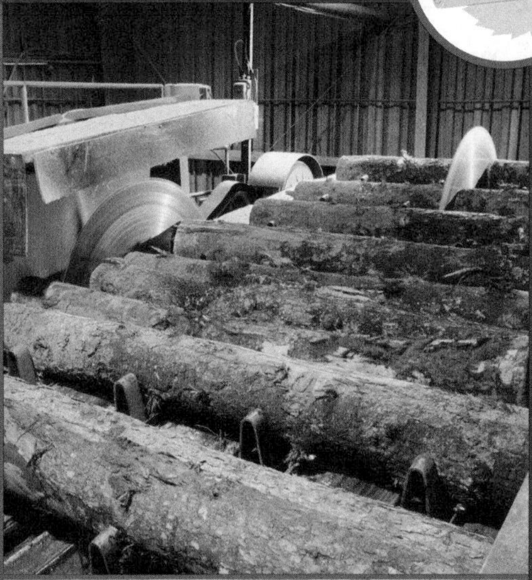

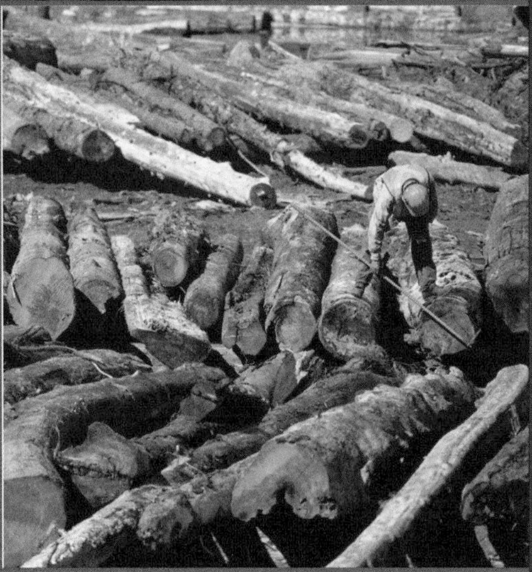

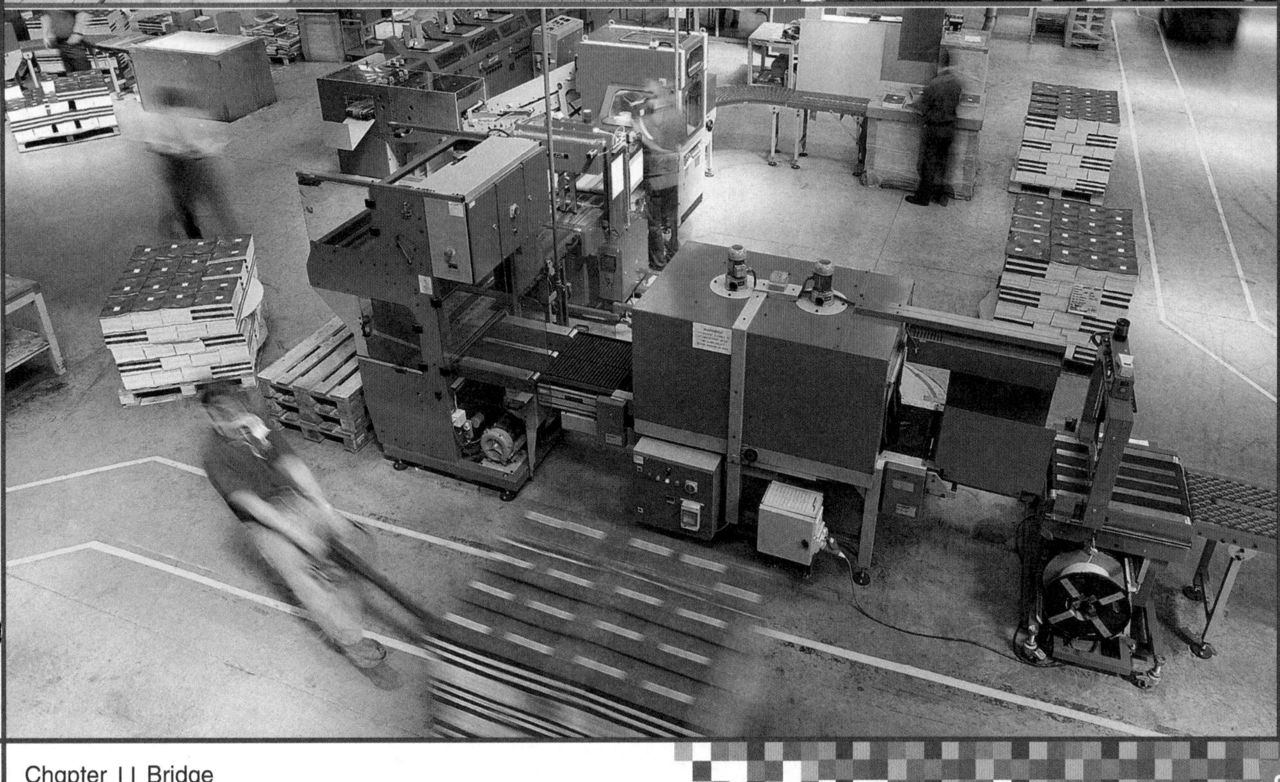

"Research Stations in the Land of Ice"
(from *Vacation Stations: Polar Explorer*, BJU Press)

Scientists go to Antarctica for many different reasons. Some go to study icebergs and glaciers. They make maps of Antarctica's coastline. Wind and tides are constantly causing Antarctica's ice to melt and freeze again. As pieces break off Antarctica's ice shelves, the coastline changes its shape. Scientists try to keep track of these changes.

Some scientists go to Antarctica to study wildlife. Penguins and seals are the most common wildlife. Other kinds of birds, such as petrels and gulls, often spend time in Antarctica. Whales can be found in the waters that surround the land.

Some scientists go to Antarctica to look for meteorites. Meteorites are dark pieces of rock that have fallen to the earth from outer space. Antarctica is one of the best places to find these rocks.

McMurdo Station is the largest research station in Antarctica. It is located on Ross Island, and it was started in 1956. It now has over one hundred buildings. It has a food supply room, a gym, and even a church. It also has a harbor and an airport. At McMurdo, people can get special training to learn how to work in a polar region. They can also use the station as a base when doing research. McMurdo is a busy place. Research teams are always coming and going.

What Is a Research Report?

Name

A **research report** gives facts about a topic. Your opinions, or how you feel about the topic, are not included. **Facts** are statements that are true and can often be checked in an encyclopedia, dictionary, or almanac.

Steps for Writing a Good Research Report

1. Choose your topic.

2. Decide the main ideas that you want to write about.

3. Read and take notes about your main ideas from books, magazine articles, encyclopedias, and the Internet.

4. Organize your information by writing an outline.

5. Write the first draft of your report from the outline.

6. Make revising changes to your report.

7. Make proofreading changes to your report.

8. Make a list of all the sources you used in your report.

9. Publish your report.

Think of an interesting country you would like to know more about. Your teacher will have suggestions of different countries for you to choose from. You will probably enjoy finding out new information about a country that you are not familiar with.

▶ Write the names of two countries you might be interested in learning more about.

_____   _____

Which country would you enjoy learning about more?

▶ Write the name of the country you have chosen in the blank. Then complete the chart.

I would like to write a report about _____ .

What I already know	What I would like to know
▶ _____	▶ _____
▶ _____	▶ _____
▶ _____	▶ _____
▶ _____	▶ _____
▶ _____	▶ _____
▶ _____	▶ _____

What Is a Research Report?

Cotter wrote a report about Ireland. Here is Cotter's final draft. Notice how each paragraph is about one main idea. Cotter did not include his opinions. He just wrote some of the facts he learned about Ireland.

Ireland: The Island Country

Ireland has green, rolling hills and rugged mountains. It is a beautiful place for tourists to visit. Ireland is an island and is slightly larger than the state of West Virginia. The grand Cliffs of Moher on the western coast drop seven hundred feet into the Atlantic Ocean.

Ireland's climate is mild. The winter season is cold and very wet. There is frequent rain and snowfall. The summer season is also wet, but warm. Ireland's skies are mostly cloudy throughout the year, and winds blow off the Atlantic Ocean daily.

The people of Ireland enjoy many traditional customs and holidays. At Christmas, the Irish display lighted candles in their windows to welcome the Holy Family. One popular holiday is St. Patrick's Day. Modern Irish people have festivals and plays to honor the memory of St. Patrick. He explained the Trinity with a shamrock leaf and drove snakes from the land.

There are several religions in Ireland today. Legends say that St. Patrick was the first person to bring Christianity to Ireland in A.D. 432. The largest religion in Ireland is Roman Catholicism, and the second largest is Protestant Presbyterianism.

Research reports use **paragraphs** to tell about the topic. The first sentence of each paragraph is called the **topic sentence** and tells one main idea. The other sentences in the paragraph are details that tell about the main idea in the topic sentence.

The Cliffs of Moher

Taking Notes

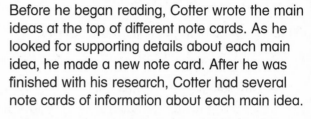

Cotter's teacher gave him four main ideas to include in his research report about Ireland. Each main idea was one paragraph in the research report. Here are the four main ideas Cotter researched:

- Geography
- Climate
- Interesting customs or holidays
- Main religions

> These are the same four main ideas that you will write about in your report.

Before he began reading, Cotter wrote the main ideas at the top of different note cards. As he looked for supporting details about each main idea, he made a new note card. After he was finished with his research, Cotter had several note cards of information about each main idea.

As Cotter read information about Ireland, he took notes to remember the facts that he found. He wrote down only enough words to remember the information. He did not copy sentences he had read. Here is an example of information Cotter read in a book called *Ireland's Beauty* by Kevin Pelham. Notice the notes Cotter took.

Most of the country has gently sloping hills that are green year round due to the high amount of annual precipitation. The country is located on an island with 1,448 kilometers of rugged coastline. The well-known Cliffs of Moher are located on the western coast of the island. In some places, these cliffs rise nearly seven hundred feet from the ocean. Low, jagged mountains surround the plain areas of the country. The North Atlantic Current directly affects the island, causing winds to blow constantly.

Ireland's Geography

1. green rolling hills
2. country is an island
3. Cliffs of Moher—famous; 700 feet high; on west coast
4. rugged mountains around plains

Ireland's Beauty, page 13

> Notice that Cotter wrote the title and page number where he found the information. These facts will help him remember the *source* of the information.

You will need to use at least two sources of information for your research report. One source should be an encyclopedia. The other sources may be nonfiction books, magazine articles, or the Internet.

Be sure to record all the information you know about the sources you use on the page your teacher gives you or on a separate sheet of paper. After you write your report, you will write a **bibliography.** A bibliography is a list of the sources of information used in the writing part of the report.

Taking Notes

Name

▶ Guided Practice

▶ **Fill in the circle next to each correct answer.**

1. The title at the top of each card should be ___.
   - ○ the name of the topic you will be researching
   - ○ one main idea about the topic you will be researching

2. When taking notes from a book, it is a good idea to ____.
   - ○ copy exactly what the author said to use in your report
   - ○ write down just enough to remember the information

3. When you are finished with your research, you should have completed ____.
   - ○ several note cards about each of the main ideas you researched
   - ○ only one note card about each main idea you researched

4. After taking notes from a source, you should always ____.
   - ○ write information about the source
   - ○ write only the author's name at the bottom of the card

5. The list of all the sources you used to write your report is called a ____.
   - ○ biography
   - ○ bibliography

▶ **Answer the questions.**

6. What are two possible sources you could look in to find information for your report?

7. What are the four main ideas you will research for your report?

▶ **Begin locating and reading information about the country of your choice. As you read, take notes on separate note cards. Don't forget to record the title of the source and the page number.**

© 2004 BJU Press. Reproduction prohibited.

Writing an Outline

After Cotter took notes about each of his main ideas, he organized his information about Ireland in an **outline.** An outline is a way to organize your ideas before you begin to write. Cotter knew that his four main ideas at the top of his note cards would become the four main points of his outline and each would be identified by a Roman numeral.

As Cotter read his note cards, he chose only the most interesting information to include in his outline. He did not use all of the details on his note cards.

Here are two of Cotter's note cards about his third main idea, *Customs and Holidays in Ireland.* The note cards are from two different sources. Notice how Cotter organized the information from these cards on his outline.

Customs and Holidays in Ireland

1. light a candle in window at Christmas, welcome the Holy Family
2. Christmas—clean house from top to bottom
3. use holly branches to decorate homes

<u>Christmas in Ireland</u>, pages 3, 5

Customs and Holidays in Ireland

1. St. Patrick's Day—festivals, plays
2. St. Patrick used shamrock as a picture of the Trinity
3. some people believe St. Patrick drove snakes out of Ireland

<u>Irish Holidays</u>, pages 16, 25

III. Customs and Holidays in Ireland

    A. Christmas—modern Irish light a candle in window to welcome the Holy Family

    B. St. Patrick's Day—have festivals and plays honoring the saint

    C. St. Patrick—legends say he explained the Trinity with a shamrock leaf and drove snakes from Ireland

▶ **Compare Cotter's note cards to his outline. Fill in the circle next to the correct answer.**

1. How many details did Cotter list altogether on these two note cards?
   ○ 3   ○ 5   ○ 6

2. How many of the details on these note cards did Cotter use in his outline?
   ○ 3   ○ 4   ○ 5

Writing an Outline

▶️ Guided Practice

▶ Read these two note cards about Ireland's geography. Choose four details
that you believe are the most important and write them in outline form.

Ireland's Geography

1. green rolling hills
2. country is an island
3. Cliffs of Moher—famous; 700 feet
   high; on west coast
4. rugged mountains around plains

Ireland's Beauty, page 13

Ireland's Geography

1. island country
2. a little larger than West Virginia
3. Cliffs of Moher by the Atlantic Ocean
4. has beautiful, lush, green landscape
   and rolling farmlands, and mountains

The World Encyclopedia, Vol. 10, page 416

I. Ireland's Geography

A. _____

_____

B. _____

C. _____

D. _____

_____

Sample Outline
I. ___ Geography
  A.
  B.
  C.
II. ___ Climate
  A.
  B.
  C.
III. Interesting Customs or
Holidays in ___
  A.
  B.
  C.
IV. Main Religions in ___
  A.
  B.
  C.

▶ Write an outline to organize the information from your note cards for
writing your research report. You might not use all the details from
your note cards. Choose the most important facts to include in your
outline. Your outline will have four main ideas. Each main idea
should have at least three supporting details.

▶ Write your outline on your own paper.

Writing the First Draft

Name _____

 Here is Cotter's outline and first draft for the first and second paragraphs of his report.

Ireland

I. Ireland's Geography
   A. A good place for tourists
   B. An island
   C. Slightly larger than West Virginia
   D. Cliffs of Moher—seven hundred feet high and on the west coast by the Atlantic Ocean
II. Ireland's Climate
   A. Mild spring and fall
   B. Wet and cold winter with lots of rain and snow
   C. Warm and wet summer
   D. Mostly cloudy skies all year
   E. Winds blowing from the Atlantic Ocean every day

> Notice that Cotter skipped lines in his draft so that he would have room to make his revising and proofreading changes later.

Ireland

Ireland has green hills and rugged mountains. It is a beautiful place for turists to visit. This country is an island. It is slightly larger than the state of west Virginia. The big Cliffs of Moher on the western coast drop seven hundred feet into the Atlantic ocean.

Ireland's climate is mild. The winter season is cold and very wet. It rains and snows a lot. I would not like to visit Ireland in the winter! The summer season is also wet, but warm. Ireland's skies are mostly cloudy throughout the year, and winds blow off the Atlantic Ocean a lot.

▶ **Use your outline to write the first draft of your research report on your own paper. Write a topic sentence for each paragraph that tells the main idea of that paragraph. Use the details from your outline to write sentences that tell about the main idea.**

English 4, Chapter 12, Lesson 114

Research Report: Revising

Name

Cotter and his partner, Stephen, talked about how to make Cotter's report better.

Here are Stephen's comments:

1. Ireland sounds like a beautiful country!
2. Your opinion about visiting Ireland should not be included in a research report.
3. Some of your sentences could be combined into compound sentences to add variety.

Cotter thought about Stephen's comments as he read his report again. He checked the thesaurus for a more exact word for *big*. He crossed out the sentence that included his opinion. He also combined some of his sentences to make them more interesting and added to his title.

Here are Cotter's first and second paragraphs of his first draft with his revisions marked.

Ireland :The Island Country

rolling
Ireland has green hills and rugged mountains. It is

Ireland
a beautiful place for turists to visit. ~~This country~~ is an

and
island. ~~It~~ is slightly larger than the state of west Virginia.

grand
The ~~big~~ Cliffs of Moher on the western coast drop seven

hundred feet into the Atlantic ocean.

Ireland's climate is mild. The winter season is cold

There is frequent rain and snowfall.
and very wet. ~~It rains and snows a lot. I would not like~~

~~to visit Ireland in the winter!~~ The summer season is also

wet, but warm. Ireland's skies are mostly cloudy

throughout the year, and winds blow off the Atlantic

daily
Ocean ~~a lot~~.

Ireland's rolling hills and stone fences

228

English 4, Chapter 12, Lesson 115

Research Report: Revising

Name _____

▶ Read your report with your partner. Write any questions or comments your partner has about the information in your report.

1. _____

2. _____

3. _____

▶ Take time to look through your note cards and read your outline again if you need to search for additional details.

▶ Revise your report using the *Revising Checklist*. Try to include answers to your partner's questions. Use proofreading marks to mark your changes.

Revising Checklist

☐ 1. Each paragraph is about one main idea.

☐ 2. All of the sentences in each paragraph tell about its main idea.

☐ 3. I used exact words.

☐ 4. All of my sentences tell facts.

☐ 5. I included enough details.

☐ 6. I combined sentences to add more variety.

Proofreading Marks

∧∨ Add

↗ Delete

≡ Capital letter

/ Lowercase

↻→ Move

Research Report: Proofreading

Name

After Cotter revised his report, he was ready to proofread it. He read his report several times to check for each item on the list—complete sentences, capital letters, punctuation marks, and misspelled words. Here is how the third and fourth paragraphs of Cotter's report looked when he was finished proofreading.

> The people of Ireland enjoy many traditional *customs* ~~customs~~ and holidays. At Christmas, the Irish display lighted candles in *their* ~~there~~ windows to welcome the Holy Family one popular holiday is St. Patrick's Day. Modern Irish people have festivals and plays to honor the memory of St. Patrick. He explained the trinity with a shamrock leaf and drove snakes from the land.
>
> There are several religions in Ireland today. Legends say that St. Patrick was the first person to bring Christianity to *Ireland* ~~Iraland~~ in A.D. 432. The largest religion in Ireland is Roman catholicism, and the second largest is Protestant Presbyterianism.

▶ **Proofread your report using the *Proofreading Checklist*. Use proofreading marks to mark your mistakes. When you are finished, you will be ready to write the final draft.**

Proofreading Checklist

☐ 1. I used complete sentences.

☐ 2. I put a capital letter at the beginning of each sentence.

☐ 3. I put a punctuation mark at the end of each sentence.

☐ 4. I used capital letters correctly within the sentences.

☐ 5. I looked for misspelled words.

Proofreading Marks

∧∨   Add

Delete

≡   Capital letter

/   Lowercase

⌒→   Move

The Bibliography

Name

A **bibliography** is a list of all the sources you used in your report. This list may include encyclopedias, books, magazine articles, or Internet sources.

- The bibliography tells others where you found the information for your report and gives proper credit to the authors.
- The bibliography lists all the information needed for locating your source. This information includes the author, title of the article and/or book, the publication location, and the publisher and date.
- A bibliography lists the sources in alphabetical order by the authors' last names.

Here is the first draft of Cotter's bibliography.

Bibliography

Beam, Ira. Irish Holidays. San Diego, CA: Agar Press, 2002.

Fowler, Dale. "Ireland." The Travel Encyclopedia. Vol. 8. Albany, NY: Children's Press, 1999.

O'Shea, Leigh. Christmas in Ireland. Dallas, TX: World Press, 2000.

General Pattern for a Book

Author(s). Title of book. Place of publication: Publisher's name, year.

General Pattern for an Encyclopedia

Author. "Title of Article." Title of encyclopedia. Volume number. Place of publication: Publisher's name, year.

The Bibliography

Name _____

▶ Guided Practice

Source 1: ● book ○ encyclopedia article

Author: _Peter Robiero_

Title: _Visiting Italy_

Encyclopedia Volume: _____

Publisher: _Vineyard Press_

Publishing Place: _Oakland, CA_   Date of Publishing: _1999_

Source 2: ● book ○ encyclopedia article

Author: _Rex Walley_

Title: _Modern Italian Customs_

Encyclopedia Volume: _____

Publisher: _Barker Press_

Publishing Place: _Chicago, IL_   Date of Publishing: _2003_

Source 3: ○ book ● encyclopedia article

Author: _Erma Neigh_

Title: _"Italy" The Travel Encyclopedia_

Encyclopedia Volume: _8_

Publisher: _World Press_

Publishing Place: _New York, NY_   Date of Publishing: _2003_

Remember

Remember to list the sources in alphabetical order by the authors' last names.

▶ Write a bibliography using the information above. See Worktext page 231 for the proper form.

1. _____

    _____

2. _____

    _____

3. _____

    _____

▶ Write the bibliography for your report. List the sources alphabetically by the authors' last names using proper form.

Chapter 12 Review

A. Fill in the circle next to the correct answer.

1. Facts are _____.
   - ○ statements that express your opinion
   - ○ statements that are true

2. The _____ is the first sentence of each paragraph and tells one main idea.
   - ○ topic sentence
   - ○ key sentence

3. The _____ is a list of the sources used in a report.
   - ○ biography
   - ○ bibliography

4. The title at the top of each note card should be _____.
   - ○ one main idea about the topic
   - ○ the title of the report

5. After taking notes from a source, you should always _____.
   - ○ write only the author of the source at the bottom of the card to give him credit
   - ○ write important information about the source at the bottom of the card

**B. Write _T_ if the statement about the stages of writing a research report is true.
Write _F_ if the statement is false.**

_____ 6. Before you revise your report, you should write the first draft.

_____ 7. After you have decided the main ideas you want to write about, you should begin taking notes.

_____ 8. You should organize your information in an outline before you decide the main ideas you want to write about.

_____ 9. Make a list of all the sources used in your report when you are ready to publish it.

_____ 10. Write the first draft of your report after organizing your information in an outline.

C. List three possible sources in which you could find information for a research report.

11. _____

12. _____

13. _____

Chapter *12* Review

D. Answer the questions using the sources given.

> Beam, Ira. <u>Irish Holidays.</u> San Diego, CA: Agar Press, 2002.

14. What is the title of this source? _____

15. What is the name of the publisher? _____

> Gillmor, David A. "Ireland." <u>The World Book Encyclopedia</u>. Vol. 10. Chicago, IL: World Book, 1994.

16. Who wrote the encyclopedia article about Ireland? _____

17. When was the encyclopedia published? _____

E. Read the note cards about Victoria Falls. Choose three details and write them in outline form.

> *Facts About Victoria Falls*
>
> 1. in Zimbabwe, Africa
> 2. sighted by missionary David Livingstone, 1855; named it for Queen Victoria of Britain
> 3. best time to visit is flood season (Feb.–Mar.)

> *Facts About Victoria Falls*
>
> 1. spray from the falls sustains small rainforest
> 2. Zambezi River, 1 mile wide at mouth of falls
> 3. height of falls, 355 ft. in center; 256 ft. on sides

I. Facts About Victoria Falls

   A. _____

   _____

   B. _____

   _____

   C. _____

   _____

Cumulative Review

A. Make a compound subject or a compound predicate by combining the pair of sentences using *and*. *(Chapter 1)*

1. Roses grow in our yard.
   Daisies grow in our yard.

   _____

2. Jenny washed the clothes.
   Jenny ironed the clothes.

   _____

B. Circle the common nouns. Mark the proper nouns that should have a capital letter using ☰. *(Chapter 3)*

3. I opened the book and read about the wilsons.

4. This family lived in new zealand.

5. Their farm was near auckland.

6. They raised cows and sold milk to pleasant pastures dairy.

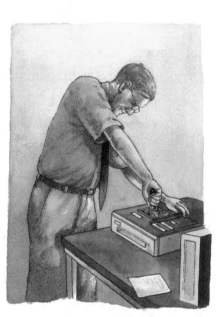

C. Write the correct possessive pronoun to replace each possessive noun. *(Chapter 9)*

7. _____ father owns his own business.
   (Caleb's)

8. He fixes _____ computers when they are broken.
   (the customers')

9. Last week, Mr. Autry fixed _____ computer.
   (my family's)

10. He replaced _____ hard drive.
    (the computer's)

11. Mr. Autry showed my mom where to save _____ files.
    (Mom's)

Cumulative Review

D. Write the word that completes each sentence. *(Chapter 10)*

hero	plot	problem	setting	solution

12. The one who does impossible acts in a tall tale is called the _____.

13. The struggle between the hero and an enemy is called the _____.

14. The way the struggle is solved is called the _____.

15. When and where the events happen is called the _____.

16. The events that happen through a story's beginning, middle, and end are called the _____.

E. Read each pair of sentences. Fill in the circle next to the correct sentence. *(Chapters 9 and 11)*

17. ○ I has visited the new library already.
    ○ I have visited the new library already.

18. ○ Our class was planning a trip to see the new library.
    ○ Our class were planning a trip to see the new library.

19. ○ Mr. McKinney is going to drive the bus.
    ○ Mr. McKinney are going to drive the bus.

20. ○ We am bringing lunches to eat in the park.
    ○ We are bringing lunches to eat in the park.

21. ○ The trash can lost it's lid.
    ○ The trash can lost its lid.

22. ○ The townspeople like their town to be clean.
    ○ The townspeople like they're town to be clean.

23. ○ We must pick up all ours trash.
    ○ We must pick up all our trash.

24. ○ Aisle look for the trash can lid.
    ○ I'll look for the trash can lid.

25. ○ I believe that bag of chips is yours.
    ○ I believe that bag of chips is your.

26. ○ I will put all my trash in the trash can.
    ○ I will put all mine trash in the trash can.

27. ○ Make sure your ready when the bus comes.
    ○ Make sure you're ready when the bus comes.

Name

An **adjective** is a word that describes a noun. Adjectives tell **what kind** or **how many.**

> *One-fifth of the Earth is covered by barren areas.*   what kind
> *Five continents contain these regions.*   how many

Adjectives often come before the noun they describe in a sentence.

> *Deserts do not receive much rainfall.*

Some adjectives come after the noun that they describe. These adjectives follow linking verbs and describe the subject of the sentence.

> *The Sahara Desert is hot.*

Diagram an adjective that comes before a noun on a line that slants below the noun it describes.

> *Large camels live in some deserts.*

subject	verb

adjective

camels	live

Large

Diagram a predicate adjective after the linking verb. Notice that the slanted line points the predicate adjective toward the subject it describes.

> *Roadrunners are fast.*

subject	linking verb \	predicate adjective

Roadrunners	are \	fast

◪ Guided Practice

▸Circle the adjective that describes each underlined noun. Decide whether the adjective tells *what kind* or *how many*. Circle the correct answer.

1. Some <u>deserts</u> are near the mountains.   what kind   how many

2. Mountains keep rain away from the hot <u>desert</u>.   what kind   how many

3. Strong <u>wind</u> forms dunes in deserts.   what kind   how many

▸Circle the six adjectives that tell *what kind* or *how many.*
Underline the noun that each adjective describes.

4. Deserts have dry climates.

5. Hot deserts have temperatures of over a hundred degrees.

6. Cold deserts receive snow instead of rain.

7. Eight deserts in the world are cold deserts.

sand dunes

▸Diagram the simple subject, the verb, and adjective from Sentence 6 above.

8. _____

Adjectives

Name

◉ Independent Practice

▶ Circle the adjective that describes each underlined noun.
Decide whether the adjective tells *what kind* or *how many*.
Circle the correct answer.

1. Many <u>kinds</u> of plants grow in the desert.   what kind   how many

2. These plants store large <u>amounts</u> of water.   what kind   how many

3. Some plants have deep <u>roots</u> to get water.   what kind   how many

4. Plants with shallow <u>roots</u> take in moisture quickly.   what kind   how many

5. Leaves are small on most <u>plants</u> in the desert.   what kind   how many

▶ Circle the four adjectives that tell *what kind* or *how many*.
Underline the noun that each adjective describes.

6. Deserts are interesting.

7. Unusual animals live in the desert.

8. Beautiful wildflowers bloom in the desert.

9. The wildflowers are gorgeous.

▶ Diagram the simple subject, the verb, and adjective of
Sentences 6, 7, 8, and 9.

10. (Sentence 6)

_____

11. (Sentence 7)

_____

12. (Sentence 8)

_____

13. (Sentence 9)

_____

desert wildflowers

② Apply and Write

▶ Write two sentences that describe the picture above. Circle the adjectives
in your sentence that tell *what kind* or *how many*.

Special Adjectives

Name _____

The words *a, an,* and *the* are special adjectives called **articles**.

Use *a* with singular nouns that begin with a consonant sound.

> *a plant*
> *a hat*

Use *an* with singular nouns that begin with a vowel sound. Some words that start with *h* begin with a consonant sound. Others begin with a vowel sound.

> *an animal*
> *an honor*

Use *the* with singular nouns to name a particular person, place, or thing and with all plural nouns.

> *the desert*
> *the dunes*

A **proper adjective** is an adjective formed from a proper noun. Proper adjectives are always capitalized.

> *American citizen*
> *Spanish language*

Diagram articles and proper adjectives on a slanted line beneath the nouns they describe.

> *The African girl smiled.*

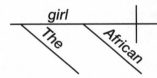

🕩 Guided Practice

▶ **Write the article *a* or *an* in each blank.**

1. _____ peanut   2. _____ alligator   3. _____ igloo   4. _____ school

▶ **Underline the correct article to complete each sentence.**

5. (The, An) saguaro cactus looks like arms reaching into the sky.

6. (The, An) barrel cactus gets its name from its barrel shape.

7. (A, An) prickly pear cactus has long thorns for protection.

8. (A, An) juice made from the aloe plant is a good medicine.

saguaro cactus

▶ **Underline the proper adjective in each sentence.**

9. The Sonoran desert is the home of the saguaro cactus.

10. My favorite place to eat is a Japanese restaurant.

▶ **Mark the letters that should be capitalized by using the proofreading mark ☰.**

11. The ambassador is mexican.   12. An italian diplomat greets him at the airport.

▶ **Diagram the simple subject, the verb, and all of the adjectives in this sentence.**

13. The new teacher is Chinese.

Special Adjectives

Name _____

Independent Practice

▶**Write the article *a* or *an* in each blank.**

1. _____ astronaut   3. _____ honor

2. _____ kitchen   4. _____ backpack

▶**Underline the correct article to complete each sentence.**

5. God made (the, an) cactus plant to store water.

6. (The, An) pleats of many cactus plants expand during times of rain.

7. The plants get smaller when (the, a) water is gone.

8. (A, An) animal gets water by eating desert plants.

9. (The, An) fruit of the saguaro cactus is used to make jam.

10. The cactus's skeleton may become (a, an) part of a house!

▶**Underline the proper adjective.**

11. Mom fixed Polish sausage for the missions banquet.

12. Mrs. Abrams made Swedish meatballs.

13. I like Mexican food the best.

14. A good Chinese dish is stir-fry.

prickly pear cactus

▶**Mark the letters that should be capitalized by using the proofreading mark ☰.**

15. The man giving a speech is german.

16. They are missionaries to the hawaiian islands.

▶**Diagram the simple subject, the verb, and all of the adjectives in this sentence.**

17. The American president is interesting.

_____

Apply and Write

▶**Write two sentences about a mission field you would like to visit. Where is it located? What language do the people speak?**

_____

_____

Adverbs

Adverbs describe verbs. They tell **how, when,** or **where** something happens. Most adverbs that tell **how** end in **ly.**

The cheetah *swiftly* moved across the field.	how
The children went *inside.*	where
They arrived at the amusement park *yesterday.*	when

An **adverb** is not always written near the **verb** that it describes in the sentence.

Slowly the snake *crawled* across the desert.
The snake *slowly crawled* across the desert.
The snake *crawled* across the desert *slowly.*

Diagram an adverb on a line that slants below the verb that it describes.

simple subject | verb
adjective   adverb

The child tiptoed softly.

child | tiptoed
The   softly

Guided Practice

▶ Circle the adverb that describes each underlined verb. Decide whether the adverb tells *how, when,* or *where.* Circle the correct answer.

1. The roadrunner quickly <u>caught</u> the rattlesnake. how when where

2. Gila monsters often <u>live</u> underneath rocks. how when where

3. The vulture <u>swooped</u> down from the sky. how when where

▶ Circle the adverb in each sentence.
Underline twice the verb that each adverb describes.

4. The Great Jerboa sleeps quietly in the daytime.

5. Tonight the Great Jerboa will hunt again.

6. It searches hungrily for seeds and insects.

7. This small rodent digs nearby in the sand.

bearded vulture

▶ Write an adverb that completes the sentence by answering the question in parentheses.

(Where?) 8. The game will be played _____.

(When?) 9. His birthday party is _____.

▶ Diagram the simple subject, the verb, and all the adjectives and adverbs in this sentence.

10. The large animal ate slowly. ―――――――――――――

Adverbs

◎ Independent Practice

▶ Circle the adverb that describes each underlined verb. Decide whether
the adverb tells *how, when,* or *where.* Circle the correct answer.

1. The dingo <u>howls</u> loudly across the Australian desert.   how   when   where

2. The fur on its back <u>stands</u> straight in times of fear or anger.   how   when   where

3. Dingoes <u>chase</u> sheep and rabbits there.   how   when   where

4. Dingoes usually <u>behave</u> like dogs.   how   when   where

▶ Circle the adverb in each sentence.
Underline twice the verb that each adverb describes.

5. Thorny devil lizards live only in the Australian deserts.

6. Thorny devils move slowly.

7. A frightened lizard tucks its head down.

8. For protection it puffs up with air.

thorny devil lizard

▶ Write an adverb that completes each sentence by answering
the question in parentheses.

(When?)   9. She _____ attends piano recitals.

(Where?) 10. Mother went _____ .

(How?)   11. Amanda _____ put the puzzle together.

▶ Diagram the simple subject, the verb, and all of the adjectives and
adverbs in each of these sentences.

12. The girl sang sweetly.

13. The five children walked slowly.

_____   _____

◑ Apply and Write

▶ Write a sentence telling how the armadillo lizard might move.
Include an adverb in your sentence.

_____

Adjective or Adverb?

Name

An **adjective** is a word that describes a noun. Adjectives tell **what kind** or **how many.** Adjectives may be written before the noun they describe or after a linking verb. The articles **a, an,** and **the** are special adjectives.

The tiny *baby* slept in the crib.

The *air* is smoky.

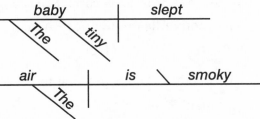

Adverbs describe verbs. They tell **how, when,** or **where** something happens. Most adverbs that tell **how** end in **ly.** Adverbs are not always written near the verbs they describe.

The cars <u>sped</u> noisily around the racetrack.

Tonight the winner <u>will celebrate</u> his victory.

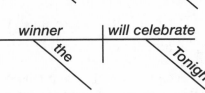

Guided Practice

▶ **Decide whether each underlined word is an adjective or an adverb. Fill in the circle next to the correct answer.**

1. Her <u>new</u> folder is on the desk.
   ○ adjective   ○ adverb

2. Jane bought it <u>yesterday</u> at the store.
   ○ adjective   ○ adverb

3. The folder is <u>purple</u>.
   ○ adjective   ○ adverb

▶ **Underline one adjective and circle one adverb in each sentence.**

4. Ramon sometimes eats two sandwiches for lunch.

5. Yesterday his sandwich was big.

6. His kind sister quickly packs their lunches.

7. Ramon carefully pours hot soup into bowls.

▶ **Diagram the simple subject, the verb, and all adjectives and adverbs in this sentence.**

8. The three kittens purr softly. ⎯⎯⎯⎯⎯⎯⎯⎯⎯⎯

Adjective or Adverb?

Name _____

◉ Independent Practice

▶**Decide whether each underlined word is an adjective or an adverb. Fill in the circle next to the correct answer.**

1. The football team practiced <u>hard</u> before the big game.
    ○ adjective   ○ adverb

2. The <u>excited</u> players listened to their coach.
    ○ adjective   ○ adverb

3. The quarterback ran <u>swiftly</u> with the ball.
    ○ adjective   ○ adverb

4. The team cheered <u>loudly</u> after the winning touchdown.
    ○ adjective   ○ adverb

5. Their uniforms were <u>muddy</u> after the game.
    ○ adjective   ○ adverb

▶**Underline the adjective that tells *what kind* or *how many*. Circle the adverb in each sentence.**

6. Mom baked three cakes today.

7. Her cakes always taste good.

8. She carefully cuts her chocolate cake.

9. Then she serves large slices for everyone.

▶**Write an adjective or adverb to complete each sentence.**

(adverb)   10. The children entered the room _____ .

(adjective) 11. A _____ piece of paper was on the floor.

▶**Diagram the simple subject, the verb, and all adjectives and adverbs in this sentence.**

12. A fat spider crawled outside.

_____

◉ Apply and Speak

▶**Add adjectives and adverbs to make your sentence interesting. Be prepared to read your sentence aloud.**

The _____ snake slithered _____ down the wall.

Comparing with er & est

Name _____

Use **er** and **est** to compare how things are alike and different.
Both adjectives and adverbs use **er** and **est** to compare.

Adjectives may be used to compare two or more **people, places,** or **things.**

Add the suffix **er** to short adjectives to compare two. Add the suffix **est** to compare more than two.

An orange is larger than a lemon.

The grapefruit is the largest citrus fruit of all.

Adverbs may be used to compare two or more **actions.**

Add the suffix **er** to short adverbs to compare two. Add the suffix **est** to compare more than two.

Nikki ran faster than Calvin did.

Jorge ran the fastest of all the runners.

Some adjectives change the spelling of the word when adding **er** or **est.** Adverbs do not change their spellings.

When an adjective **ends in a consonant and y,** change **y** to **i** before adding **er** or **est.**

| heavy | heavier | heaviest |

When an adjective ends with an **e,** drop the **e** before adding **er** or **est.**

| strange | stranger | strangest |

When an adjective has **only one vowel and ends in a consonant, double the final consonant** before adding **er** or **est.**

| big | bigger | biggest |

◀ Guided Practice

▶Write the **er** and **est** forms of each adjective or adverb.

1. funny _____ _____

2. slow _____ _____

3. cool _____ _____

roadrunner

▶Underline the correct adjective or adverb in each sentence.

4. The red racer snake moves the (faster, fastest) of any desert snake.

5. The temperature in desert regions is (hotter, hottest) than in mountain regions.

6. The cactus is a (sturdier, sturdiest) plant than a pine tree because it stores water.

▶Write the adjective or adverb form of the word in parentheses to compare the animals.

7. A dingo is a _____ desert animal than an armadillo lizard. (loud)

8. The roadrunner runs the _____ of any bird in the desert. (fast)

Comparing with
er & est

⊙ Independent Practice

▶ **Write the *er* and *est* forms of each adjective or adverb.**

1. great _____ _____
2. rainy _____ _____
3. big _____ _____
4. high _____ _____
5. late _____ _____

▶ **Underline the correct adjective or adverb in each sentence.**

6. The camel is (larger, largest) than a horse.

7. Camels can survive (long, longer) without drinking water than people.

8. No animal can travel (farther, farthest) than a camel in the desert.

9. Camels are (stronger, strongest) than donkeys.

10. Camels' heads are (higher, highest) than most animals.

Bactrian camels

▶ **Write the adjective or adverb form of the word in parentheses.**

11. It is _____ for a camel to walk on sand than for a horse. (easy)

12. Camels have the _____ eyelashes of all desert animals. (thick)

13. Camels drink the _____ of any mammal. (fast)

⊘ Apply and Write

▶ **Many stories have been written about camels living in the desert. What other information do you know about camels? What have you read about them in stories? Write at least two sentences about camels.**

_____

_____

dromedary camels

Comparing with More & Most

Name _____

Use **more** with long adjectives to compare two people, places, or things. Use **most** with long adjectives to compare more than two.

> *In-line skates are more expensive than roller skates.*
> *Skateboards are the most expensive.*

Use **more** with longer adverbs and adverbs that end in **ly** to compare two. Use **most** with longer adverbs and adverbs that end in **ly** to compare more than two.

> *Leslie picked the puppy up more carefully than the mother dog did.*
> *She lifted the smallest puppy the most carefully.*

More and *most* are never used with *er* or *est* in writing the same word.

Guided Practice

▶ **Fill in the circle next to the correct answer.**

1. ○ Camels are probably the most famous of all desert animals.
   ○ Camels are probably the more famous of all desert animals.

2. ○ The Bactrian camel has larger humps than the dromedary camel.
   ○ The Bactrian camel has more larger humps than the dromedary camel.

3. ○ Camels are the more useful way to carry heavy loads in the desert.
   ○ Camels are the most useful way to carry heavy loads in the desert.

▶ **Write the correct adjective or adverb form for the word in parentheses.**

4. Camels are _____ than horses at surviving in the desert. (skillful)

5. Camels drink water _____ than cows do. (fast)

6. Items made from camel hair are the _____ in the desert. (plentiful)

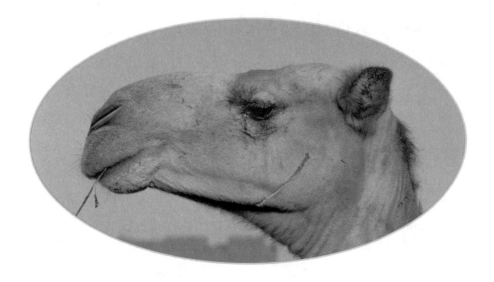

Comparing with More & Most

Independent Practice

▶ **Fill in the circle next to the correct answer.**

1. ○ Camel races are the most popular races in the Middle East.
   ○ Camel races are the more popular races in the Middle East.

2. ○ Some people think that camel meat is more delicious than beef.
   ○ Some people think that camel meat is most delicious than beef.

3. ○ Bactrian camels have longest fur than Arabian camels.
   ○ Bactrian camels have longer fur than Arabian camels.

4. ○ Camels can move more steadily than horses in the hot sand.
   ○ Camels can move most steadily than horses in the hot sand.

Arabian camel

▶ **Write the correct adjective or adverb form for the word in parentheses.**

5. The Arabian Desert is the _____ home for dromedary camels. (common)

6. This desert has some of the _____ roads in the world. (ancient)

7. Nomads live in this desert _____ than in American deserts. (frequently)

▶ **Proofread the paragraph. Find the three mistakes using *more* and *most* to compare. Use the proofreading marks to delete the mistakes and add the correct words.**

I went to the camel exhibit at the zoo. They were the more curious animals I have ever seen. One camel was most hateful than the other. He spit his food at the visitors. We tried to keep our distance. The second camel was considerater than his buddy. He came to the fence to admire the visitors!

Proofreading Marks
∧∨ Add
 ℓ   Delete

Apply and Speak

▶ **What did you learn about camels in this lesson?**
Share your thoughts as your teacher leads the discussion.

Special Forms for Good & Bad

Name _____

The words **good** and **well** are often confused in sentences. **Good** is always used as an **adjective**. **Well** is an **adverb** unless it is talking about someone's health.

Rita made a *good* grade on her book report.	adjective
Chad plays the piano *well*.	adverb
The teacher does not feel *well* today.	adjective

Special Adjectives That Compare

One	Two	More than Two
good	better	best
bad	worse	worst

Special Adverbs That Compare

One	Two	More than Two
well	better	best
badly	worse	worst

Guided Practice

▶**Write *good* or *well* to complete each sentence.**

1. Dr. White is a _____ doctor.

2. He does his job _____.

3. A _____ surgeon is hard to find.

▶**Underline the correct adjective form.**

4. Mom makes the (good, best) spaghetti of anyone I know.

5. The chocolate cake is (better, best) than the coconut cake.

6. The weather is (worse, worst) this week than last week.

7. That was the (bad, worst) storm we've had in years.

▶**Underline the correct adverb form.**

8. He wrote (badly, worst) with his broken arm.

9. Thomas ran (worse, worst) in the second race.

10. The singer performed (well, worst) in her recital.

11. Sarah likes volleyball the (best, worst) of all sports.

Special Forms for *Good & Bad*

◉ Independent Practice

▶ **Write *good* or *well* to complete each sentence.**

1. They had a _____ time at the birthday party.

2. Margo ran _____ in the race.

3. The parents thanked the principal for his _____ work.

4. Are you a _____ listener?

5. Tim did his homework _____ .

▶ **Underline the correct adjective form to compare in each sentence.**

6. The barber gave Tony a (good, best) haircut.

7. It was (worst, better) than his last haircut.

8. The last haircut was the (bad, worst) one he'd ever had.

9. It was (good, worse) than the one Tony gave himself.

▶ **Underline the correct adverb form.**

10. The storm (bad, badly) damaged the roof of our house.

11. He coughed (worse, worst) today than yesterday.

12. An eagle flies (good, better) than a rooster.

13. The trip went (good, well).

14. He hits (good, best) with a wooden bat.

▶ **Proofread the paragraph. Find the three mistakes using *good* and *well*. Use proofreading marks to delete the mistakes and add the correct words.**

> Mike likes to read mystery stories. If the story is written good, he can usually figure out the clues. "A well detective," says Mike, "has to put the clues together to solve the case." Mike believes that the best cases involve a detective who asks questions good and has a good mind for solving problems.

Proofreading Marks

∧∨ Add
∘⌐ Delete

◑ Apply and Write

▶ **Write one sentence using *good* correctly and one sentence using *well* correctly.**

_____

_____

Suffixes

Name _____

A **suffix** is a word part added to the end of a base word. Adding a suffix makes a new word with a different meaning.

> color + ful = colorful

Some adjectives change the spelling of the word when adding a suffix. Adverbs do not change their spellings.

When an adjective **ends in a consonant and y,** change **y** to **i** before adding **er** or **est.**

> scary   scarier   scariest

When an adjective ends with an **e,** drop the **e** before adding **er** or **est.**

> large   larger   largest

When an adjective has **only one vowel and ends in a consonant, double the final consonant** before adding **er** or **est.**

> thin   thinner   thinnest

Some words change their part of speech and their spelling when a suffix is added.

> penny + less = penniless   mud + y = muddy
> noise + y = noisy   beauty + ful = beautiful

Guided Practice

▶Underline the word in each sentence that has a suffix. Circle the suffix.

Jesus Christ died for the sins of mankind.

John 3:16

1. Miranda is a reporter for the local newspaper.

2. Once a thief made an agreement to talk with her.

3. He said that he was not guilty of any crimes.

4. Miranda knew that he was not being truthful with her.

5. Miranda told the hopeless man about Christ's love and forgiveness.

▶Add a suffix to the word in parentheses to complete each sentence. See page 347 for a list of suffixes.

6. It would be _____ if you would do the dishes. (help)

7. A fox is a _____ animal. (trick)

8. Nails are _____ without a hammer. (use)

9. Mr. Nelson is the _____ of those new homes. (build)

10. The weatherman said that tomorrow will be a _____ day. (rain)

Suffixes

Name

⊙ Independent Practice

▶ **Underline the word in each sentence that has a suffix. Circle the suffix.**

1. She is frequently late for school.

2. The Pilgrims made a new settlement in Massachusetts.

3. It is foggy today.

4. He was tired after a sleepless night.

5. My new dress is washable.

6. God wants us to be thankful in all things.

▶ **Add a suffix to the word in parentheses to complete each sentence.
See page 347 for a list of suffixes.**

7. Jonathan is a _____ person. (thought)

8. The roses in Mrs. Smith's garden are _____ . (beauty)

9. We were very _____ after the race. (thirst)

10. The chickens ran _____ around the yard. (wild)

11. The players were filled with _____ after the game. (excite)

12. You will be _____ in school if you study. (success)

13. The sky is _____ today. (cloud)

14. We are _____ for our food and homes. (thank)

15. Are your new shoes _____ ? (comfort)

② Apply and Write

▶ **Many adjectives that describe weather have suffixes. Write about today's weather.
Underline the adjectives that contain suffixes.**

_____

_____

A. Circle the adjective that describes each underlined noun.
Decide whether the adjective tells *what kind* or *how many*.
Circle the correct answer.

1. David's rock collection has many <u>types</u> of rocks.   what kind   how many

2. Some of his <u>rocks</u> are large, and some are only pebbles.   what kind   how many

3. Some rocks have smooth <u>surfaces</u>.   what kind   how many

4. David's favorite <u>one</u> has gold flecks in it.   what kind   how many

5. Several <u>rocks</u> came from the desert of New Mexico.   what kind   how many

B. Underline the correct article to complete each sentence.

6. Lynn got (a, an) new camera for her birthday.

7. (The, A) directions for using the camera were easy to follow.

8. (The, An) film was loaded first.

9. Next Lynn put (the, a) batteries in the camera.

10. She focused her camera on (a, an) beautiful red rose.

C. Circle the adverb that describes the underlined verb.

11. Maria and Katie <u>will swim</u> at the pool today.

12. Maria <u>swims</u> fast in swimming races.

13. The girls <u>walk</u> carefully around the edge of the pool.

14. They <u>dry</u> themselves quickly before leaving.

D. Write the *er* and *est* forms of each adjective or adverb.

15. hard _____   _____

16. big _____   _____

17. rainy _____   _____

E. Write the correct adjective or adverb form for the word in parentheses.

18. The pie tasting contest is the _____ booth at the fair. (popular)

19. The cherry pie was _____ than the apple pie. (delicious)

20. Pumpkin pie was bought _____ than blueberry pie. (frequently)

21. People were the _____ about the vinegar pie than any other pie. (curious)

22. The _____ pie was Aunt Carol's blueberry pie. (outstanding)

F. Write *good* or *well* to complete each sentence.

23. Donna is a _____ softball player.

24. She pitches the ball _____.

25. She is also a _____ batter.

26. Her team had a _____ season this year.

27. Donna hopes they will play _____ next season.

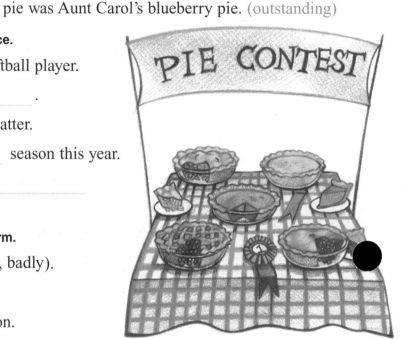

G. Underline the correct adjective or adverb form.

28. Yesterday the cut on my arm hurt (bad, badly).

29. The cut is (worse, worst) today.

30. I hope the cut will get (good, well) soon.

31. We have the (better, best) doctor in town!

H. Diagram the simple subject, the verb, and all adjectives and adverbs in this sentence.

32. A big lion roared loudly.

_____

Cumulative Review

A. Underline the correctly spelled noun or abbreviation in each sentence. *(Chapter 3)*

1. Aaron has an appointment to see the (Doctor, doctor) tomorrow.
2. Our school hosted a visit from (Gov., Gvnr.) Sanchez.
3. The Bible assures us that God is our (Father, father).
4. Every (Saturday, saturday) my dad makes pancakes for breakfast.
5. School will be out in (June, june).
6. (Msr., Mr.) Miller is our basketball coach.
7. My uncle plays for the (Chicago bears, Chicago Bears).
8. All of the (wives, wifes) got flowers on (Mother's Day, mother's Day).
9. We gathered (bunchs, bunches) of wildflowers in the field.
10. A family of (mice, mouses) lives behind the wall.

B. Match the words to the correct part of a friendly letter *(Chapter 4)*

_____ 11. *Dear Adrian,*
_____ 12. Name of the person writing the letter
_____ 13. *Your friend,*
_____ 14. Main part of the letter
_____ 15. Address of the person writing the letter

> A. body
> B. closing
> C. greeting
> D. heading
> E. signature

C. Underline the words that can form contractions. Write the contractions. *(Chapter 5)*

16. I have decided to take piano lessons.
17. My mom thinks that is a good idea.
18. I have not played before.
19. I cannot imagine anyone who does not want to learn.

D. Underline twice the correct form of the helping verb. *(Chapter 5)*

20. The horse (has, have) won the race.
21. Five horses (does, do) graze in that field.
22. They (is, are) sleeping in the stable now.

Cumulative Review

E. Correct the double negative by deleting or replacing one of the underlined negatives. Write your new sentence. *(Chapter 5)*

23. My dog, Ginger, <u>doesn't</u> like <u>no</u> cats.

_____

F. Underline the correct homophone. *(Chapter 9)*

24. We (ate, eight) dessert at (ate, eight).

25. We sang our favorite (him, hymn) for (him, hymn).

26. It didn't cost a (sent, scent, cent) when she (sent, scent, cent) me stickers with a fruity (sent, scent, cent).

27. The beautiful pink (flour, flower) on that cake is made of (flour, flower).

28. Everybody (nose, knows) you can sing through your (nose, knows).

G. Complete each sentence with the correct form of the verb in parentheses. *(Chapter 11)*

29. Heidi just _____ me a secret. (tell)

30. I had _____ to her house for dinner. (come)

31. Jeremy has _____ three inches this year. (grow)

32. A peach _____ from the tree. (fall)

33. Yesterday Dad _____ me five dollars. (give)

H. Choose the correct verb in parentheses to complete each sentence. *(Chapter 11)*

34. _____ you do fifty sit-ups? (May, Can)

35. _____ those glasses on the table, please. (Sit, Set)

36. Juan _____ me how to speak Spanish. (taught, learned)

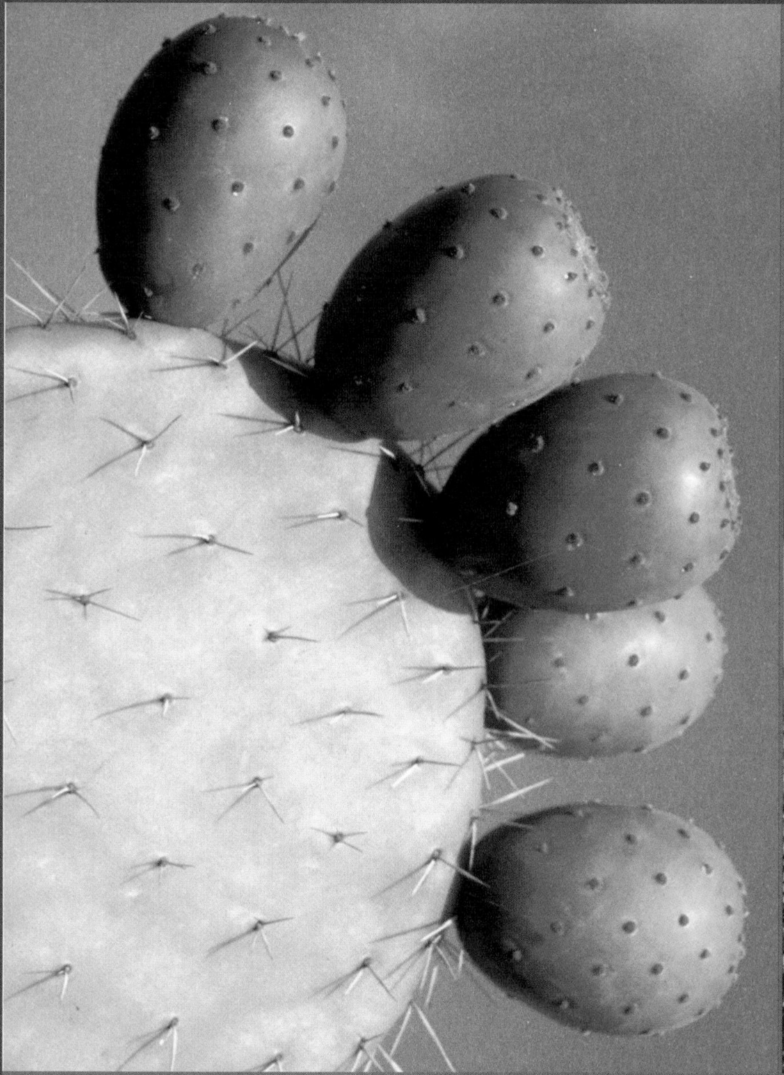
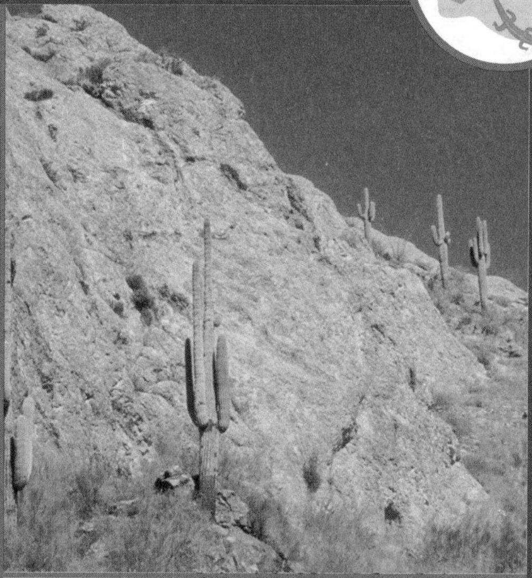
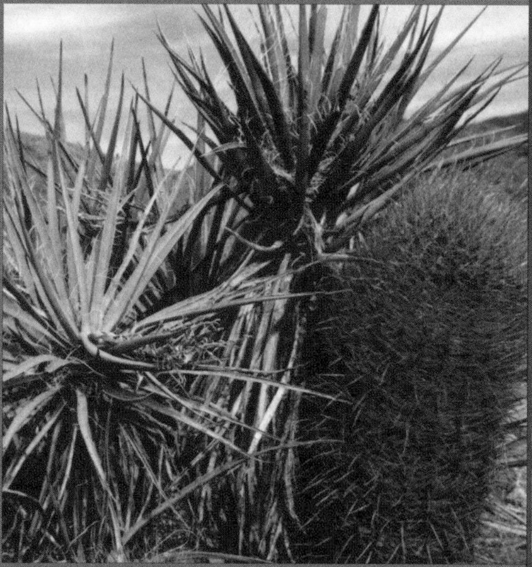
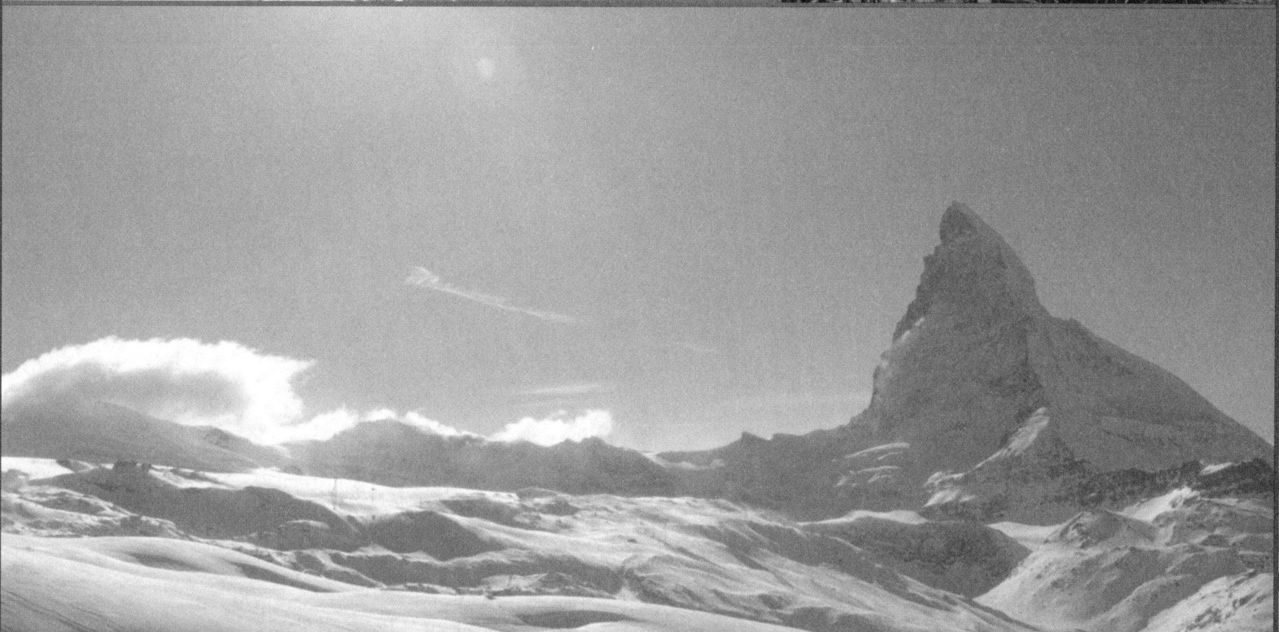

Excerpt from *Arby Jenkins Meets His Match*
by Sharon Hambrick

My hands shook as I tore the envelope open and read the letter silently:

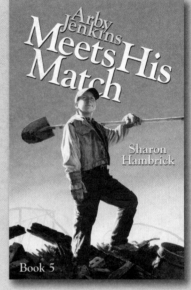

Book 5

A JourneyForth book from
BJU Press

AMERICAN MEMORIES
627 Maple Avenue
Westminster, CO 80031

AMERICAN MEMORIES
627 Maple Avenue
Westminster, CO 80031

Dear Mr. Jenkins:

We are pleased to inform you that you have been selected as the winner of this year's essay competition. Your essay, "Mr Watson, American Hero," will be published in the May edition of our magazine. I am pleased to inform you that I will be able to present you with a plaque and a five-hundred-dollar check when I visit your area next month. I have already contacted the Greenhaven Herald, and they have agreed to cover the event.

Sincerely,

Anna Leigh Harrison
Editor

I handed Mom the letter. She read it and a smile crept over her face. She wrapped me up in a hug. "You're great," she said.

Two Kinds of Letters

Friendly letters are not the only kinds of letters. People often write **business letters** too. Many business letters are written to request information or to order a product.

Some business letters are written to give information. Some are written to express opinions.

Friendly Letter

> 1339 Spake Circle
> Atlanta, GA 30311
> December 3, 2004
>
> Dear Hunter,
>   You'll never guess what our class is doing! We're setting up an electric train in one corner of the assembly room.
>   Someone gave the school an old Lionel train with ten cars, an engine, and a caboose. Our teacher ordered plans for a train table, and we're building it after school. Everything should be ready by the end of this week. I wish you could see it!
>   Will you be coming to Atlanta during your Christmas vacation? Write and let us know. We all miss you!
>   Your friend,
>   Tony

Business Letter

> Hope Christian School
> 1052 Petty Road
> Atlanta, GA 30311
> November 15, 2004
>
> American Plywood Association
> 1119 A Street
> Tacoma, WA 98401
>
> Dear Sir or Madam:
>
>   Our school was given an old Lionel model train. My students and I are interested in constructing a table for the train. I understand your company publishes instructional material for building this type of table. Please send me your patterns and directions for building a model train table. I am enclosing a check for $5.00.
>
>   Sincerely,
>   Alan M. Verhoff
>   Alan M. Verhoff

Two Kinds of Letters

Name

A **friendly letter** is written to someone you know. However, a **business letter** is usually written to someone whom you do not know. The two sample letters were written for different purposes. The friendly letter from Tony to Hunter was written to tell him about the train table that the students in his class were building. The business letter from Tony's teacher to the American Plywood Association was written to order instructions for building the table.

▶ **Compare the two letters on page 259. Fill in the circle next to each correct answer.**

1. Which letter contains more details about the train?
   ○ the friendly letter
   ○ the business letter

2. Which letter contains only facts?
   ○ the friendly letter
   ○ the business letter

3. Which letter is more conversational in tone?
   ○ the friendly letter
   ○ the business letter

4. Which letter has two addresses?
   ○ the friendly letter
   ○ the business letter

5. Which letter's greeting is written to someone the writer does not know?
   ○ the friendly letter
   ○ the business letter

6. Which letter's closing is more formal in tone?
   ○ the friendly letter
   ○ the business letter

 Apply and Write

▶**Kaylene wants to order some gospel tracts from the American Tract Society. Write two sentences that she could use in her business letter to the society.**

Lionel

Looking at Business Letters

Name _____

Amanda and Allie have written business letters to the forestry commission in their state.

▶ **Imagine that you are the forester who reads their letters.**
Think about how you would answer these questions about each letter.

1. Why is this student writing to our commission?

2. What does she want me to do for her?

3. Will she appreciate the help that I give her?

---

113 Creekside Road
Greer, SC 29651
February 11, 2005

South Carolina Forestry Commission
P.O. Box 21707
Columbia, SC 29221

Dear Sir or Madam:

    I am working on a report about forests for school, and I would like to learn more about flowers that grow in the forest. Please send one copy of your booklet *Flowers of the Forest* and one copy of *Our Woodland World* to my address. I am enclosing a money order for $3.50 to cover the cost of the booklets, postage, and handling.

                      Sincerely,

                      Amanda Brenner

                      Amanda Brenner

February 11, 2005

South Carolina Forestry Commission
P.O. Box 21707
Columbia, SC 29221

Dear Forester:

    Our class has to study forests and stuff like that this year. I don't want to spend a lot of time in the library, so send me all your books and charts on forests. Send pictures and posters too. I need it right away!

                      So long,

                      allie

                      Allie

Looking at Business Letters

Name

One letter **wastes words.**

One letter has an **impolite tone.**

One letter **does not give enough facts.**

One letter uses **precise wording.**

One letter has a **polite tone.**

One letter gives **plain facts.**

Allie's letter:

Wasting Words

- "Our class has to study forests and stuff like that . . ."
- "I don't want to spend a lot of time . . ."

Impolite Tone

- "Dear Forester:"
- "Send me all your books . . ."
- "I need it right away!"
- "So long."

Not Enough Facts

- Does not mention which books, charts, and pictures she needs
- Does not include her address

Amanda's letter:

Precise Wording

- Makes request without giving unnecessary details

Polite Tone

- "Dear Sir or Madam:"
- "Please send one copy. . ."
- "Sincerely,"

Plain Facts

- Mentions names of booklets
- Mentions amount of money enclosed

God wants our speech to be kind and appropriate.

Prov. 25:11   Eph. 4:29

Joel is ordering a copy of *Boomerangs: How to Make and Throw Them.* Each copy costs $2.95 plus $1 for postage and handling.

▶**Work with your teacher to rewrite the greeting, body, and closing of Joel's letter using precise words, a polite tone, and plain facts.**

Dear Man or Lady:

    My friend Kyler and I want to make boomerangs. Our brothers have the same birthday. We are going to surprise them and give them boomerangs for their birthdays. I've heard that you have a book that costs $2.95. Send me the book. I'll send you the money if we like the book.

              Bye for now,

              Joel

Parts of a Business Letter

Remember

Good Business Letters
Use precise wording.
Use a polite tone.
Give plain facts.

A good business letter also has **proper form.** Every business letter should have the six parts that this letter has.

Heading
(writer's address)

Inside Address
(address of the company to whom you are writing)

Greeting

Body

Closing

Signature

147 Clifton Drive
Canton, OH 44706
March 28, 2005

Educational Services
Red Mill Papers Association
500 West Main Street
Erie, PA 16512

Dear Sir or Madam:

    I am doing a project in my history class on the history of printing. I am especially interested in the first moveable-type printing press invented by Gutenberg. Please send me a copy of your free pamphlet on the history of printing.

    I would also like to receive a catalog of your booklets. Thank you for your help.

Yours truly,

Mark Nagato

Mark Nagato

A friendly letter has only five parts. What additional part is included in a business letter?

Your address in the **heading** tells the person who receives the letter where to send his reply. The heading also includes the date.

The **inside address** shows who should receive the letter. In large companies, the envelope is often thrown away, so the recipient's name or department name in the inside address is important. Street names are usually not abbreviated in business letters.

In the **greeting,** write *Sir or Madam* if you do not know the name of the person who should receive the letter. Use a colon (:) after the greeting.

Choose a formal **closing** such as *Sincerely* or *Yours truly* and put a comma after it.

Include your first and last name in your **signature.** Most business letters are typed, but they may also be handwritten neatly. If the letter is typed, you should sign your name by hand in the space above the typed name.

replica of the Gutenberg press

Parts of a Business Letter

Name ____________________

▶ **Read the business letter and proofread it for mistakes in form. Use proofreading marks to mark the three mistakes.**

115 Rose Avenue
Owatonna, MN 55060
April 16, 2005

Dear Sir or Madam,

Jo's Antiques and Doll Accessories
1704 Richland Street
Kansas City, MO 64148

I have one of your Victorian Miss dolls. I hear that you sell additional outfits for your dolls. Would you please send me a catalog of all the doll clothes that you sell? If there is a cost for the catalog, please let me know, and I will be glad to pay for it. Thank you for your service.

Sincerely:

Alena Torres
Alena Torres

Proofreading Marks

- ∧∨ Add
- Delete
- ≡ Capital letter
- / Lowercase
- Move

Business Letter: Planning

Thomas was interested in collecting coins. His teacher, Mr. Adams, had shown him some coins he had collected through the American Numismatic Association (ANA). Mr. Adams even had some Roman coins from Bible times. He showed Thomas a newsletter that he got from the ANA.

Thomas found out that he could write to the ANA and request a coin-collecting guide. He copied the address of the ANA from the newsletter. Thomas used a planning chart to plan his business letter.

Purpose:

Why am I writing this letter?

To ask for a coin-collecting guide

Audience:

To what business am I writing?

To whom or to what department in the company will I address the letter?

What is the company's address?

American Numismatic Association

Education Department

818 Cascade Avenue

Colorado Springs, CO 80903

Details:

What facts do I need to include in my letter?

Interested in collecting coins
 (mostly Roman coins)

Would like a coin-collecting guide

Enclosing $3.00 and a self-
 addressed envelope with two stamps

Finding Addresses

Where can you go to find addresses for businesses?

If the company is near you, look in your local telephone directory.

If the company is far away, check in their advertisements or brochures.

If searching the Internet, type the company's name or a keyword from its name in a search engine.

Your Business Letter

What information would you like to know? Where could you write to get this information? Here are some suggestions of possible places to write to and information or items to request:

1. Department of Natural Resources (state information)

2. Local chamber of commerce (museums)

3. Magazine (sample copy)

Business Letter: Planning

Name

▶Use this chart as you plan what you will say in your business letter.

Purpose:

Why am I writing this letter?

_____

_____

_____

_____

_____

_____

_____

Audience:

To what business am I writing?

To whom or to what department in the company will I address the letter?

What is the company's address?

_____

_____

_____

_____

_____

_____

_____

Details:

What facts do I need to include in my letter?

_____

_____

_____

_____

_____

_____

▶Save your chart for use in **Lesson 135.**

Name

Here is the rough draft of Thomas's letter to the American Numismatic Association:

167 Woodberry Drive

Sedona, AZ 86336

March 18 2005

American Numismatic Association

Education Department

818 Cascade avenue

Colorado Springs, CO. 80903

Dear Sir or Madam,

    I am interested in collecting coins from Bible times. I am especially interested in roman coins. My teacher collects coins. Would you please send me your coin-collecting guide? I am inclosing $3.00 for the guide and a self-addressed envelope with two stamps.

Sincerely,

Thomas Farley

Thomas used his planning chart as he drafted his letter. Notice that he indented the first line of the paragraph in the body of the letter.

When drafting your business letter, remember the four *P*s:

1. Precise wording
2. Polite tone
3. Plain facts
4. Proper form

▶**On your own paper, draft a business letter to the company of your choice.**

Name

When Thomas finished drafting his letter, he let Chloe read it. Chloe had some suggestions to help Thomas improve the letter. Here are the changes Thomas made.

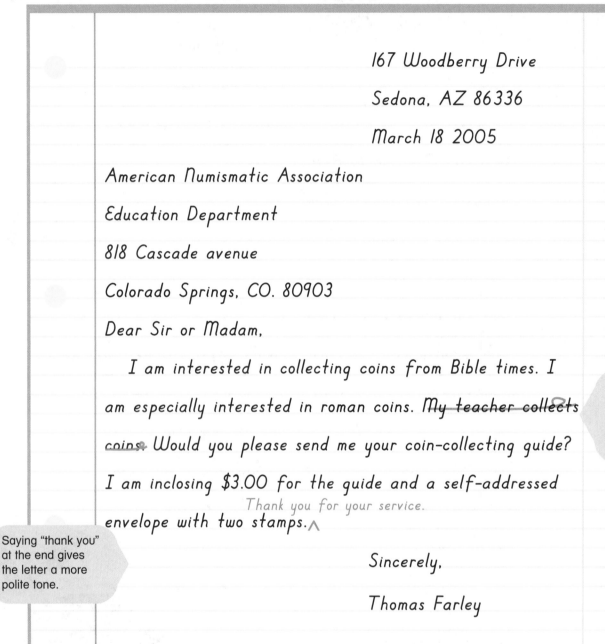

167 Woodberry Drive

Sedona, AZ 86336

March 18 2005

American Numismatic Association

Education Department

818 Cascade avenue

Colorado Springs, CO. 80903

Dear Sir or Madam,

    I am interested in collecting coins from Bible times. I am especially interested in roman coins. ~~My teacher collects coins.~~ Would you please send me your coin-collecting guide? I am inclosing $3.00 for the guide and a self-addressed envelope with two stamps. ∧ *Thank you for your service.*

                           Sincerely,

                           Thomas Farley

Chloe did not think Thomas needed to include this fact.

Saying "thank you" at the end gives the letter a more polite tone.

▶ Use this *Revising Checklist* and proofreading marks to help you revise your business letter.

Revising Checklist

☐ 1. My letter uses precise wording. I did not waste words.

☐ 2. My letter has a polite tone. I used *please* and *thank you.*

☐ 3. My letter gives plain facts. It tells what the recipient needs to know and includes no unnecessary details.

Proofreading Marks

∧∨   **Add**

    Delete

≡   **Capital letter**

/   **Lowercase**

   Move

Business Letter: Proofreading

Name _____

Thomas addressed a business envelope to the ANA.

Return Address

Thomas Farley
167 Woodberry Dr.
Sedona, AZ 86336

USA 75

Mailing Address

American Numismatic Association
Education Department
818 Cascade Ave.
Colorado Springs, CO 80903

▶ Proofread the addresses on this envelope.
Use proofreading marks to mark the four mistakes.

Jackson Lewis
102 Pine St.
Delmar De 19940

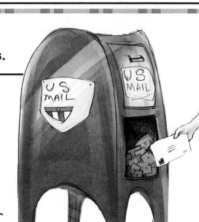

Mr. David Grayson
Eastview science Center
8308 Laurel Ct
Jackson, MS 39206

▶ Write your address on the lines for the return address. For the mailing address, write the address of the place you are sending your letter.

USA 75

Business Letter: Proofreading

After Thomas revised his letter, he proofread it using the *Proofreading Checklist.* Which mistakes did Thomas find in the letter? Which proofreading marks did he use to mark his mistakes?

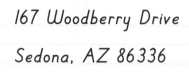

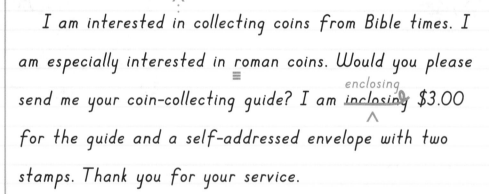

167 Woodberry Drive

Sedona, AZ 86336

March 18͜ 2005

American Numismatic Association

Education Department

818 Cascade ≡avenue

Colorado Springs, CO͜80903

Dear Sir or Madam͜

    I am interested in collecting coins from Bible times. I am especially interested in ≡roman coins. Would you please send me your coin-collecting guide? I am ~~inclosing~~ *enclosing* $3.00 for the guide and a self-addressed envelope with two stamps. Thank you for your service.

Sincerely,

Thomas Farley

Proofreading Checklist

☐ 1. I used correct business letter form.

☐ 2. I put a capital letter at the beginning of each sentence.

☐ 3. I put a punctuation mark at the end of each sentence.

☐ 4. I used capital letters correctly within the sentences.

☐ 5. I used commas and colons correctly in the heading, inside address, greeting, and closing.

☐ 6. I looked for misspelled words.

Proofreading Marks

∧∨   Add

✎   Delete

≡   Capital letter

/   Lowercase

↻→   Move

A. Write the letter of the correct answer in the blank.

_____ 1. Always followed by a colon in a business letter

_____ 2. Gives the date that the letter was written

_____ 3. "Sincerely,"

_____ 4. The part of the letter that gives the facts

_____ 5. The address of the person or business receiving the letter

_____ 6. Always written by hand in a typed business letter

A. body
B. closing
C. greeting
D. heading
E. inside address
F. signature

B. Fill in the circle next to the correct answer.

7. Which is not one of the purposes for business letters?
   ○ to request information
   ○ to express an opinion
   ○ to give friendly news about your family

8. Which is not an appropriate greeting for a business letter?
   ○ Dear Sir or Madam:
   ○ Dear Bob,
   ○ Dear Mr. Nazelli:

9. Which is not an appropriate closing for a business letter?
   ○ Yours truly,
   ○ Sincerely,
   ○ Love,

10. Which is an example of an impolite tone?
   ○ Send a brochure as soon as possible.
   ○ Please send me a brochure at the address above.
   ○ I would appreciate your sending me a brochure.

11. Which is an example of imprecise wording?
   ○ I would like any information you have about the African rainforest.
   ○ Please send me the free book *At Home in the Tundra.*
   ○ If you have any stuff about different habitats, please send it all.

12. Most business letters are ___.
   ○ typed
   ○ handwritten

C. Read the letter. Then fill in the circle next to the answer that completes each sentence.

9584 Oak tree Lane
Richmond, VA 23233
April 7, 2005

Wildlife Stamp Association
5800 Blanche Avenue
Washington, D.C.

Dear Sir or Madam:

    I am interested in collecting stamps with wildlife on them. I would appreciate your sending me any information you have about stamp collecting. I am especially interested in receiving your free beginning stamp collector's album. Please send it to me at the above address. Thank you for your service.

Sincerely:

Amy Wong

Amy Wong

13. This letter is a _____ letter.
   - ○ friendly
   - ○ business

14. The tone of Amy's letter is _____.
   - ○ polite
   - ○ demanding

15. The letter gives _____.
   - ○ plain facts
   - ○ too many unimportant details

16. Amy has left out an important part of the address in the _____.
   - ○ heading
   - ○ inside address

17. The letter has a capitalization mistake in the _____.
   - ○ heading
   - ○ greeting

18. The letter has a punctuation mistake in the _____.
   - ○ greeting
   - ○ closing

Cumulative Review

A. Make a compound sentence by combining the pair of sentences with a comma and a joining word. *(Chapter 1)*

1. You can do your homework now.
   You can wash the dishes.

   _____

B. Write the simple subject and verb on each diagram. If the verb is a linking verb, draw a slanted line and write the predicate adjective or predicate noun. *(Chapter 5)*

2. The flowers look beautiful.

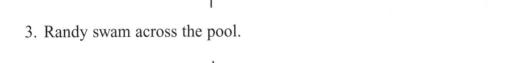

3. Randy swam across the pool.

   _____|_____

C. Underline the correct form of the helping verb twice. *(Chapter 5)*

4. The band members (has, have) practiced all month.

5. They (is, are) giving a concert Friday night.

6. The band director (has, have) prepared them well.

D. Circle the direct object in each sentence. *(Chapter 5)*

7. Daniel threw the ball over the fence.

8. Sammy caught it with his glove.

9. Fiona brought soda for everyone.

E. Diagram the simple subject, action verb, and direct object of each sentence *(Chapter 5)*

10. The deer ate our garden vegetables.

   _____|_____|_____

11. Dad built a tall fence.

   _____

Cumulative Review

F. Fill in the circle next to each correct answer. *(Chapter 7)*

12. To find out about the bank robbery last weekend, you should look at a(n) ____.
    ○ encyclopedia   ○ newspaper   ○ book about detectives

13. To check the meanings of *stoop,* you should look in a(n) ____.
    ○ encyclopedia   ○ newspaper   ○ dictionary

14. If you don't know the author or title of a book but want to find a book about karate, how would you search for the book?
    ○ by subject   ○ by title   ○ by author

15. The books of an encyclopedia are called ____.
    ○ articles   ○ volumes   ○ issues

16. To find out when John Adams became president, you should look in a(n) ____.
    ○ encyclopedia   ○ magazine   ○ dictionary

17. To find out where camping sites are located in the state of Colorado, you should look in a(n) ____.
    ○ encyclopedia   ○ newspaper   ○ atlas

G. Answer the questions using the bibliography. *(Chapter 12)*

> Ledbetter, Sam. <u>Coon Hunting</u>. Atlanta, GA: Down Home Press, 2002.

18. What is the title of this book? _____

19. What is the name of the publisher? _____

H. Underline the correct article to complete each sentence. *(Chapter 13)*

20. You can make (a, an) puppet.
21. Use (a, the) paper bags that are sold in the grocery store.
22. Pick (a, an) easy face to draw.
23. Draw (a, the) eyes on the top flap of the bag.
24. Draw (a, an) mouth on and under the flap.

**I. Decide whether each underlined word is an adjective or an adverb.
   Fill in the circle next to the correct answer.** *(Chapter 13)*

25. They ate <u>spicy</u> hamburgers for lunch.   ○ adjective   ○ adverb
26. Kate's hamburger was <u>burnt</u>.   ○ adjective   ○ adverb
27. Kate <u>politely</u> asked for another hamburger.   ○ adjective   ○ adverb
28. The cook <u>carefully</u> prepared another hamburger.   ○ adjective   ○ adverb

Prepositions

A **preposition** shows the relationship between a noun or pronoun and other words in the sentence. The preposition always comes before the object noun or pronoun.

> *The Sullivans hiked to the lighthouse.*
> *We went with them.*

Common Prepositions

about	at	down	of	through
above	before	for	off	to
across	behind	from	on	under
after	below	in	out	until
along	beside	inside	outside	up
around	by	near	over	with

▶ Guided Practice

▶Underline the preposition in each sentence.

1. Lighthouses are built over oceans.

2. Lighthouses warn sailors of dangerous waters.

3. The first lighthouse was built in Egypt.

4. The Pharos Lighthouse used fires for light.

5. The light was four hundred feet above the ground.

▶Underline the preposition that makes sense in each sentence.

6. I read a story (about, across) lighthouses.

7. The keeper and his family lived (beside, against) the lighthouse.

8. A severe storm beat the waves (against, with) the lighthouse.

9. The lighthouse keeper tended the lights (after, at) the top.

10. He guided ships safely (before, to) the shore.

11. One night he saw the shape (of, after) a sinking ship.

12. The lighthouse keeper ran quickly (in, down) the stairs.

13. He shined his flashlight (with, across) the choppy waves.

14. The keeper pulled the struggling men to safety (against, with) ropes.

Prepositions

Name

◉ Independent Practice

▶ **Underline the preposition in each sentence.**

1. Lighthouses usually consist of stone, wood, brick, or steel.

2. Tower-shaped lighthouses have many steps leading to the top.

3. Some lighthouses are built on platforms.

4. Metal skeletal towers are built in the sea.

5. Some lighthouses have *day marker* patterns so mariners can recognize them in the daytime.

6. Light lists are publications that distinguish one lighthouse from another.

▶ **Underline the preposition that makes sense in each sentence.**

7. The first American lighthouse was built (at, in) 1716.

8. It was built (under, in) Boston Harbor.

9. It was destroyed (by, about) the British in the Revolutionary War.

10. The Americans rebuilt it (through, after) the war.

11. This lighthouse has had (about, from) sixty different keepers.

12. The fuel (over, for) the first American lighthouses was whale oil, kerosene, and lard oil.

13. The keeper spent most (of, beside) his day tending to the lamps in the lighthouse.

14. One keeper watched some sheep struggle (before, in) the sea.

15. There are many interesting stories (to, about) this lighthouse.

about
above
before
beside
by
for
from
in
of
on
over
through
to

◉ Apply and Write

▶ **Describe what your day might be like if you were a lighthouse keeper one hundred years ago. Underline any prepositions you use.**

Boston Harbor Lighthouse

Object of the Preposition

The noun or pronoun that follows the preposition in a sentence is called the object of the preposition.

> *The foghorn (at the lighthouse) alerts ships (on foggy days.)*

preposition = at
object of the preposition = lighthouse

preposition = on
object of the preposition = days

A prepositional phrase begins with a preposition and ends with the object of the preposition and includes all the words between them.

> *Lighthouses are kept (by the U.S. Coast Guard.)*

by the U.S. Coast Guard = prepositional phrase
by = preposition
U.S. Coast Guard = object of the preposition

▶ Guided Practice

▶**Circle the object of the preposition in each prepositional phrase.**

1. down the basement stairs
2. inside the large circle
3. around the next corner
4. under the bed
5. beside the white fence
6. with my friend

▶**Put parentheses around each prepositional phrase. One sentence has two prepositional phrases. See page 348 in the Grammar Handbook for a list of common prepositions.**

7. The Federal Lighthouse Service started in 1789.

8. Congress wanted a national system for American lighthouses.

9. In 1939, the U.S. Lighthouse Service joined with the Coast Guard.

10. Years ago lighthouses were run by keepers.

11. Today, a system of automation controls most lighthouses around the world.

Fresnel lens

Object of the Preposition

Name _____

◯ Independent Practice

▶ Circle the object of the preposition in each prepositional phrase.

1. about that time
2. after dark
3. before breakfast
4. across a wide river

5. near the Atlantic Ocean
6. through the rain
7. up the tall ladder
8. from a new student

▶ Put parentheses around each prepositional phrase.
Two sentences have two prepositional phrases.

9. The Cape Hatteras Lighthouse was built in North Carolina.

10. The top of the lighthouse is 208 feet high.

11. Ships can see its light for miles.

12. It stands in an area called the Graveyard of the Atlantic.

13. Many ships have crashed from the strong currents.

14. Builders finished the lighthouse in 1873 and painted it
    with a striped day marker pattern.

15. The land around Cape Hatteras Lighthouse has eroded.

16. People were afraid the lighthouse would collapse into the ocean.

17. Across the state, money was collected.

18. People hauled the lighthouse farther away from the sea.

19. Now the lighthouse will be here for a long time.

Cape Hatteras Lighthouse

◯ Apply and Write

▶ The Cape Hatteras National Seashore on North Carolina's Outer Banks has
not been developed into cities or neighborhoods. This area includes
camping, miles of beaches, a large wildlife refuge, and six lighthouses. If
you took a vacation there, what would you like to do? Write about it.
Underline any prepositional phrases in your sentences.

_____

_____

_____

Using Prepositional Phrases

Name _____

A **prepositional phrase** begins with a **preposition** and ends with **the object of the preposition** and includes all of the words between them. Prepositional phrases give more information about other parts of the sentence.

California's lighthouses are built (on rough shores.)

on rough shores = prepositional phrase
on = preposition
shores = object of the preposition

Prepositional phrases expand sentences and make them more interesting.

These lighthouses are not very old.
These lighthouses (in California) are not very old.
These lighthouses (in California) are newer than lighthouses (in other parts) (of the country.)

Guided Practice

▶ **Put parentheses around the prepositional phrase in each sentence. One sentence has two prepositional phrases. See page 348 of the Grammar Handbook for a list of common prepositions.**

1. California lighthouses are frequently covered in fog.

2. The Point Reyes Lighthouse is in a foggy area.

3. Each year, it is in fog for nine months.

4. Point Reyes is the windiest promontory in America.

5. Point Reyes extends into the ocean.

Point Reyes Lighthouse in California

▶ **Add a prepositional phrase to expand each sentence.**

6. The clown laughed. _____

_____

7. The dog barked. _____

_____

Using Prepositional Phrases

◎ Independent Practice

▶ **Put parentheses around the prepositional phrase in each sentence. One sentence has two prepositional phrases.**

1. Many shipwrecks occurred at Point Reyes.

2. After fourteen shipwrecks a lighthouse was built.

3. The lighthouse was constructed in 1870.

4. It was built near the water's edge.

5. Many steps lead down the cliff to the lighthouse.

6. The keepers have a long climb to the tower.

▶ **Add a prepositional phrase to expand each sentence.**

7. My dad works. _____

8. Mrs. Wang traveled. _____

9. The light shone. _____

10. The man waved. _____

✐ Apply and Write

▶ **The Point Reyes Lighthouse sits on rocky land. Write how the lighthouse keeper's job at this lighthouse would be more difficult than at a lighthouse located on a smooth, sandy beach. Put parentheses around any prepositional phrases in your sentences.**

_____

_____

_____

_____

More Practice with Prepositions

Name _____

A **preposition** is a word that shows the relationship between a noun or pronoun and other words in the sentence. The **preposition** begins a **prepositional phrase.** An **object of the preposition** ends the phrase.

> *The lighthouse keeper walked (up the stairs.)*

up the stairs = prepositional phrase
up = preposition
stairs = object of the preposition

Guided Practice

▶ **Put parentheses around each prepositional phrase.**

1. Alligator Reef Light Station was built in the Florida Keys.

2. Men fastened its iron tower into the sea floor.

3. The tower looks like a skeleton of iron.

4. The powerful winds of hurricanes have not toppled this lighthouse.

▶ **Write a preposition that makes sense in each sentence. See page 348 of the Grammar Handbook for a list of common prepositions.**

5. The Matinicus Rock Lighthouse was built _____ an island.

6. The ground _____ the lighthouse is rocky.

7. The keepers traveled inland _____ boat to get supplies.

8. Life was hard whenever bad weather came _____ the island.

Matinicus Rock Lighthouse in Maine

More Practice with Prepositions

Name

◎ Independent Practice

▶**Put parentheses around each prepositional phrase.**

1. Abbie Burgess saved her family as a girl.

2. She began helping her father in the lighthouse when she was fourteen.

3. Once her father was off the island.

4. A terrible storm raged around their house.

5. Abbie lit the lamps in the towers.

6. Mrs. Burgess and the three younger sisters were rescued by Abbie.

7. Their entire house was drawn into the sea by storm.

8. Her hens were saved from the raging sea.

9. After the storm, people praised Abbie's courage.

▶**Write a preposition that makes sense in each sentence. See page 349 in the Grammar Handbook for a list of common prepositions.**

10. The Matinicus Rock Lighthouse was built _____ 1827.

11. The powerful waves crashed _____ the rocky coast.

12. The lighthouse guided ships _____ the storms.

13. The mariners were thankful _____ the light.

14. Now the lighthouse is run _____ the Coast Guard.

✐ Apply and Write

▶**Write a sentence using the word *in* as a preposition.**

_____

_____

Independent Clauses

An **independent clause** has a subject and a predicate. It expresses a complete thought and can stand alone. It is a sentence.

subject   predicate

Many lighthouses | are open to the public.

A **fragment** is a group of words that does not express a complete thought. A fragment is not a sentence because it is missing either a subject or a predicate.

The tower on the lighthouse = missing a predicate

Built on the rocks = missing a subject

Guided Practice

▶ **Decide whether each group of words is an independent clause or a fragment. Fill in the circle next to the correct answer.**

1. The Split Rock Lighthouse overlooks Lake Superior.
   ○ independent clause   ○ fragment

2. Have visited the lighthouse.
   ○ independent clause   ○ fragment

3. Tourists often visit the lighthouse.
   ○ independent clause   ○ fragment

4. A tower fifty-four feet high.
   ○ independent clause   ○ fragment

5. Are shorter than this lighthouse.
   ○ independent clause   ○ fragment

Split Rock Lighthouse in Minnesota

▶ **Write an independent clause (sentence) by adding a subject or predicate to each fragment.**

6. an old ship _____

_____

7. fell during a storm _____

_____

8. visit the lighthouse _____

Independent Clauses

Name

◉ Independent Practice

▶ **Decide whether each group of words is an independent clause or a fragment. Fill in the circle next to the correct answer.**

1. The Split Rock Lighthouse was built in 1910.
   ○ independent clause   ○ fragment

2. Ships traveled frequently on the Great Lakes.
   ○ independent clause   ○ fragment

3. Became the leading industrial nation.
   ○ independent clause   ○ fragment

4. Very dangerous winds.
   ○ independent clause   ○ fragment

5. Storms proved the need for a lighthouse.
   ○ independent clause   ○ fragment

▶ **Write an independent clause (sentence) by adding a subject or predicate to the fragment.**

6. the lighthouse keeper _____

7. built the lighthouse _____

8. the water _____

② Apply and Write

▶ Write a postcard to a friend describing your favorite lighthouse. Check your sentences to make sure they are all complete sentences and not fragments.

Dependent Clauses

Name

An **independent clause** has a subject and a predicate. It expresses a complete thought and can stand alone. It is a sentence.

> *I am ten years old.*

A **dependent clause** is a group of words that has a subject and a predicate but cannot stand alone as a sentence. A dependent clause does not express a complete thought. A dependent clause is another type of fragment.

> *When I am ten years old.*

A dependent clause begins with a **joining word,** such as *although, because, since, until, when,* and *where.*

> *Because* Sarah is sick.
> *Until* Sarah feels well.

◪ Guided Practice

▶ Write *IC* if the clause is an independent clause.
Write *DC* if the clause is a dependent clause.
Circle the joining word in each dependent clause.

_____ 1. White cliffs are near Cape Blanco Lighthouse.

_____ 2. Because the lighthouse is located in Oregon.

_____ 3. Where the Oregon coastline is ragged.

_____ 4. It is the tallest lighthouse in Oregon.

_____ 5. James Langlois was the keeper for forty-two years.

_____ 6. When the war started.

_____ 7. The lighthouse is popular.

_____ 8. Because visitors were given a tour by the keeper.

Cape Blanco Lighthouse
by Lisa Anne Miller

Dependent Clauses

Name _____

◎ Independent Practice

▶ Write *IC* if the clause is an independent clause.
Write *DC* if the clause is a dependent clause.
Circle the joining word in each dependent clause.

_____ 1. The Cape Blanco Lighthouse protected the mainland.

_____ 2. Since the United States was fighting World War II.

_____ 3. The lighthouse escaped damage.

_____ 4. When bombs fell into the forest.

_____ 5. The Japanese plane was not noticed.

_____ 6. Because it had come from a submarine.

_____ 7. The pilot saw the lighthouse.

_____ 8. When the enemy planned the attack.

_____ 9. Until the war ended.

_____ 10. The lighthouse returned to its original purpose.

◰ Apply and Write

▶ Some lighthouses were difficult to build because of their locations on rocky land. Write a sentence explaining one of the dangers that a construction crew might face.

_____

_____

Another Type of Fragment

A **clause** is a group of words that has a subject and a predicate. An **independent clause** expresses a complete thought. It can stand alone as a sentence.

> The <u>keeper</u> <u>lit</u> the wick.

A **dependent clause** does not express a complete thought. It cannot stand alone.

> Unless the <u>lighthouse</u> <u>is automated</u>.

A dependent clause begins with a **joining word** such as *although, because, since, until, when,* or *where.* A dependent clause is another type of fragment. You can change this type of fragment into a sentence by removing the joining word.

fragment = *Since* the <u>captain</u> <u>saw</u> the lighthouse.
sentence = *The* <u>captain</u> <u>saw</u> the lighthouse.

▶ Guided Practice

▶ Write *IC* if the clause is an independent clause.
Write *DC* if the clause is a dependent clause.
Rewrite each dependent clause as an independent clause (sentence).

_____ 1. The Cape Flattery Lighthouse is important.

Cape Flattery Lighthouse

_____ 2. Since the lighthouse was built on Native American lands.

_____ 3. Taloosh Island was used for many years by the Makah Indians.

_____ 4. The lighthouse was built where the Makahs had *potlatch* ceremonies.

_____ 5. Construction on the lighthouse was slow.

_____ 6. When the lighthouse was finished after one and one-half years.

Another Type of Fragment

Independent Practice

▸Write *IC* if the clause is an independent clause.
Write *DC* if the clause is a dependent clause.
Rewrite each dependent clause as an independent clause (sentence).

_____ 1. The Cape Flattery Lighthouse had several different keepers.

_____ 2. Although its location was lonely.

_____ 3. The first four keepers had a short stay.

_____ 4. Because they were afraid of the Native Americans.

_____ 5. Until the telephone was invented in 1876.

_____ 6. Since visitors did not come often.

_____ 7. The keepers were frequently unhappy living at the lighthouse.

_____ 8. One time the keepers became angry with each other.

_____ 9. When they began to fight.

_____ 10. Coffee was thrown by the keepers.

Apply and Speak

▸Think about how God wants Christians to solve their disagreements. How could you complete the dependent and independent clauses in this sentence? Share it with your teacher.

When I _____, God wants me to _____.

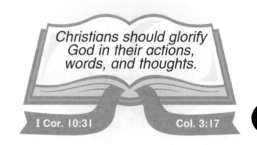

Christians should glorify God in their actions, words, and thoughts.

I Cor. 10:31   Col. 3:17

Using Commas

A **comma** is used to show a pause in writing. If a sentence is read aloud, there is a natural pause in your voice. This helps the listener to understand more clearly what is being spoken or written.

Comma Uses

1. **in dates between the number of the day and the year**

June 15, 2004

2. **between a city and state**

Thomasville, North Carolina

3. **in a series**

The children ran, skipped, and walked on the playground.

4. **in a compound sentence before the joining word**

I wanted to order dessert, but I was too full.

5. **in dialogue**

"The telephone is ringing," she announced.

6. **in a direct address**

Dad, may I go to the park?
I wonder, Kyle, if the game is going to be cancelled.
We hope you have a wonderful birthday, Nancy.

7. **after introductory words, such as *yes, no,* and *well***

Yes, I will go with you.   Well, let me think about it.

8. **after a long introductory phrase of five or more words**

In the early morning hours, the city seems to sleep.

Guided Practice

▶**Fill in the circle next to each sentence that is written correctly.**

1. ○ Before Bethany's surprise birthday party, we had a storm.
   ○ Before, Bethany's surprise birthday party we had a storm.

2. ○ I think Mom, that I would like vanilla ice cream.
   ○ I think, Mom, that I would like vanilla ice cream.

▶**Proofread the sentences. Insert a comma where it is needed in each sentence using ⌄.**

3. Where did you leave your homework Zachary?

4. "Let's go to the park" said Travis.

5. No I don't know the answer to that question.

6. Roscoe you need a bath!

7. After the toddler's long nap he was happy.

English 4, Chapter 15, Lesson 148

Using Commas

Name

◯ Independent Practice

▶**Fill in the circle next to each sentence that is written correctly.**

1. ◯ Well, our trip was very exciting.
   ◯ Well our trip, was very exciting.

2. ◯ There is a huge, zoo in Houston Texas.
   ◯ There is a huge zoo in Houston, Texas.

3. ◯ Brian, have you ever been there before?
   ◯ Brian have you ever been there, before?

4. ◯ No, I don't believe that I have seen it.
   ◯ No I don't believe, that I have seen it.

5. ◯ After walking into the zoo, you see signs about the exhibits.
   ◯ After walking into the zoo you see signs, about the exhibits.

6. ◯ Jaws, a ferocious crocodile, was my favorite animal.
   ◯ Jaws a ferocious, crocodile was my favorite animal.

▶**Proofread the sentences. Insert a comma where it is needed in each sentence using the ⟁. Two sentences need more than one comma.**

7. In the middle of the night I heard a scraping noise.

8. Were you scared Andrea?

9. "Yes I was at first" answered Andrea.

10. After hearing the sound again I went to find my parents.

11. Wake up Dad!

12. He got up calmed me down and tucked me back in bed.

13. Andrea did you ever figure out what the noise was?

14. Yes it was the wind dragging tree branches across my windows.

◢ Apply and Write

▶**Write a sentence using *yes, no,* or *well* at the beginning of the sentence.**

_____

▶**Write a sentence using a person's name in a direct address.**

_____

▶**Write a sentence using this introductory phrase:** In the afternoon after school

_____

Chapter *15* Review

Name

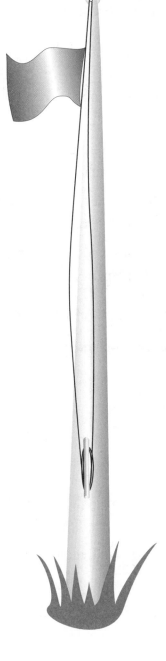

A. Underline the preposition in each sentence.

1. My mother's cabinets in the kitchen are organized.

2. The pots and pans are under the stove.

3. The dish cabinet is beside the sink.

4. She has a cereal cabinet above the stove.

5. The pantry is near the refrigerator.

6. The food inside the pantry is neat.

B. Circle the object of the preposition in each prepositional phrase.

7. along the wall

8. up the flagpole

9. under the bed

10. about sunrise

11. on the sailboat

12. through the field

13. from the outside

14. around the yard

C. Put parentheses around each prepositional phrase.

15. Raphael's family went camping at the park.

16. They set up the tent near some water.

17. Raphael saw a deer across the creek.

18. It was hiding behind a tall tree.

19. Raphael and his father swam until suppertime.

20. Then his mother called for them.

D. Proofread the sentences. Insert a comma where it is needed in each sentence using the ⌃. Two sentences need more than one comma.

21. Meredith will be a missionary in Madrid Spain.

22. In my morning devotional time I will pray for her.

23. We prayed for safety good health and a fruitful ministry.

24. "Mom let's pray for Meredith right now" I said.

25. As part of her schooling Meredith will learn the language of the people.

Christians should share the good news of salvation.

Mark 16:15   II Tim. 4:2

© 2004 BJU Press. Reproduction prohibited.

E. Decide whether each group of words is an independent clause or a fragment. Fill in the circle next to each correct answer.

26. A large pink rose in the flower garden.
    ○ independent clause   ○ fragment

27. The rose bushes need pruning and fertilizing.
    ○ independent clause   ○ fragment

28. The rose trellis is white.
    ○ independent clause   ○ fragment

29. Pricked her finger on a thorn.
    ○ independent clause   ○ fragment

30. Sherida put a dozen roses in a vase.
    ○ independent clause   ○ fragment

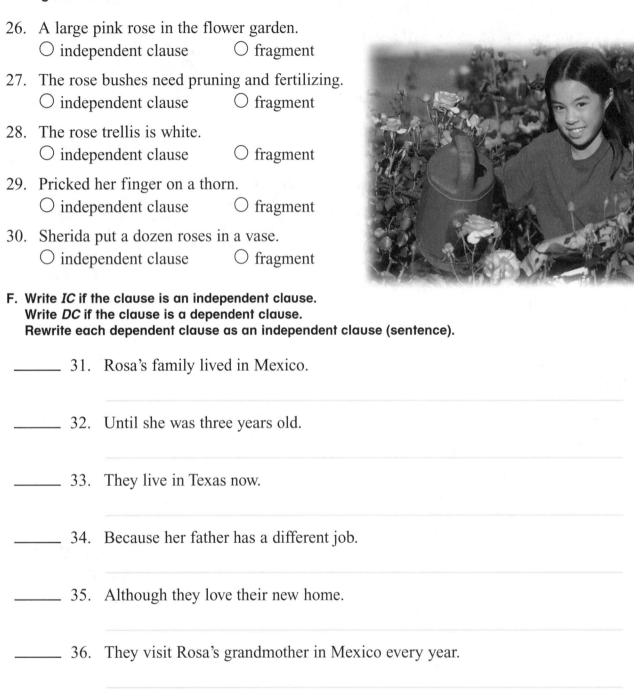

F. Write *IC* if the clause is an independent clause.
Write *DC* if the clause is a dependent clause.
Rewrite each dependent clause as an independent clause (sentence).

_____ 31. Rosa's family lived in Mexico.

_____ 32. Until she was three years old.

_____ 33. They live in Texas now.

_____ 34. Because her father has a different job.

_____ 35. Although they love their new home.

_____ 36. They visit Rosa's grandmother in Mexico every year.

_____ 37. Rosa wants to be a doctor in Mexico.

Cumulative Review

A. Write _S_ if the group of words is a sentence.
   Write _F_ if the group of words is a fragment. *(Chapter 1)*

_____   1. You may go to the park.

_____   2. On the swings.

_____   3. Let's swing high into the air.

B. Underline the verb twice that best completes each sentence. *(Chapters 5 and 11)*

   4. Dad (is, be) on top of the house.

   5. There (is, are) two kittens on the roof.

   6. They (has, had) climbed a tree and jumped onto the roof.

   7. The kittens (does, did) not know how to jump back to the tree.

   8. Jacob (brung, brought) a basket to hold the kittens.

   9. Dad (told, telled) Jacob to take the kittens inside.

C. Fill in the circle next to the best way to search for a particular book in a library's electronic catalog. *(Chapter 7)*

   10. You know the title of the book but don't know the author's name.
        ○ title   ○ author   ○ subject

   11. You don't know the title of the book or the author's name.
        ○ title   ○ author   ○ subject

   12. You know the author's name but don't know the title of the book.
        ○ title   ○ author   ○ subject

D. Read these paragraphs from an article about alligators and crocodiles. Fill in the circle next to the three outline parts that are not correct. *(Chapter 7)*

Alligators and Crocodiles	
Two animals that are frequently confused are the alligator and the crocodile. The skin of both animals is rough, with bumps. The toes of each are webbed. Both animals like warm water for the entire year. These two reptiles look different at their heads. The alligator's head is broader. Its snout is round, but the crocodile's snout has a point. There is another difference, but you may not want to get close enough to check it. The crocodile's upper jaw has a groove for the fourth tooth of the lower jaw. The crocodile looks as if it is smiling.	○ alligators and Crocodiles ○ I. How they are alike ○ A. Reptiles ○ B. Skin and feet ○ C. Habitat ○ 2. How they are different ○ A. Heads ○ b. Snouts ○ C. Teeth

Cumulative Review

E. Match each description to the correct part of a book. *(Chapter 7)*

_____ 13. Look at the ___ to find the year a book was published.

_____ 14. Look at the ___ to find the author of a book.

_____ 15. Look at the ___ to find which page in a history book
          tells about Harriet Tubman.

_____ 16. Look at the ___ to find which chapter
          in a history book tells about the Civil War.

_____ 17. Look at the book's ___ to find what a word means in
          a history book.

> A. glossary
> B. copyright page
> C. index
> D. title page
> E. table of contents

**F. Circle the correct pronoun to replace the underlined word(s).
     Write *S* if the correct answer is a subject pronoun.
     Write *O* if the correct answer is an object pronoun.** *(Chapter 9)*

_____ 18. <u>Ashley</u> plays soccer.   her   she

_____ 19. Her sister Courtney plays <u>soccer</u> too.   them   it

_____ 20. Courtney passes the ball to <u>Brooke</u>.   her   she

_____ 21. <u>The girls</u> practice every day.   they   them

G. Fill in the circle next to the word that completes the sentence. *(Chapter 13)*

22. Jared's bag is _____ than my bag.   ○ heavier   ○ heavyer
23. I clean my bag ___ often than Jared.   ○ most   ○ more
24. You sang ___ this morning.   ○ good   ○ well
25. No one could have done it _____.   ○ gooder   ○ better

**H. Complete the information about research reports using the words
     from the word bank.** *(Chapter 12)*

paragraphs	research report	facts	opinions	topic sentence	details

A _____ gives facts about a topic. Your _____ ,
or how you feel about the topic, are not included. _____ are statements
that are true and can often be checked in an encyclopedia, dictionary, or almanac.

Research reports use _____ to tell about the topic. The first
sentence of each paragraph is called the _____ and tells one main
idea. The other sentences in the paragraph are _____ that tell about
the main idea in the topic sentence.

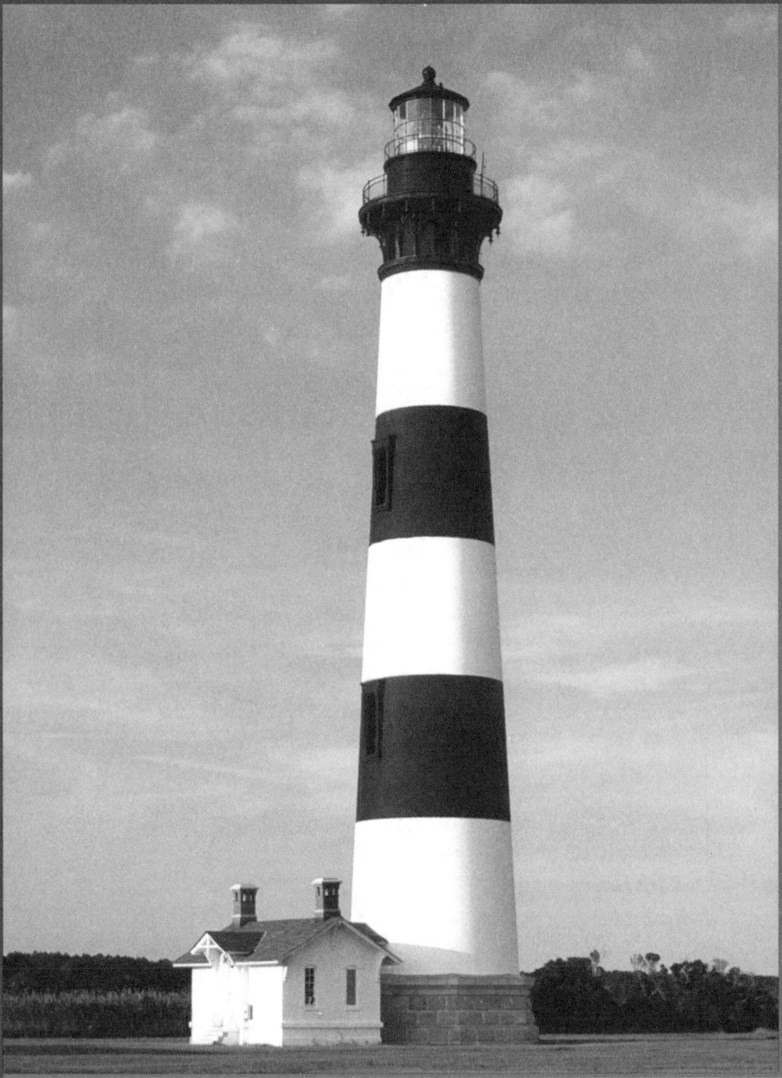

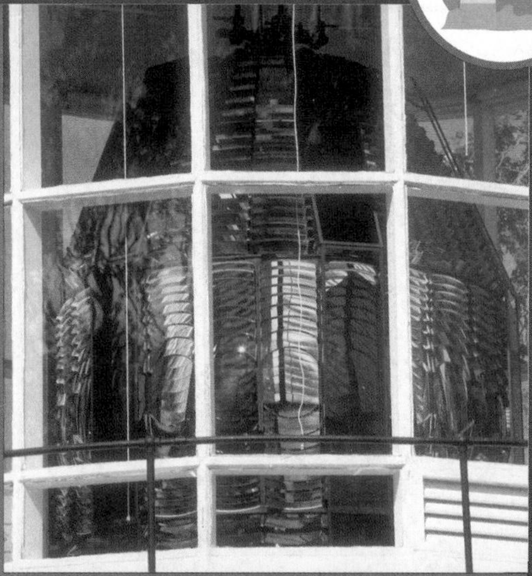

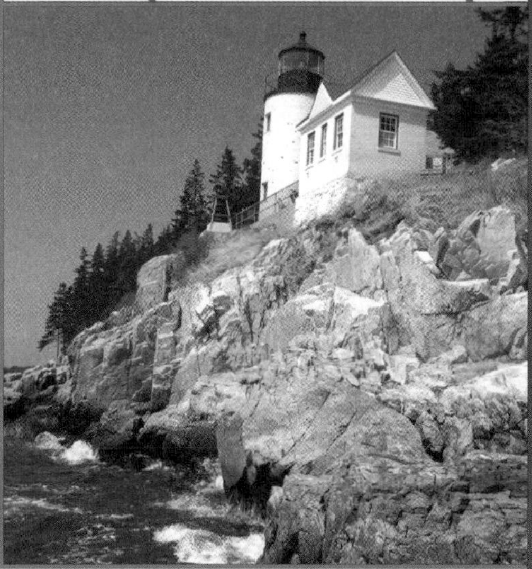

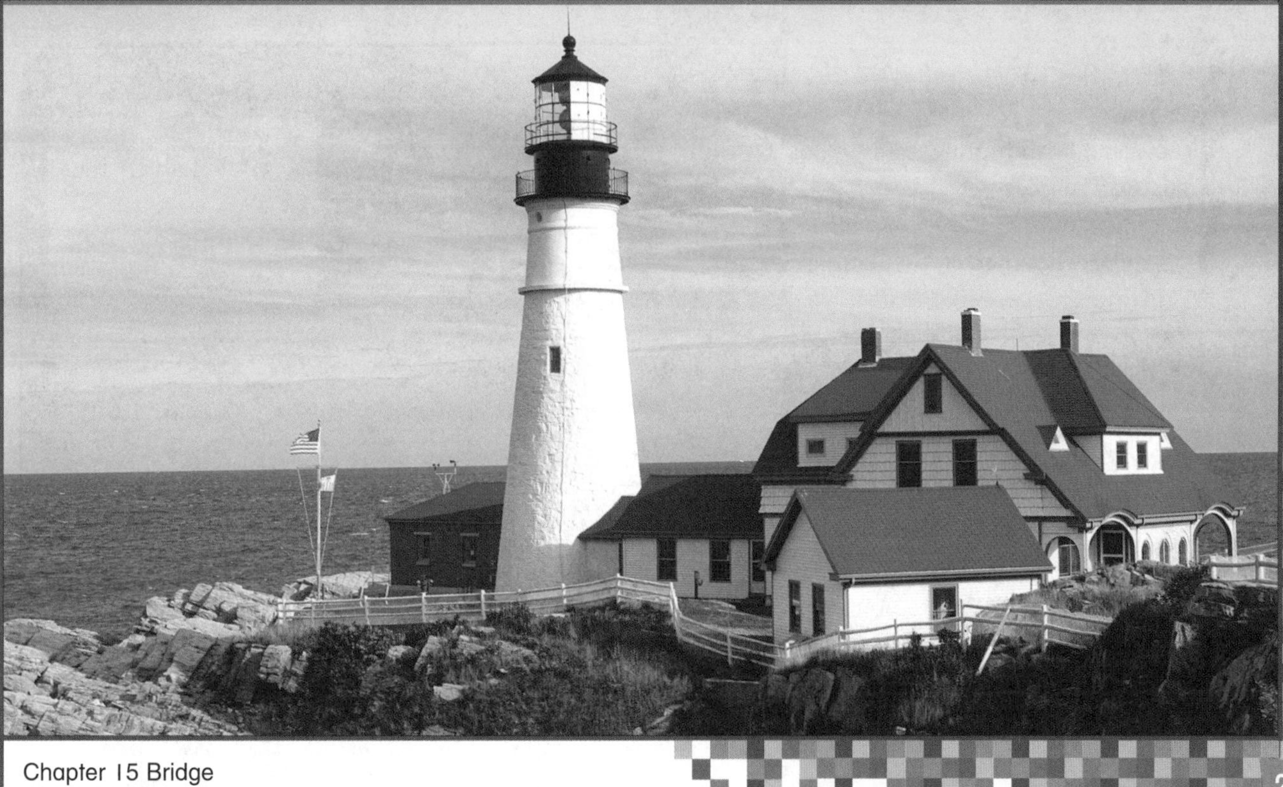

Literature Link

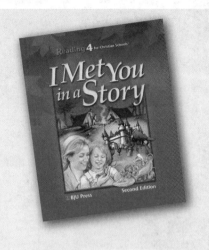

"Cherry Time" by Wendy Harris
from *I Met You in a Story,* BJU Press

Burdened cherry limbs

Battleground of man and bird

Bucket against beak.

Poems from *Spring: an Alphabet Acrostic*
by Steven Schnur

Hair swaying, each girl leaps
On one foot
Past the first
Space,
Crouches and springs
Once, twice, three
Times, returns and
Collects her marker, then jumps
Home.

Nestled under the
Eaves, a
Song-filled ark of
Twigs and grass.

Using a Thesaurus

Poets are people who love words. They love the sounds words make, the way words look on the page, and the beautiful descriptions they can make by putting certain words together. Where do poets find their words?

The thesaurus is an important tool for poets. Sometimes one word fits better than another word with a poem's sound or rhythm. A thesaurus helps the poet find interesting, unusual, and appropriate words to use in his poem. Here is the thesaurus entry for the word *shake*.

shake *verb*
to move or make move up and down or back and forth in short, quick movements
I felt the ground shake during the earthquake.
quiver, rock, tremble, vibrate

*Aspen leaves shake
in a gentle mountain breeze
above slim white trunks.*

After writing this poem, the poet decided that she wanted a more unusual word than *shake* in the first line. She wanted a word that would describe the motion of the leaves more exactly than *shake*. Which synonym from the entry would you choose to replace *shake*?

The poet thought that *quiver* or *tremble* would work best in her poem. Since the breeze was gentle, the motion of the leaves would be small and slight. *Rock* and *vibrate* made her think of greater motion. She finally decided that she liked the word *quiver* best in her poem.

*Aspen leaves quiver
in a gentle mountain breeze
above slim white trunks.*

Guided Practice

▶ **Use the thesaurus to find a more interesting or unusual word to replace the underlined word. Write the new word in the blank.**

1. The <u>brave</u> sun pushed through the clouds.

   _____

2. Horses <u>pull</u> the logs through the fields.

   _____

3. The flower grows in the <u>cold</u> mountain air.

   _____

4. The monkey's noises made us <u>laugh</u>.

   _____

Using a Thesaurus

Name

◉ Independent Practice

▶Read each sentence. Use the thesaurus to find a more interesting
or unusual word to replace the underlined word. Write the new word in the blank.

1. A <u>hot</u> desert wind blew in through the window. _____

2. Will you help me <u>find</u> my lost cat? _____

3. The main character in this book makes me <u>angry</u>. _____

4. Be careful not to <u>hurt</u> your sister in that rough game. _____

5. Is that a <u>real</u> diamond? _____

▶Read the following poems. Use the thesaurus to find an appropriate
word to replace the underlined word. Write the new word in the blank.

6. The rain will <u>hit</u> the garden stones
   And on the roof its music drones.

   _____

7. Blither, blather, says the creek.
   Splitter splatter, hear it <u>say</u>.
   Gab and blabber, nothing more,
   Always gossiping to the shore.

   _____

8. Turtles have scaly faces,
   <u>Carry</u> their homes on their backs,
   And they rarely win races—
   These are all turtle facts!

   _____

9. Sunset clouds creep
   Into the evening sky
   Like spilled paint blobs
   In <u>bright</u> colors.

   _____

10. Two horses <u>run</u>,
    Manes and tails streaming behind
    Like flames of red fire.

    _____

11. In the shade of rocks
    We watch the chipmunks feast,
    <u>Happy</u> with breadcrumbs.

    _____

Learning About Haiku

There are many different kinds of poems. Often poems have some kind of sound pattern, sounds placed in such a way through the poem that they hold the poem together. Some poems rhyme. Some poems do not rhyme, but they include other sound effects such as *alliteration* and *onomatopoeia.* Other poems have a certain number of beats per line.

Here are some examples of haiku.

Canary

When my canary
flew away, that was the end
of spring in my house.

City Winter

Crazy confetti
whirling in a soft glow is
snow in the streetlight.

One kind of poem, the **haiku,** is based on a pattern of syllables. Although your ear cannot hear rhyme or rhythm when you read a haiku aloud, each line of the poem has a certain number of syllables. The Japanese wrote the first haiku many years ago.

▶ **Count the syllables in each line of each poem.**

Haiku poetry describes something in nature. Haiku always brings a specific picture, or **image,** to the reader's mind.

Haiku

First line = 5 syllables
Second line = 7 syllables
Third line = 5 syllables

▶ **Choose one of the haiku poems from above.**
Draw a picture that goes with the poem.

Haiku: Planning

Name

The best poems are written about things that are familiar to us. Poems are written about objects we have seen, places we have been, or feelings we have experienced. But poems often try to tell about those places, objects, or experiences in a new way.

Look at the pictures on this page. Do any of them look like something you have seen before? Is there one that reminds you of some other place or some other object? Which one interests you the most?

▶ **Choose one of the following pictures as the topic for your own haiku.**
Circle the picture of your choice.

Name

Lee decided to write about the spring flowers in his mother's garden. He thought that the flowers looked similar to a crowd of people. Here is the rough draft of Lee's haiku.

> *The Crowd*
> *Spring flowers, yellow, purple,*
> *pretty colurs crowd around*
> *little green blades of grass.*

Look at the picture you have chosen. Does the object in the picture remind you of anything else? What words or phrases would you like to include in your haiku? Remember that you are limited to a total of seventeen syllables, so every word has to count.

▶ **Write a short phrase about your topic in the middle oval. Fill in the outside ovals with words you might like to include in your haiku.**

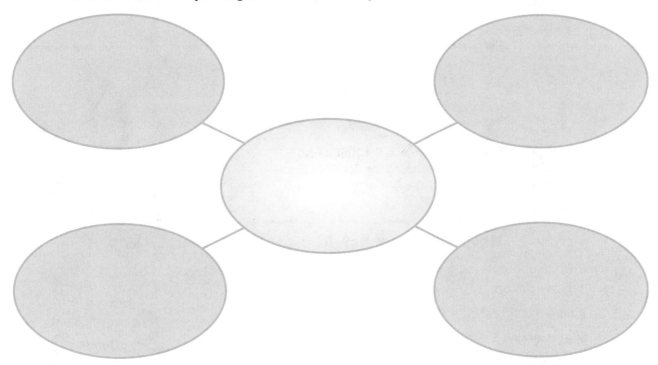

▶ **Draft your haiku on your own paper. Try to use at least some of the words from your web. Remember to keep the correct number of syllables in each line.**

Haiku

First line = 5 syllables
Second line = 7 syllables
Third line = 5 syllables

Haiku: Revising & Proofreading

Name _____

When Lee showed his haiku to Alison, he noticed that it did not have the right number of syllables in each line. He had seven syllables in the first line, seven in the second, and six in the third. Lee knew that a haiku should have only five syllables in the first and third lines. He would have to change some of the words in his poem.

Lee decided on some different colors for the flowers in the first line. *Blue* and *pink* have only one syllable each. He used his thesaurus to find a one-syllable word to replace *little*. He also found a more interesting word than *pretty* in the thesaurus.

The Crowd

blue, pink,
Spring flowers, ~~yellow, purple~~
∧
pleasing
~~pretty~~ colors crowd around
∧
short
~~little~~ green blades of grass.
∧

The Crowd

Spring flowers, blue, pink,

colors
pleasing ~~colurs~~ crowd around
∧

short green blades of grass.

When the time came to proofread his haiku, Lee noticed that *colors* was misspelled. He corrected the mistake.

Not all of the usual proofreading rules apply to haiku. Capitalization at the beginning of lines and punctuation at the end of lines may vary in haiku poetry. A haiku does not have to be a complete sentence.

▶ **Read your haiku to your partner. Revise the haiku and then proofread it using the proofreading marks. Use these checklists to help you.**

Revising Checklist

☐ 1. My haiku follows the five syllable, seven syllable, five syllable pattern.

☐ 2. I used exact and interesting words.

☐ 3. My haiku gives a specific picture of an object in nature.

Proofreading Checklist

☐ 1. I used correct spelling.

☐ 2. I used correct grammar.

☐ 3. My haiku makes sense.

Proofreading Marks

∧∨ Add
∿ Delete
≡ Capital letter
/ Lowercase
○→ Move

English 4, Chapter 16, Lesson 154

Learning About
Acrostic Poems

Name

Poets often experiment with writing different kinds of poems. Haiku have the syllable pattern of 5, 7, 5 for the three lines. In an **acrostic** each line begins with a letter in a keyword, often someone's name.

> *My German shepherd*
> *Always gets in trouble for*
> *Jumping up*
> *On our sofa and barking—*
> *Ruff! Ruff!*

In his poem "Major," Eric used the name of his dog as the keyword in his acrostic poem. He wrote about one of Major's familiar actions that always gets him in trouble.

In her poem "Summer," Danielle described the things she likes about a season of the year. Both writers chose a keyword that was interesting and familiar to them.

When you write an acrostic poem, start by writing the letters of the keywords vertically down the left side of the page. Then write the lines of your poem across the page, beginning each line with a letter of the keyword.

> *Soft breeze rustling*
> *Up in the trees,*
> *Mornings with no school,*
> *Making me feel lazy,*
> *Evenings of playing outside,*
> *Racing the wind on my bike.*

Tips for Writing Acrostic Poems

1. Choose a keyword that would make a good poetry topic. Choose a word that interests you and one that you would enjoy writing about.

2. Think about words you could use in your poem before you begin writing it. Look at the letters in the keyword. What words beginning with those letters could you use to tell about your topic? Sometimes the letters in your keyword can help you think of creative and colorful words.

3. Be careful about choosing keywords with unusual letters in them. It might be hard to think of a word beginning with *X* or *Z* that fits into your poem.

Acrostic Poem: Planning

Name

The first step in writing your acrostic poem is choosing your keyword. You may want to write an acrostic poem about yourself, a family member, or a pet, using a proper name as the keyword. Or you may want to write about a month or a season of the year, using its name as the keyword.

Here are some other suggestions with some ideas for keywords in parentheses.

Ideas

1. Write about a flower (rose, tulip).
2. Write about your favorite holiday (Easter, Christmas).
3. Write about a color (purple, black).
4. Write about your favorite food (cupcakes, tacos).
5. Write about an activity you like to do (swimming, baseball).

▶ **Write your keyword on the line. Leave some space after each letter. Beneath each letter of the keyword, list words beginning with that letter that you could use to tell about your topic.**

Keyword:

Name

Here is the rough draft of Danielle's poem about summer.

Soft breeze blowing

Up in the trees,

Mornings with no school,

Making me feel lazy,

Evnings of playing,

Riding my bike.

This is Danielle's first try before she made any changes or fixed mistakes. Notice that Danielle made one of her lines flow into the next with no pause *(Soft breeze blowing / Up in the trees).* The rest of her lines have a pause at the end of them. Poems with very few pauses at the ends of the lines move quickly. Poems with many pauses at the ends of lines move more slowly.

Danielle's poem moves slowly, helping to communicate the lazy mood of a long summer day.

What is your poem about? An energetic animal? A quiet, thoughtful person? An active kind of sport? A beautiful flower? Do you think that the lines of your poem should move quickly or slowly?

▶ **Write your keyword vertically down a piece of paper, leaving a blank line after each letter. Check carefully to make sure that you spelled the keyword correctly. Look at your word list for words to use in your poem.**

▶ **Draft your acrostic poem.**

Acrostic Poem: Revising & Proofreading

Name

Danielle shared her poem with Eric. Eric thought the poem was very good. His only suggestion for revision was to add some colorful words. Danielle thought of the word *rustling* to replace *blowing*. *Rustling* had more appeal to her senses, because it made her think of a sound.

She then looked at the list of words she thought of during the planning stage and found another *r* word—*racing*. Putting that idea together with the breeze in the beginning of her poem, she came up with a more colorful description for bike-riding: *racing the wind on my bike*.

> Soft breeze ~~blowing~~ *rustling*
> ∧
> Up in the trees,
>
> Mornings with no school,
>
> Making me feel lazy,
>
> Evnings of playing,
>
> *Racing the wind on*
> ~~Riding~~ my bike.
> ∧

> Soft breeze rustling
>
> Up in the trees,
>
> Mornings with no school,
>
> Making me feel lazy,
>
> *Evenings*
> ~~Evnings~~ of playing,
> ∧
>
> Racing the wind on my bike.

Next, Danielle proofread her acrostic poem. She wasn't sure about the spelling of *evenings,* so she checked a dictionary. What proofreading marks did she use to correct the misspelling?

▶ **Read your acrostic poem to your partner.**
  Revise the poem and then proofread it.
  Use these checklists to help you.

Revising Checklist

☐ 1. My acrostic poem has a keyword that is spelled correctly.
☐ 2. My acrostic poem tells about the keyword.
☐ 3. My acrostic poem has exact and interesting words.
☐ 4. The movement (fast or slow) of my acrostic poem goes with my topic.

Proofreading Checklist

☐ 1. I used correct spelling.
☐ 2. I used correct grammar.
☐ 3. My acrostic poem makes sense.
☐ 4. Each line of my acrostic poem begins with a capital letter.

Proofreading Marks

∧∨ Add
⌒ Delete
≡ Capital letter
/ Lowercase
○→ Move

 is part of the illustration.

Name

A. Write the letter of the correct answer in the blank.

		A. acrostic poem
		B. haiku

_____ 1. Follow a pattern of syllables

_____ 2. Has a keyword that determines its pattern

_____ 3. Are always about nature

_____ 4. Capitalizes the first word in every line

_____ 5. May be long or short

_____ 6. Are always three lines long

B. Fill in the circle next to the correct answer.

7. A thesaurus is _____ for poets.
   ○ often helpful
   ○ not very useful

8. A poet could use a thesaurus to find words with the correct number of _____ to fit in a haiku.
   ○ letters
   ○ syllables

9. _____ are not necessary in a haiku.
   ○ Correctly spelled words
   ○ Complete sentences

10. A haiku should give a _____ picture of an object in nature.
    ○ specific
    ○ hidden

11. The keyword in an acrostic poem should be one that _____ the poet.
    ○ puzzles
    ○ interests

12. The keyword in an acrostic poem should be written _____ on the page.
    ○ horizontally
    ○ vertically

13. Which keyword do you think would be easiest to use in an acrostic poem?
    ○ hot dog
    ○ candy
    ○ quesadillas

C. Read the haiku. Fill in the circle next to the correct answer.

14. What object from nature is mentioned in this haiku?
- ○ barn
- ○ tractor
- ○ apples

> *Harvest*
> Red barn in autumn,
> gren tractor gleaming nearby,
> big ripe apples.

15. Which line has an incorrect number of syllables?
- ○ line 1
- ○ line 2
- ○ line 3

16. Which word would be the best substitute for *big* in the pattern for this haiku?
- ○ massive
- ○ large
- ○ gigantic

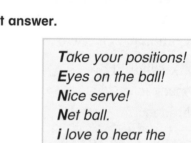

17. Which line contains a misspelled word?
- ○ line 1
- ○ line 2
- ○ line 3

D. Read the acrostic poem. Fill in the circle next to the correct answer.

18. The author of this poem probably _____.
- ○ won a tennis tournament
- ○ likes to play and watch tennis
- ○ does not enjoy tennis

> *T*ake your positions!
> *E*yes on the ball!
> *N*ice serve!
> *N*et ball.
> *i* love to hear the
> *S*ound of the game.

19. The poem includes pauses at the ends of _____.
- ○ all of the lines
- ○ a few of the lines
- ○ many of the lines

20. Which line has a capitalization mistake?
- ○ line 1
- ○ line 5
- ○ line 6

Cumulative Review

A. Underline the words that have prefixes. Fill in the circle next to the correct meaning of the word you underlined. *(Chapter 5)*

1. The jeweler would not accept an imperfect diamond.
   ○ not perfect   ○ perfect again

2. We will precook the ham today and serve it cold tomorrow.
   ○ not cook   ○ cook before

3. Barrett became entangled in the branches.
   ○ tangled before   ○ tangled in

4. Dad said the commercial was all nonsense.
   ○ not having sense   ○ into sense

B. Underline each word that has a suffix. Circle the suffix. *(Chapter 13)*

5. The penniless boy went for a job.

6. We will try to complete the course more quickly.

7. They won't fish on a stormy day.

8. The farmer will milk his cows at 5:00 A.M.

9. Those are the most comfortable shoes I've ever worn!

10. A job well done will bring much fulfillment.

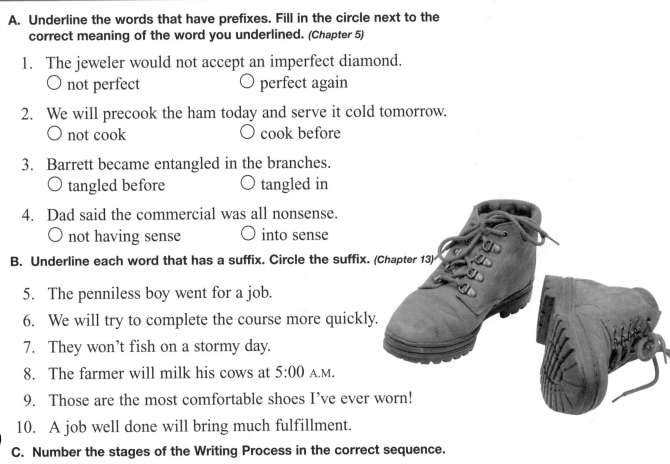

C. Number the stages of the Writing Process in the correct sequence. *(All writing chapters)*

_____ 11. Add, delete, or change details to improve the writing.

_____ 12. Choose your topic and plan the events or details to include.

_____ 13. Write a neat final copy.

_____ 14. Check for correct spelling and punctuation.

_____ 15. Write the first draft.

D. Put parentheses around each prepositional phrase. One sentence has more than one prepositional phrase. *(Chapter 15)*

16. In 1880 a boy was wading in the pool at Jerusalem.

17. He wandered into the tunnel.

18. He found an inscription on the wall.

19. The inscription was written in Hebrew.

20. It told about Hezekiah's tunnel.

21. No one had seen the inscription for many years.

E. Decide whether the underlined clause is dependent or independent. *(Chapter 15)*

22. I visited the Grand Canyon <u>when I was four years old</u>.
    ○ dependent   ○ independent

23. <u>Because I was so young</u>, I don't remember much about the trip.
    ○ dependent   ○ independent

24. When I am older, <u>I plan to go back to the Grand Canyon</u>.
    ○ dependent   ○ independent

25. <u>I will visit Mexico</u> after I see the Grand Canyon.
    ○ dependent   ○ independent

26. I will help the missionaries <u>while I am in Mexico</u>.
    ○ dependent   ○ independent

F. Fill in the Venn diagram with the information from the T-chart. *(Chapter 6)*

Car	Truck
4 tires	4 tires
trunk	bed
4 doors	2 doors
carries more people	carries more things
gas pedal	gas pedal

Different   **Alike**   **Different**

Car   Truck

Writing Handbook

Using a Thesaurus

A *thesaurus* contains a list of synonyms, words that have similar meanings. You can use a thesaurus to find a more exact word or a more interesting word when you write. A poet may use a thesaurus to find a word that fits better with his poem's sound or rhythm.

The *entry words* are arranged in alphabetical order. *Guide words* can help you locate a word. Each entry gives a *definition* and uses the word in a *sample sentence.* A list of *synonyms* that can be used to replace the entry word is provided. The entry also tells the *part of speech,* how the word is used in the sentence. Some entries include an *antonym,* a word that has the opposite meaning of the entry word.

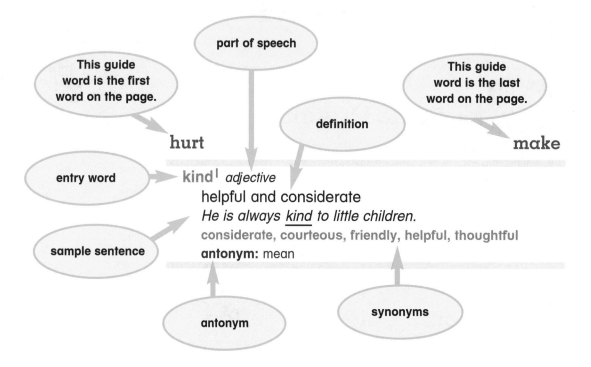

The following sentence tells the reader what the bus driver is like. Changing the word *kind* will give a more precise meaning to each sentence. When choosing a synonym, be careful not to change the meaning of the sentence.

*That bus driver is always **kind** when we ride his bus.*

*That bus driver is always **considerate** when we ride his bus.*
*That bus driver is always **courteous** when we ride his bus.*
*That bus driver is always **friendly** when we ride his bus.*
*That bus driver is always **helpful** when we ride his bus.*
*That bus driver is always **thoughtful** when we ride his bus.*

afraid *adjective*
 filled with fear
 He is <u>*afraid*</u> *to climb the tower.*
 fearful, frightened, nervous, scared, uneasy,
 worried **antonym:** confident

angry *adjective*
 showing strong feeling that comes from
 believing that one has been treated badly
 We were <u>*angry*</u> *with her for telling our secret.*
 aggravated, annoyed, enraged, fuming,
 furious, irate, offended, resentful, wrathful
 antonym: calm

answer *noun*
 a reply to a question, statement, or
 invitation
 My <u>*answer*</u> *is "no."*
 reply, response **antonym:** question

ask *verb*
 to put a question to; to look for an
 answer to
 <u>*Ask*</u> *the librarian for help.*
 inquire, interrogate, petition, question, request
 antonym: answer

attack *verb*
 to set upon with violent force
 The armies <u>*attack*</u> *the city.*
 afflict, assault, harm, invade, raid
 antonym: defend

bad *adjective*
 not good
 Christa is having a <u>*bad*</u> *day.*
 awful, dreadful, horrible, horrid, hurtful, rotten,
 terrible **antonym:** good

before *adverb*
 earlier; at any time in the past
 I read that book <u>*before*</u>*.*
 already, earlier, previously, prior to
 antonym: after

beg *verb*
 to ask for in a humble way
 They <u>*beg*</u> *for mercy.*
 ask, demand, entreat, plead
 antonyms: demand, urge

big *adjective*
 of great size
 An elephant is a <u>*big*</u> *animal.*
 enormous, gigantic, grand, great, huge, large,
 massive **antonym:** little

bother *verb*
 to give trouble to
 Please don't <u>*bother*</u> *your brother when he*
 is doing homework.
 annoy, disturb, harass, interrupt, irritate,
 pester, provoke **antonym:** comfort

brave *adjective*
 having or showing courage
 <u>*Brave*</u> *men rescued the boy from the cave.*
 bold, confident, courageous, daring, heroic,
 valiant **antonym:** cowardly

break *verb*
 to come apart or take apart
 Don't <u>*break*</u> *the branch on the tree.*
 crack, crush, damage, fracture, separate,
 shatter, smash, wreck **antonym:** repair

bright *adjective*
 giving off much light; strong in color
 The <u>*bright*</u> *sun shone through the branches.*
 brilliant, illuminating, luminous, radiant,
 shining, vivid **antonym:** dull

build *verb*
 to make or form something by putting
 parts or materials together
 Let's <u>*build*</u> *a fence.*
 construct, form, shape **antonym:** destroy

buy *verb*
 to give money to get goods or services
 We will <u>*buy*</u> *candy at the store.*
 obtain, purchase **antonym:** sell

calm *adjective*
 peacefully quiet
 She spoke in a <u>*calm*</u> *voice.*
 peaceful, placid, serene, still, tranquil,
 undisturbed **antonyms:** excited, angry, troubled

careful *adjective*
 taking time to think before acting
 Be <u>*careful*</u> *about crossing the street.*
 cautious, prudent, vigilant, watchful
 antonym: careless

carry *verb*
to take from one place to another
The men carry furniture into the house.
haul, lug, move, tote, transport

change *verb*
to make or become different
Let's change the color of the room.
alter, replace, shift, substitute, switch, transform, vary **antonym:** remain

clean[1] *adjective*
free from dirt, stain, or germs
The kitchen floor is clean.
immaculate, neat, pure, sanitary, spotless, stainless, tidy **antonyms:** soiled, dirty

clean[2] *verb*
to get rid of dirt, stain, or germs
You should clean a wound to prevent infection.
cleanse, disinfect, purify, sanitize, wash
antonym: soil

cold *adjective*
having a low temperature; feeling no warmth
This house is cold.
chilly, cool, frigid, frosty, frozen, icy
antonym: hot

collect *verb*
to bring or come together in a group
The girls collect stickers.
accumulate, compile, gather, obtain, reserve, store **antonym:** scatter

copy *verb*
to make to be like or look like something else
Please copy this letter.
duplicate, replicate, reproduce

cry *verb*
to shed tears because of pain or a strong feeling
I sometimes cry when I am hurt.
bawl, mourn, sob, wail, weep, whimper
antonym: laugh

cut *verb*
to tear into strips or pieces
Cut the paper.
chop, dice, gash, rip, shred, slice, snip, tear

dangerous *adjective*
threatening harm or injury; unsafe
The ocean is dangerous in stormy weather.
hazardous, perilous, risky **antonym:** safe

dark *adjective*
without light or with very little light
Today was a dark winter day.
cloudy, dim, dull, overcast **antonym:** light

destroy *verb*
to ruin completely; wipe out
The fire will destroy the village.
annihilate, demolish, devastate, ruin, wreck
antonym: make

different *adjective*
not being the same
The sea horse is different from other fish.
distinct, unique, unlike, unusual **antonyms:** same, alike

dirty *adjective*
soiled
My shirt was dirty after I played with the dog.
filthy, grimy, muddy, nasty, polluted
antonym: clean

disappear *verb*
to pass out of sight
The chocolate cookies always disappear first.
fade, vanish **antonym:** appear

do *verb*
to perform or make; carry out
What will you do this summer?
achieve, complete, perform, practice, undertake

easy *adjective*
needing very little work
It's easy to ride a bicycle.
effortless, simple, uncomplicated
antonym: difficult

empty *adjective*
   containing nothing
   The house was empty.
   deserted, unoccupied, vacant, void
   antonym: full

enough *adjective*
   as many or as much as needed
   Is there enough food for everyone?
   adequate, plenty, sufficient
   antonym: insufficient

fair *adjective*
   not favoring one more than another
   The judge made a fair decision.
   consistent, honest, impartial, just, lawful,
   legal, right **antonym:** unfair

fake *adjective*
   not genuine; false
   The criminal tried to spend fake money.
   artificial, counterfeit, false, fraudulent, phony
   antonym: real

fat *adjective*
   too heavy; plump
   That is a very fat cat.
   bulky, chubby, enormous, large, massive,
   obese
   antonym: thin

fear *noun*
   a bad feeling caused by danger or pain
   The nightmare filled me with fear.
   alarm, dismay, dread, fright, terror

find *verb*
   to come upon by accident or to look for
   and discover
   Did you find my keys?
   discover, encounter, locate, recover
   antonym: lose

finish *verb*
   to bring to an end
   When will you finish your homework?
   accomplish, complete, conclude, terminate
   antonyms: start, begin

fix *verb*
   to secure or repair
   Could you fix the broken faucet?
   mend, repair, restore **antonym:** break

funny *adjective*
   causing laughter or amusement
   The funny clown made us laugh.
   amusing, comical, hilarious, humorous
   antonym: serious

get *verb*
   to receive; to gain
   She will get a bike for her birthday.
   acquire, gain, obtain, receive **antonym:** give

give *verb*
   to make a present of; to hand over
   We give money to the missionaries.
   contribute, donate, grant, offer, present,
   provide, supply **antonyms:** get, receive

gloomy *adjective*
   a dark or discouraging state of mind
   or atmosphere
   He has a gloomy look on his face.
   bleak, depressing, dismal, dreary, somber
   antonym: cheerful

go *verb*
   to pass from one place to another
   We go to Washington every year.
   depart, leave, move, proceed, race, run, travel
   antonyms: stay, remain

good[1] *adjective*
   high in quality
   Earthworms are good for our soil.
   fabulous, favorable, helpful, right, suitable,
   superb, terrific, useful, wonderful **antonym:**
   bad

good[2] *adjective*
   having a pleasant taste or smell
   The cookies are good.
   delicious, delightful, scrumptious, tasty
   antonym: bad

great *adjective*
   superior in quality
   George Washington was a great leader.
   awesome, excellent, exceptional, fantastic,
   grand, important, magnificent, outstanding,
   wonderful **antonyms:** terrible, awful

group *noun*
a number of persons or things together
The state of Hawaii is made up of a group of islands in the Pacific Ocean.
clump, cluster, collection, bunch, gathering, set, team **antonym:** individual

grow *verb*
to become larger in size
The trees grow every year.
develop, increase, mature **antonym:** shrink

guard *verb*
to keep from harm
Soldiers guard the entrance to the palace.
defend, keep, protect, shield, watch

happy *adjective*
having a cheerful spirit
The happy children played and sang.
carefree, cheerful, content, glad, joyful, jubilant, satisfied **antonym:** sad

hard *adjective*
requiring great effort
You have a hard job to do.
complicated, difficult, tough, trying
antonym: easy

hate *verb*
to dislike very much
I hate asparagus.
abhor, despise, detest, dislike, loathe
antonym: love

hide *verb*
to put or keep out of sight
Let's hide the presents.
conceal, cover **antonym:** show

high *adjective*
having or being at a great height
Dad looked down from the high balloon.
elevated, towering **antonym:** low

hit *verb*
to give a blow to
I will hit the nail hard.
pound, smack, smite, strike

hold *verb*
to take and keep in the hands or arms
Hold the rope tightly.
clasp, clutch, grasp, grip **antonym:** release

honest *adjective*
truthful
An honest person will return a lost wallet.
respectable, sincere, trustworthy, upright
antonym: deceitful

hot *adjective*
having a lot of heat
Don't touch the hot stove.
burning, fiery, scorching, sweltering
antonym: cold

hurry *verb*
to go faster
We can finish on time if we hurry.
accelerate, hustle, rush

hurt *verb*
to cause pain or injury
Don't fall and hurt yourself.
damage, harm, impair, injure, wound
antonym: help

important *adjective*
having great value, meaning, or significance
He gave me an important message.
impressive, influential, meaningful, momentous, significant, valuable
antonym: unimportant

job *noun*
a chore, usually done on a regular schedule; occupation
My job is to teach English.
career, chore, duty, employment, livelihood, profession, task, trade, work

join *verb*
to come together; to become one of a group
He will join the pieces.
attach, combine, connect, fasten, link
antonym: disconnect

jump *verb*
to rise off the ground by using the legs
Some grasshoppers can jump very high.
bounce, hop, leap, spring up

kind¹ *adjective*
helpful and considerate
He is always <u>*kind*</u> *to little children.*
considerate, courteous, friendly, helpful, thoughtful **antonym:** mean

kind² *noun*
a group of the same or similar things
Swans are a <u>*kind*</u> *of water bird.*
category, group, sort, type

laugh *verb*
to make sounds and movements to express happiness or amusement
The clown makes him <u>*laugh*</u>*.*
chuckle, giggle, snicker **antonym:** cry

let *verb*
to permit; allow
She <u>*let*</u> *him talk.*
allow, consent, permit **antonym:** forbid

lift *verb*
to raise into the air
She will <u>*lift*</u> *the box.*
elevate, hoist, raise **antonym:** lower

like *verb*
to be fond of
Which outfit do you <u>*like*</u>*?*
enjoy, favor, prefer **antonym:** dislike

little *adjective*
small in size or quantity
Our <u>*little*</u> *table seats only three people.*
miniature, minute, petite, short, tiny
antonym: big

live *verb*
to make one's home
I <u>*live*</u> *in a brick house.*
abide, dwell, inhabit, occupy, reside

look¹ *verb*
to use the eyes to see; to seek
<u>*Look*</u> *at the beautiful sunset.*
behold, gaze, glance, observe, peer, stare, view, watch

look² *verb*
to search for
<u>*Look*</u> *up the word in the dictionary.*
check, hunt, investigate, search, seek, survey

make *verb*
to bring into being; put together
I will <u>*make*</u> *a gift for you.*
build, construct, create, form, mold, produce, shape **antonym:** destroy

many *adjective*
a large number of; a lot of
He has <u>*many*</u> *friends.*
countless, multiple, numerous **antonym:** few

move *verb*
to change or cause to change location
Can you <u>*move*</u> *your chair?*
budge, relocate, scoot, shift, transfer, transport

neat *adjective*
in clean condition, not messy
He has a <u>*neat*</u> *desk.*
orderly, organized, tidy **antonym:** messy

needed *adjective*
impossible to do without
We don't have the <u>*needed*</u> *tools to fix the car.*
essential, necessary, required
antonym: unnecessary

new *adjective*
recently made, built, formed, or grown
Don't walk on the <u>*new*</u> *grass.*
fresh, immature, recent **antonym:** old

nice *adjective*
very pleasing
What a <u>*nice*</u> *girl she is!*
fine, good, kind, pleasant, pleasing
antonyms: nasty, mean

noise *noun*
a sound or an unpleasant or unexpected sound
The <u>*noise*</u> *outside kept me awake.*
clamor, commotion, racket, sound, uproar

old *adjective*
having lived or existed for many years
An <u>*old*</u> *man lives next door.*
aged, ancient, elderly **antonym:** young

part *noun*
something that along with other things makes a whole
Would you like a part of my dessert?
section, segment, piece, portion
antonym: whole

perfect *adjective*
completely free from mistake
Jessica's recital was perfect.
accurate, faultless, flawless, precise
antonym: defective

pick *verb*
to decide on or prefer something
Our teacher will pick the team captains.
choose, decide, elect, select **antonym:** overlook

polite *adjective*
having or showing good manners
He is always polite to visitors.
courteous, gracious, mannerly, tactful
antonym: impolite

pretty *adjective*
delightful to look at, listen to, or think about
That is a pretty painting.
beautiful, gorgeous, lovely, marvelous, pleasing, wonderful **antonym:** ugly

promise *verb*
to give one's word to do or not to do something; to make an oath
I promise to obey my parents.
agree, commit, declare, guarantee, pledge, vow

protect *verb*
to keep from harm
She wore sunglasses to protect her eyes from the glare.
guard, preserve, shield **antonym:** attack

proud¹ *adjective*
overly satisfied with oneself
He is too proud to ask for help.
arrogant, conceited, haughty, vain
antonym: humble

proud² *adjective*
feeling pleased over something made, done, or owned
I am proud of the A I got on my test.
pleased, satisfied, fulfilled, contented, delighted, ecstatic, excited **antonym:** ashamed

pull *verb*
to grasp something and cause it to move forward or toward oneself
Pull the rope harder.
drag, jerk, tow, tug **antonym:** push

push *verb*
to press against something in order to move it
He tried to push the rock into the hole.
press, shove, thrust **antonym:** pull

put *verb*
to set or cause to be in a certain location or condition
Put the lamp on the desk.
establish, install, lay, place, set
antonym: remove

quick *adjective*
moving or acting with speed; done in a short amount of time
Mom made a quick trip to the grocery store.
fast, rapid, speedy, swift **antonym:** slow

quiet *adjective*
making little or no noise
A farm is quiet in the early morning hours.
calm, hushed, peaceful, restful, silent, still, tranquil **antonym:** noisy

real *adjective*
true
These are real diamonds.
actual, authentic, genuine **antonym:** fake

reason *noun*
cause or explanation
What is her reason for going to church?
cause, goal, intention, motive, purpose
antonym: result

reliable *adjective*
able to be depended upon
She is a reliable person and will complete the job.
dependable, faithful, responsible, trustworthy
antonym: unreliable

replace *verb*
to take or fill the place of
Replace the silk roses with real roses.
exchange, substitute, supersede, supplant, switch

rich *adjective*
having great wealth
That man is rich.
affluent, prosperous, wealthy
antonym: poor

right *adjective*
something that is true
Yes, that is the right answer.
accurate, correct, exact, proper, true
antonym: wrong

rough¹ *adjective*
having a surface that is not even or smooth
Rough dirt roads can be hard on a car.
bumpy, coarse, jagged, rugged, uneven
antonym: smooth

rough² *adjective*
requiring great bodily, mental, or spiritual strength
He had a rough day.
difficult, severe, tough, trying, burdensome

run *verb*
to move quickly on foot
The children run at recess.
canter, dash, gallop, jog, race, sprint
antonym: walk

sad *adjective*
filled with sorrow
He was sad when it was time to leave.
depressed, gloomy, sorrowful, unhappy
antonym: happy

same *adjective*
being exactly like something else
These two bowls are the same.
equivalent, identical **antonym:** different

save *verb*
to keep or set aside for use in the future; store up
It is wise to save money.
conserve, reserve **antonym:** spend

say *verb*
to speak out loud
Can you say that more clearly?
communicate, declare, exclaim, express, remark, speak, state, utter

scary *adjective*
causing fear or alarm
Wasn't that a scary book?
alarming, fearful, frightening, horrifying, terrifying **antonym:** pleasant

serious *adjective*
not smiling or happy
He had a serious expression on his face.
earnest, grave, grim, somber, solemn
antonym: funny

shake *verb*
to move or make move up and down or back and forth in short, quick movements
I felt the ground shake during the earthquake.
quiver, rock, tremble, vibrate

shiny *adjective*
reflecting light
Mother has a shiny jewel in her ring.
bright, brilliant, glistening, radiant
antonym: dull

short *adjective*
taking a small amount of time
The boss held a short meeting.
abrupt, brief, condensed, quick **antonym:** long

shout *verb*
to say something in a loud voice; cry out
Don't shout in the library.
cheer, holler, scream, shriek, yell
antonym: whisper

show *verb*
to put in sight; allow to be seen
Please show your science project to the judge.
demonstrate, display, exhibit, present, reveal
antonym: hide

smart *adjective*
having or requiring a quick mind
You have to be <u>smart</u> to answer that question.
bright, clever, ingenious, intelligent, shrewd, skillful **antonym:** unintelligent

smell *noun*
scent
I caught the <u>smell</u> of onions cooking.
aroma, fragrance, odor, stench, stink

smile *verb*
showing happiness, amusement, pleasure, or friendliness by an expression on the face
I <u>smile</u> when they congratulate me.
beam, grin **antonym:** frown

some *adjective*
a number or quantity not known or named
I have <u>some</u> baseball cards.
several, few, many

special *adjective*
different from what is usual or common
Christmas is a <u>special</u> day.
exceptional, extraordinary, particular, unusual
antonym: ordinary

start *verb*
to begin an action or movement
The game will <u>start</u> after lunch.
begin, commence, embark, initiate
antonym: finish

stop *verb*
to cease moving
We will <u>stop</u> soon.
break, cease, halt, pause
antonyms: begin, go

strange *adjective*
not known before; different
They came to a <u>strange</u> land.
bizarre, different, odd, peculiar, unfamiliar, unusual, weird **antonym:** ordinary

strict *adjective*
firm or severe
Aunt Sarah is very <u>strict</u> about bedtime.
firm, grave, severe, stern
antonyms: flexible, lenient

strong *adjective*
having much power, energy, or strength
The <u>strong</u> elephant lifted the tree trunk.
fortified, great, mighty, muscular, powerful, sturdy **antonym:** weak

sure *adjective*
feeling certain about someone or something; having no doubt
I'm <u>sure</u> he's coming to the party.
certain, confident, positive
antonym: uncertain

surprise *verb*
to cause to feel astonishment or wonder
I will <u>surprise</u> my mother on her birthday.
amaze, astonish, shock, startle

take *verb*
to capture, seize, or win
Let the horse <u>take</u> the apple from your hand.
grab, grasp, seize, snatch, sneak, steal
antonym: give

teach *verb*
to help someone learn
I will <u>teach</u> her how to read.
direct, educate, guide, inform, instruct, show, train **antonym:** learn

thin *adjective*
having little space between opposite sides or surfaces; skinny
That board is too <u>thin</u> for our project.
gaunt, lean, scrawny, slender, slight, slim
antonym: thick

think *verb*
to use one's mind to make decisions or judgments
<u>Think</u> before you act.
consider, contemplate, imagine, meditate, muse, ponder, reflect

throw *verb*
to send through the air with a swift motion of the arm
<u>Throw</u> the ball to Lance.
cast, fling, hurl, pitch, toss **antonym:** catch

tie *verb*

to fasten or bind with a cord or rope

Let's tie the twigs together with string.

bind, fasten, hold, secure, wrap

antonyms: loosen, untie

tired *adjective*

exhausted in body or mind

He's so tired that he can't keep his eyes open.

exhausted, fatigued, sluggish, weary

antonym: alert

travel *verb*

to go from one place to another

She may travel through Europe.

journey, sojourn, tour

trip *noun*

a journey from one place to another

We took a trip of one thousand miles.

excursion, journey, vacation, voyage

trouble *noun*

a difficult or dangerous situation

The flood caused trouble for the city.

affliction, danger, difficulty, distress, grief, misery **antonym:** safety

ugly *adjective*

not pleasant to look at

The monster had an ugly face.

gross, grotesque, hideous, homely, repulsive, unattractive

antonyms: beautiful, pretty

understand *verb*

to get or grasp the meaning of

Do you understand the question?

comprehend, discern, grasp, know

antonym: confuse

usual *adjective*

seen or happening all of the time

I ate my usual breakfast.

customary, expected, normal, ordinary, regular, typical **antonym:** unusual

very *adverb*

in a high degree

I am very happy.

absolutely, extremely, fully, genuinely, truly

antonym: slightly

walk *verb*

to move on foot at an easy, steady pace

Let's walk through the woods.

amble, march, plod, saunter, step, stroll, strut, trudge **antonym:** run

want *verb*

to have a desire for

I want a bicycle.

crave, desire, wish

waste *verb*

to spend or use up foolishly

Don't waste the whole day watching television.

misspend, squander **antonym:** save

weak *adjective*

not having strength, power, or energy

He was weak after his illness.

feeble, frail, powerless **antonym:** strong

wet *adjective*

full of moisture

Her shoes were wet from the rain.

damp, drenched, humid, saturated, soaked, soggy **antonym:** dry

whole *adjective*

having all its parts; complete

Did you eat a whole pizza?

complete, entire, total, undivided **antonym:** part

work *noun*

what a person does to accomplish something or to earn money

His work was to paint the house.

chore, duty, effort, employment, job, labor, livelihood, occupation, profession, task, toil, trade **antonym:** play

worker *noun*

someone who works

She is a diligent worker.

employee, laborer

The Writing Process

The *Writing Process* is the stages or the steps that a writer follows as he writes. At each stage, the writer has an activity to do. Sometimes a writer repeats the stages until he is satisfied with his writing.

1 Planning:
Getting Ready to Write

2 Drafting:
Writing Your Ideas in Sentences

3 Revising:
Improving Your Writing

4 Proofreading:
Finding and Correcting Mistakes in Your Writing

5 Publishing:
Sharing Your Writing with Someone

Planning: *Getting Ready to Write*

- **Choose your topic**—*What will you write about?*

- **Find out your reason for writing**—*Why are you writing?*

- **Find out your audience**—*Whom are you writing for?*

- **Find out your format**—*How will it look?*

When you know the answers to these questions, you can explore your topic and organize your ideas and information. You can group your ideas and details with a graphic organizer. This will help you choose which details you will write about and in what order you will write them.

Some graphic organizers include the following:

- **Events/Details Chart** *(See sample on page 326.)*

- **Time-Order Chart** *(See sample on page 327.)*

- **Venn Diagram** *(See sample on page 328.)*

- **Opinion Chart** *(See sample on page 329.)*

- **Word Web** *(See sample on page 330.)*

- **Plot Pyramid** *(See sample on page 331.)*

- **Outline** *(See sample on page 332.)*

Drafting: *Writing Your Ideas in Sentences*

In this stage you put your ideas into sentences and write them on paper. This is the first version of your writing. Sometimes it is called a *rough draft* or *first draft.*

Look at your plan as you write. If you think of other details, you can add them. Don't worry about mistakes. You can fix misspelled words and details that are out of order later.

If you are writing a paragraph, begin with an interesting sentence that tells the *main idea.* This is your *topic sentence.* Be sure to include only the *details* that belong with your topic sentence. Sometimes you will need to write an ending sentence for your paragraph. This sentence tells what you think or feel about your topic.

3

Revising: *Improving Your Writing*

During this stage you make your writing better. Read your writing to yourself. Look at the details you included. Ask yourself whether the details are in the right order and whether they are about your topic. Change the order of your details if they are confusing or out of order. Cross out any detail that does not belong.

Ask yourself whether you can make your writing clearer by using more exact words. Ask yourself whether you can make it more interesting by using more colorful words. Use your thesaurus on pages 313–21 to find better words.

Read your writing to someone else (your partner, your teacher, your parent). Ask your partner to make suggestions and to ask questions about your writing. If he doesn't understand something, try to make your writing clearer. Think about his suggestions. Make any changes that *you* think are important to make.

Most writers do not write perfectly the first time. In the revising stage, they make their writing better by rewriting, reordering, or adding or deleting words.

Proofreading: *Finding and Correcting Mistakes in Your Writing*

At this stage, you need to look for mistakes in capitalization, punctuation, indenting, and spelling. It is hard to look for different types of mistakes at one time. Read your writing several times and check for one or two types of mistakes at a time. You can use a proofreading checklist to help. Here is a paragraph that has been proofread using the proofreading marks.

similar

Many things about Nebraska and South Carolina are similar. My School in Nebraska is a lot like my old school in South carolina. We study all the same subjects and we even use the same kind of textbooks. Similarly, our neighborhood here in Nebraska reminds me of our neighborhood in South Carolina. There our house was on a

cul-de-sac

culdasak, and our house here is too. Like the neighbors in South Carolina, the neighbors here in Nebraska are friendly, and there are some kids my own age. South Carolina had a good church for us to attend, and Nebraska does also.

Proofreading Marks

∧∨ Add
⤴ Delete
≡ Capital letter
/ Lowercase
⊙→ Move

Publishing: *Sharing Your Writing with Someone*

Finally, copy your writing neatly and correct all the mistakes you found during the proofreading stage. Now you can share your writing with someone. There are many ways to share your writing: you may give it to your teacher, display it on a bulletin board, put it in a book, read it aloud, record it, or mail it to a friend or relative.

Graphic Organizers

How do you begin? Sometimes graphic organizers are used to plan your writing. If you have many ideas, graphic organizers can help you organize them. As you gather information, these organizers can help you arrange the details before you begin writing. Use the graphic organizer that works best for the type of writing you will be doing.

Events/Details Chart

When you write about a personal experience, it is important that you recall the main events of the experience. But you must also include details to help your audience see and hear what happened. Use an *events/details chart* to help you plan. Once you have chosen your topic, begin by listing the main events of the experience. Then add details for each event, such as specific places, colors, sounds, and people's words and movements. The details will make the events seem more real to your readers. You may also plan an opening that gets the reader's attention and a closing that tells what you learned or how you felt about the experience.

Events	Details
1. Saw Great-Grandma sitting outside her room	▸ felt afraid ▸ silky blue robe ▸ gray hair in a long braid
2. She smiled at me	▸ shaky voice ▸ smile full of love ▸
3. Took her out onto the deck	▸ in her wheelchair ▸ talked to Dad in Bengali ▸
4. Read Bible to her	▸ asked me to read ▸ read Psalm 23 ▸ quoted the psalm in Bengali
5. Ended our visit	▸ squeezed my hand ▸ Dad prayed ▸ took her back to her room

Time-Order Chart

Use a *time-order chart* to help you sequence. When you write instructions, begin by telling the topic and the materials needed. Write one step in each box. Then add details that make each step clearer and more exact. Choose a time-order word such as *first, next,* or *finally* to begin each step.

Time-Order Words	Steps	Details
First	Break the graham cracker in half	▶ put the chocolate bar on one ▶ ▶
Next	Hold the marshmallows over the fire	▶ on the stick ▶ till they get done ▶
Then	Take the marshmallows off the stick	▶ with your fingers ▶ lay them on top of the chocolate ▶
Finally	Smash the other half of the graham cracker on top	▶ like a sandwich ▶ ▶

Venn Diagram

A *Venn diagram* helps you categorize information for a compare-contrast essay. Before completing the Venn diagram, it is helpful to make lists of characteristics of your two subjects. A Venn diagram consists of two overlapping ovals, with one oval representing each subject. In the middle part of the diagram, where the ovals overlap, list the characteristics that the two subjects have in common (likenesses). In the outer parts of each oval, list the characteristics that are unique to each subject (differences).

Horses	Donkeys
short ears	long ears
carry loads	short mane
good for riding	carry loads
neighing sounds	braying sounds
live in herds	good for riding
long mane	live in herds
Bible talks about them	Bible talks about them

Horses
short ears
long mane
neighing sounds

good for riding
carry loads
live in herds
Bible talks about them

Donkeys
long ears
short mane
braying sounds

Opinion Chart

An *opinion chart* helps you organize the reasons for your opinion before writing a book review. Your opinion is *how* you think or feel about something. A reason tells *why* you think or feel the way you do. Some reasons are stronger than others. As you think about the characters, setting, plot, and lessons taught in your book, you can formulate specific reasons for your opinion. Write your opinion and the two strongest reasons that support your opinion. For each reason, write two or three examples from the book that support that reason.

My Opinion of the Book

I liked it, thought it was good

Reason 1

It was exciting

Reason 2

It taught important lessons

Examples from the Book

Nick and Anthony find
    cabin in the mountains
    for clubhouse
Smugglers also using cabin
Get locked inside
Fire in cabin
Thunderstorm

Examples from the Book

Kindness—Nick and old man
Forgiveness—Anthony when
    dog gets hurt in fire
Loving others

My Recommendation

Good book if you like adventure

Word Web

A *word web* can be used to plan a character before you write a story. Write the character's name in an oval in the center of your paper. Write details about the character around the center oval. Circle each detail. Draw a line from each detail to the topic in the center. You can describe each detail. Circle the descriptions and draw a line from the descriptions to the detail. Choose the details you will include in your writing. Number the details in the order that you want to write about them.

A word web can also help you plan words to use in a poem about a certain topic. Write the topic in the center oval. Write words that go with that topic in the surrounding ovals.

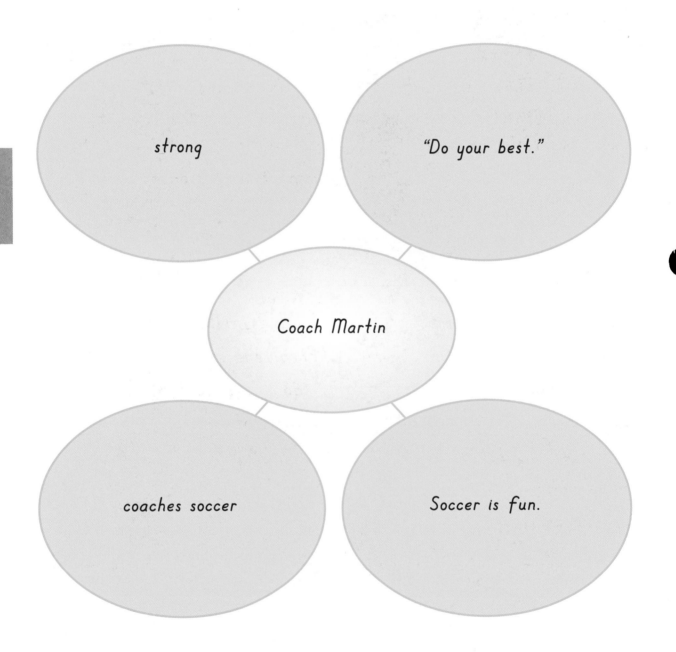

strong

"Do your best."

Coach Martin

coaches soccer

Soccer is fun.

English 4, Graphic Organizers

Plot Pyramid

Tall tales have a beginning, a middle, and an end. The *plot* is the sequence of events in make-believe stories such as a tall tale. The *Beginning* introduces the hero and other main characters and tells about the setting. The *Problem* marks the point at which the tall tale moves from the beginning to the middle. The problem in a tall tale is usually a struggle between the hero and a powerful enemy. The *Middle* tells more about the problem and tells how the hero tries to solve the problem. The *Solution* marks the point at which the tall tale moves from the middle to the end. The solution in a tall tale is usually an impossible act performed by the hero. The *End* tells what happens after the problem is solved.

Middle

Tom tosses orange juice at bee
Bee gets mad and comes closer

Problem

Giant bee comes after him

Solution

Tom blindfolds bee and cuts off stinger

Beginning

Tom Toughguy eats biscuits on his porch in Georgia

End

Bee leaves
Tom builds huge fire

© 2004 BJU Press. Reproduction prohibited.

Outline

Before beginning a research report, you must read, take notes, and then organize your research. An *outline* helps you organize the information from your note cards before you begin to write. Your main ideas will be your main points, labeled with Roman numerals. Gather your note cards about each main idea and choose the most interesting details to include beneath each main point. Decide in what order to tell about these details. Use capital letters to label the details under each main point.

Customs and Holidays in Ireland

1. light a candle in window at Christmas, welcomes the Holy Family
2. Christmas—clean house from top to bottom
3. use holly branches to decorate homes

Christmas in Ireland, pages 3, 5

Customs and Holidays in Ireland

1. St. Patrick's Day—festivals, plays
2. St. Patrick used shamrock as a picture of the Trinity
3. some people believe St. Patrick drove snakes out of Ireland

Irish Holidays, pages 16, 25

Ireland

I. Ireland's Geography
  A. A good place for tourists
  B. An island
  C. Slightly larger than West Virginia
  D. Cliffs of Moher, seven hundred feet high and on the west coast by the Atlantic Ocean

II. Ireland's Climate
  A. Mild spring and fall
  B. Wet and cold winter with lots of rain and snow
  C. Warm and wet summer
  D. Mostly cloudy skies all year
  E. Winds blowing from the Atlantic Ocean every day

III. Customs and Holidays in Ireland
  A. Christmas—modern Irish light a candle in window to welcome the Holy Family
  B. St. Patrick's Day—have festivals and plays honoring the saint
  C. St. Patrick—legends say he explained the Trinity with a shamrock leaf and drove snakes from Ireland

IV. Main Religion in Ireland
  A. St. Patrick—first to bring Christianity in A.D. 432
  B. Largest religion—Roman Catholicism
  C. Second largest religion—Protestant Presbyterianism

English 4, Graphic Organizers

Writing Models

Personal Narrative

A *personal narrative* is a true story about the writer's own experience.

How to Write a Personal Narrative

- Write about an experience that you had.

- Choose an exciting, scary, fun, or unusual experience that you remember clearly.

- Include details about when, where, and how the experience happened.

- Include details about what you saw, heard, smelled, tasted, or felt so that the reader can picture your experience.

- Include dialogue to make the people in your narrative come alive.

- Make your ending sentence tell what you learned or how you felt about the experience.

My New Friend

Last year I went with my dad to visit his grandmother at Berrydale Nursing Center. I didn't know I was going to make a new friend. I only knew I felt nervous. My great-grandmother was sitting outside the door of her room wearing a silky blue robe. Her gray hair was pulled back into a long braid. When she saw me, she smiled and said, "This must be Shibu." Her voice was soft and shaky, but her smile was full of love. I didn't feel nervous anymore.

My dad wheeled her wheelchair out onto the deck. She talked to my dad in Bengali. It is the language of her people in India. I could not understand, so I just kept quiet. Then my great-grandmother turned to me and said in English, "Shibu, will you read?" She handed me the Bible in her lap, and I saw that it was open to the Twenty-third Psalm. I read it out loud. When I finished, she began to speak in Bengali. She quoted the whole psalm for me in her own language. Then she smiled again and gave my hand a squeeze. My dad prayed, and we took Great-Grandma back to her room.

Now I write letters to my great-grandmother. She writes back right away. Sometimes she writes a sentence in Bengali at the end, and I ask my dad to read it for me. Great-Grandma is ninety years old, but I feel as if she is one of my best friends.

Instructions in a Friendly Letter

Instructions give directions or explain how to do or make something. The directions should be in order. When writing instructions in a friendly letter, be sure to include all of the parts of the letter: the heading, the greeting, the body, the closing, and the signature.

How to Write Instructions in a Friendly Letter

- Complete a time-order chart.
- In the heading of the letter, write your address and the date. (Begin at the top center of your paper.)
- Write an appropriate greeting and the name of the person to whom you are writing.
- In the body of the letter, introduce the topic in an interesting way.
- List materials needed for the activity before giving the steps.
- Write each step of the instructions in order.
- Use time-order words such as *first, second, third, then, next, finally,* and *afterward* to show the order.
- Conclude the instructions in an encouraging way.
- Write an appropriate closing. (Begin at the bottom center of your paper.)
- Sign your name. (Begin at the bottom center of your paper under the closing.)

1452 Lilac Circle
Denver, CO 80260
October 23, 2004

Dear Jason,

I'm glad you liked the s'mores we had at the picnic. If you'd like to try making one yourself, here's how to do it. You will need a graham cracker, part of a chocolate bar, two big marshmallows, a stick, and a bonfire.

First, break the graham cracker in half. Lay the chocolate bar on one half. Next, hold the marshmallows on a stick over the fire until they get soft and slightly brown on the outside. Then slide the marshmallows off the stick with your fingers and lay them on top of the chocolate. Finally, press the other half of the graham cracker on top to make a sandwich.

Almost everybody likes s'mores, even though they're a little sticky! Have a fun time making them.

Your friend,
Parker

English 4, Writing Models

Envelope

You can mail your letter after you correctly address an envelope. Lists of state postal abbreviations and other abbreviations you may want to use are on pages 344–45 of your Grammar Handbook. An envelope has two addresses.

The *return address* is written in the top left corner of the envelope and tells who is sending the letter. The letter will be returned to this address if it cannot be delivered.

The *mailing address* is written in the center of the envelope and tells who will receive the letter.

You must place a stamp in the top right corner of the envelope. The stamp is payment for sending the letter.

How to Address an Envelope

- Write your name and address in the top left corner. (This is the *return address*.)

- Write the name and address you are sending the letter to in the center of the envelope. (This is the *mailing address*.)

- Place a stamp in the top right corner.

Return Address →

Parker Johnson
1452 Lilac Circle
Denver, CO 80260

Mailing Address →

Jason Vanderkellen
7 Kenton Rd.
Lawrence, KS 66049

Compare-Contrast Essay

When you *compare* two subjects, you tell how they are alike. When you *contrast* two subjects, you tell how they are different. A *compare-contrast essay* compares and contrasts subjects.

How to Write a Compare-Contrast Essay

- Choose two people, places, or things to compare and contrast.
- Make a list of characteristics for each subject.
- Organize these characteristics using a Venn diagram.
- In the first paragraph, write an *introduction* to tell what the essay is going to be about.
- Write the second paragraph comparing the two subjects.
- Write the third paragraph contrasting the two subjects.
- Use comparing and contrasting words to connect the ideas in your paragraphs.
- In the fourth paragraph, write a *conclusion* to sum up your feelings about both subjects.

The Piano and the Organ

At our house we have a piano and an organ. I can play both of them a little bit. They look similar, but they have a lot of differences.

The piano and the organ have some likenesses. They both have keyboards with black and white keys. You play them both by pressing these keys to get different notes. They both also have a pedal that changes their volume. Both the piano and the organ are often used in churches.

Pianos and organs have a lot in common, but they are very different instruments. The organ is electric, and it must be plugged in and turned on before you can play it. However, the piano does not need to be plugged in. You can just sit down and play it. Our organ has two short rows of keys, but our piano has only one long row. The organ has stops that make it sound like many different types of instruments like bells or flutes. In contrast, the piano has only one type of sound. The organ has many pedals that play different bass notes. But our piano has only three pedals, and they do not play notes.

I'm glad we have both a piano and an organ. I like the way both of them sound. Even though the piano is easier for me to play, I enjoy trying to play the organ sometimes too.

Book Review

A *book review* uses persuasion to convince someone to agree with the writer's opinion of a book.

How to Write a Book Review

- Choose a book you have recently read and that you remember well.
- Evaluate the book, asking yourself questions about its characters, setting, plot, and the lessons it teaches.
- Complete an opinion chart.
- Tell the title, author, and your opinion near the beginning of the review.
- Explain the first reason that supports your opinion. Give two or three examples from the book that support the reason.
- Explain the second reason that supports your opinion. Give specific examples from the book to support this reason.
- Remember to use details about the characters, setting, and plot in the examples.
- Use a time-order word to begin each reason.
- End the essay with a recommendation to the reader.

Summer of the Secret Cabin

Opinion

Do you want to read a story about secrets, forgotten letters, and adventure? Then *Summer of the Secret Cabin* by Mason Hyde is a terrific book for you.

Reason 1

First, it is a very exciting book. Nick and Anthony find a deserted cabin in the mountains and decide to use it for a clubhouse. But soon they discover that a ring of smugglers is also using the cabin. One night the boys even get locked inside! Do you think they escape? Do the smugglers get caught? Read the book to find out.

Reason 2

Second, this is a book that will teach you important lessons. Nick has to learn a lesson about kindness when he meets an old man who needs his help. Anthony learns about forgiveness when his dog gets hurt in a fire in the cabin. Reading this book taught me how important it is to love others.

Recommendation

I would recommend this book to anyone who likes adventure. You won't have any trouble getting into the story, but you might have trouble putting it down!

Tall Tale

A *tall tale* is a story so far-fetched that no one would ever believe it. It tells about a hero with a larger-than-life problem and how he solves it by doing an impossible act. Tall tales use colorful descriptions to bring pictures to the reader's mind.

How to Write a Tall Tale

- Develop the hero by asking yourself questions about his size, brainpower, strength, and abilities.

- Develop the other main characters using word webs.

- Plan the problem, the solution, and a setting in which that problem could happen.

- Plan the plot using a plot pyramid.

- Write the beginning of the story. Introduce the main characters and tell about the setting and the problem.

- Write the middle of the story. Tell more about the problem and ways the characters try to solve the problem.

- Write the end of the story. Tell the solution to the problem and what happens after the problem is solved.

- Include dialogue and colorful descriptions to make the story come alive.

The Biggest Bee in the South

It was a hot summer morning in Georgia. Tom Toughguy was eating breakfast out on his porch. Every morning Tom ate five hundred biscuits dripping with honey. He was just about to pop the last three biscuits into his mouth when he heard a terrible sound like a chainsaw.

"Whoa!" he yelled. "That's the biggest bee I've ever seen!"

A gigantic bee was flying toward him. It was buzzing so loudly that Tom had to cover his ears. The bee was about the size of an elephant. Its stinger was as long as a telephone pole. That bee was mad because Tom had used up all the honey in its hive.

Tom tossed his glass of orange juice at the bee. That would have drowned most bees. But it just made this one madder. The bee came closer and closer.

"You won't get me!" said Tom. Then he unfolded his big red napkin. He threw it over the bee's head. Quick as a lightning flash, he tied the napkin's edges in a knot.

The bee could not see out of its blindfold! It flew around in circles. It bumped into Tom's house. It smacked into a tree.

Tom took his knife and chopped off the bee's stinger. That made the bee so upset that it just gave up and went home. Tom chopped the stinger up into small pieces and used it for firewood. People all over the South could see the smoke from that bonfire.

English 4, Writing Models

Research Report (on a country)

A *research report* gives facts about a topic. A research report about a country might include information about its geography, its climate, interesting customs or holidays, and its main religions. Your opinion or how you feel about the topic is not included in the report. At the end of a research report is a *bibliography,* a list of the sources you used in your report. The bibliography tells others where you found your information and gives proper credit to the authors.

How to Write a Research Report

- Choose a country for your topic.

- Find information in an encyclopedia and/or nonfiction books about this country.

- Read and take notes about the country's geography, climate, customs and holidays, and main religions.

- Organize your notes into an outline.

- Draft your report, beginning each paragraph with a topic sentence that tells one of the main ideas in your outline.

- Write supporting sentences in each paragraph, using the details in your outline that tell about each main idea.

- Write a title for the report.

- Write a bibliography, a list of sources used.

Ireland: The Island Country

Ireland has green, rolling hills and rugged mountains. It is a beautiful place for tourists to visit. Ireland is an island, and it is slightly larger than the state of West Virginia. The grand Cliffs of Moher on the western coast drop seven hundred feet into the Atlantic Ocean.

Ireland's climate is mild. The winter season is cold and very wet. There is frequent rain and snowfall. The summer season is also wet, but warm. Ireland's skies are mostly cloudy throughout the year, and winds blow off the Atlantic Ocean daily.

The people of Ireland enjoy many traditional customs and holidays. At Christmas, the Irish display lighted candles in their windows to welcome the Holy Family. One popular holiday is St. Patrick's Day. Modern Irish people have festivals and plays to honor the memory of St. Patrick. He explained the Trinity with a shamrock leaf and drove snakes from the land.

There are several religions in Ireland today. Legends say that St. Patrick was the first person to bring Christianity to Ireland in A.D. 432. The largest religion in Ireland is Roman Catholicism, and the second largest is Protestant Presbyterianism.

How to Write a Bibliography

- Gather the following information about each source that you used: the author, the title of the article and/or book, the publisher, and the publication location and date.

- List the sources in alphabetical order by the author's last name (last name, first name).

- Follow the appropriate format for a bibliographical entry (see below).

Bibliography Format

General pattern for a book

Author(s). <u>Title of book</u>. Place of publication: Publisher's name, year.

General pattern for an encyclopedia

Author. "Title of Article." <u>Title of Encyclopedia</u>. Volume Number. Place of publication: Publisher's name, year.

General pattern for a magazine

Author. "Title of Article." <u>Title of Magazine</u>. Date: Page(s).

General pattern for an online article

Author. "Title of Article." <u>Journal Title</u> volume. issue number (date). Date Accessed. Network address.

Bibliography

Beam, Ira. <u>Irish Holidays</u>. San Diego, CA: Agar Press, 2002.

Fowler, Dale. "Ireland." <u>The Travel Encyclopedia</u>. Vol. 8. Albany, NY: Children's Press, 1999.

O'Shea, Leigh. <u>Christmas in Ireland</u>. Dallas, TX: World Press, 2000.

Smith, Erica. "St. Patrick's Day." <u>The Statesville Journal</u>. Mar. 12, 1999: 25.

Water, Jill. "Landforms of Ireland." <u>The Travel Journal</u> 3. Apr. 2002. May 7, 2004 <http://geographysites.edu/ireland.htm>.

Business Letter

A *business letter* is usually written to someone that you do not know. Business letters may be written to request information, order a product, give information, or express an opinion. Business letters include a heading, an inside address, a greeting, body, closing, and signature. Remember to mail business letters in a business-size envelope.

How to Write a Business Letter

- Decide on a purpose and an audience for your business letter. Locate the address of the company in a telephone directory or a brochure or on the Internet.

- Plan facts and details that need to be included in your letter.

- In the heading, write your address and the date at the top center of your paper.

- Write the inside address (the address of the company to whom you are writing).

- Write an appropriate greeting and the name of the person to whom you are writing. If you do not know the person's name, write *Dear Sir or Madam.*

- In the body, write your letter in one or two brief paragraphs, using precise wording, a polite tone, and plain facts.

- Write an appropriate closing at the bottom center of your paper.

Heading (the writer's address)

Inside Address (the address of the company to which you are writing)

Greeting

Body

Closing

Signature

147 Clifton Drive
Canton, OH 44706
March 28, 2005

Educational Services
Red Mill Papers Association
500 West Main Street
Erie, PA 16512

Dear Sir or Madam:

I am doing a project in my history class on the history of printing. I am especially interested in the first moveable-type printing press invented by Gutenberg. Please send me a copy of your free pamphlet on the history of printing.

I would also like to receive a catalog of your booklets. Thank you for your help.

Yours truly,

Mark Nagato

Mark Nagato

Commonly Misspelled Words

again	found	o'clock	through
a lot	friend	off	tired
always		often	together
another	getting	once	tomorrow
answer	girl	other	too
anything	goes	our	
around	going	outside	until
	guess		upon
beautiful		people	usually
because	happened	please	
before	heard	practice	very
believe		pretty	
brought	I'm	probably	we'll
	instead		we're
caught	into	ready	when
children	its	really	where
coming	it's	receive	while
could		right	whole
cousin	knew		would
	know	said	wouldn't
decide		school	write
different	letter	since	
done	library	some	your
don't	listen	someone	you're
down	little	something	
		sometimes	
early	maybe	soon	
enough	might	sure	
every	minute	surprise	
everybody	money	swimming	
everyone	morning		
	mother's	than	
family		their	
favorite	neighbor	there	
field	none	they	
finally	nothing	thought	
first		threw	

Grammar Handbook

State Postal Abbreviations

The United States Postal Service gives abbreviations for the states as two capital letters with no periods.

State	Abbr.	State	Abbr.
Alabama	AL	Montana	MT
Alaska	AK	Nebraska	NE
Arizona	AZ	Nevada	NV
Arkansas	AR	New Hampshire	NH
California	CA	New Jersey	NJ
Colorado	CO	New Mexico	NM
Connecticut	CT	New York	NY
Delaware	DE	North Carolina	NC
District of Columbia	DC	North Dakota	ND
Florida	FL	Ohio	OH
Georgia	GA	Oklahoma	OK
Hawaii	HI	Oregon	OR
Idaho	ID	Pennsylvania	PA
Illinois	IL	Rhode Island	RI
Indiana	IN	South Carolina	SC
Iowa	IA	South Dakota	SD
Kansas	KS	Tennessee	TN
Kentucky	KY	Texas	TX
Louisiana	LA	Utah	UT
Maine	ME	Vermont	VT
Maryland	MD	Virginia	VA
Massachusetts	MA	Washington	WA
Michigan	MI	West Virginia	WV
Minnesota	MN	Wisconsin	WI
Mississippi	MS	Wyoming	WY
Missouri	MO		

English 4, Abbreviations

More Abbreviations

Months

January	Jan.
February	Feb.
March	Mar.
April	Apr.
August	Aug.
September	Sept.
October	Oct.
November	Nov.
December	Dec.

May, June, and *July* have no abbreviations because they are short words.

Days of the Week

Sunday	Sun.
Monday	Mon.
Tuesday	Tues.
Wednesday	Wed.
Thursday	Thurs.
Friday	Fri.
Saturday	Sat.

Titles of People

Titles are special words used with people's names to show respect. The names and titles of people are capitalized. Abbreviations are used for most titles. The title *Miss* does not have an abbreviation.

adult man	Mr.
married adult woman	Mrs.
adult woman	Ms.
unmarried adult woman	Miss
doctor	Dr.
ordained preacher	Rev.
president	Pres.
senator	Sen.
governor	Gov.
professor	Prof.
captain	Capt.

Address Abbreviations

Apartment	Apt.
Avenue	Ave.
Boulevard	Blvd.
Circle	Cir.
Court	Ct.
Drive	Dr.
Lane	La.
Post Office	P.O.
Road	Rd.
Street	St.

Contractions

A **contraction** is two words that are put together and shortened to make one word. An **apostrophe** (') takes the place of any letter or letters that are left out of the new word. Some contractions are formed by combining pronouns and verbs. Some contractions are formed by combining verbs and the word *not*.

Pronoun + Verb = Contraction

I	+	will	=	I'll		he	+	is	=	he's
you	+	will	=	you'll		she	+	is	=	she's
he	+	will	=	he'll		it	+	is	=	it's
she	+	will	=	she'll		here	+	is	=	here's
they	+	will	=	they'll		what	+	is	=	what's
we	+	will	=	we'll		that	+	is	=	that's
you	+	are	=	you're		I	+	have	=	I've
we	+	are	=	we're		you	+	have	=	you've
they	+	are	=	they're		we	+	have	=	we've
						they	+	have	=	they've

I + am = I'm

Common Contractions with *Not*

is not	isn't	has not	hasn't	do not	don't
are not	aren't	have not	haven't	does not	doesn't
was not	wasn't	had not	hadn't	did not	didn't
were not	weren't	could not	couldn't	should not	shouldn't
would not	wouldn't	cannot	can't	will not	won't

Two Exceptions

Won't is formed from the words *will* and *not*. Notice that *can't* is formed from one word, *cannot*.

Prefixes & Suffixes

A **prefix** is a group of letters added to the beginning of a base word to make a new word with a different meaning or use.

Prefix	Prefix Meaning	Example	Example Meaning
en	in	enclose	to close in
im *in*	into	implant indoors	to plant into inside the doors of a building
im *in* *non*	not	immature inaccurate nonessential	not mature not accurate not essential
dis *un*	not or opposite of	disagree unwrapped	to not agree or the opposite of *agree* not wrapped or the opposite of *wrapped*
mis	bad/wrong	misbehave	to behave badly
pre	before	preview	to view before
re	again or back	reread	to read again

Note: The prefix *im* is added only to words beginning with *b*, *m*, and *p*.

A **suffix** is a word part added to the end of a base word. Adding a suffix makes a new word with a different meaning.

Suffix	Suffix Meaning	Example	Example Meaning
er	person who	painter	a person who paints
ful	full of	careful	full of care; caring
ly	in a certain way	quickly	with quickness or speed
less	without	fearless	without fear
ment	the result of	agreement	a result of agreeing
y	being like or having	thirsty	having thirst
able *ible*	able to be	comfortable flexible	able to have comfort able to bend without breaking

Prepositions

A **preposition** shows the relationship between a noun or pronoun (the object of the preposition) and other words in the sentence. The preposition always comes before the object of the preposition.

The Sullivans hiked to the lighthouse.

We went with them.

Common Prepositions

about	beside	on
above	by	out
across	down	outside
after	for	over
along	from	through
around	in	to
at	inside	under
before	near	until
behind	of	up
below	off	with

Homophones

Homophones are words that sound alike but have different meanings and usually different spellings.

ate past tense of *eat*: *We ate hot dogs for lunch.*

eight a number; 8: *There are eight children on each team.*

bill money: *I have a dollar bill.*

bill statement of money owed: *The power company sent me a bill for the month.*

bill beak: *The duck had an orange bill.*

blew action of the wind: *The wind blew the door shut.*

blue a color: *She wore a blue skirt.*

can to be able to: *I can play the flute.*

can metal container: *I opened a can of vegetables.*

dear loved or respected: *A dear friend gave me a gift.*

deer an animal: *The deer leaped over the brook.*

fair honest: *The referee will make sure the game is fair.*

fair a carnival: *Did you go to the fair?*

fare toll: *The taxi fare was not very expensive.*

file collection of papers: *Please put that document in your file.*

file tool for smoothing: *I will file my nails.*

flour processed grain: *Dad mixed flour into the cookie dough.*

flower colorful plant petals: *This flower is a daisy.*

for purpose: *I wrote a story for my teacher.*

for destination: *I am going for a walk.*

four a number; 4: *I used four sentences.*

hair grows on the head: *Andy has red hair.*

hare rabbit: *The hare twitched his long ears.*

heal cure: *My cut will heal itself quickly.*

heel bottom of the foot: *My heel is sore.*

hear understand by listening: *Can you hear him talking?*

here in this place: *Please come sit here.*

him a masculine pronoun: *I sat next to him.*

hymn a song to God: *We sang my favorite hymn.*

hoarse husky-voiced: *He could not sing because he was hoarse.*

horse an animal: *The cowboy rode a horse.*

hole tear, opening: *There was a hole in my jacket.*

whole entire: *The whole town was there to see it.*

its the possessive form of *it*: *Return the book to its shelf.*

it's contraction of *it is*: *I think it's going to rain.*

knew was aware of: *I knew the answer.*

new just made or bought: *Mike has new shoes.*

new different: *We have a new teacher.*

knot a twist or tangle: *My shoelaces are in a knot.*

not negation of a word: *I will not forget the assignment.*

knows is aware of: *He knows about the surprise party.*

nose organ of smelling: *My nose is stuffy.*

lock a curl of hair: *A lock of hair fell on her forehead.*

lock a fastener: *Dad put a lock on the front door.*

might power: *Our God is a God of might.*

might will possibly happen: *We might have to cancel the game.*

mint plant with a fresh flavor: *You can crush mint leaves to make tea.*

mint place where coins are made: *We visited the Denver Mint.*

pair couple; two similar things: *I bought a pair of shoes.*

pare cut or peel: *Will you pare the apples for the pie?*

pear juicy, grainy fruit: *The pear was sweet and juicy.*

plain ordinary; without anything added: *Grandpa wore a plain red tie.*

plane airplane: *We flew on a plane.*

rest sleep: *I did not get enough rest last night.*

rest the remainder: *The rest of us will wait here.*

right opposite of *left: My house is the brown one on the right.*

right correct: *How many did I get right on my paper?*

write to make letters or words: *Please write neatly.*

write compose: *I will write my story about a bear.*

sea body of water: *The sea was still and blue.*

see to look: *I see birds flying.*

sent past tense of *send: I sent the letter to him.*

cent penny: *The groceries cost seven dollars and one cent.*

scent a smell: *Hunting dogs can track their prey by scent.*

shed a building: *Dan put the lawnmower back in the shed.*

shed to take off: *Snakes shed their skin.*

stair a step: *The toddler climbed up on the stair.*

stare to gaze steadfastly: *It is not polite to stare.*

tail part attached to the back of an animal: *The puppy wagged his tail.*

tale a story: *"Paul Bunyan" is a tall tale.*

their possessive form of *they: I'm going to their house.*

there at that place: *The ball bounced over there.*

they're contraction of *they are: They're going to come with us.*

to direction of or toward: *We drove to Washington.*

too also: *I can play the piano too.*

too very: *You played too long.*

two a number; 2: *He has two pens.*

way path: *Which way should we go?*

way habit of doing things: *That is the way we do it.*

weigh to measure the heaviness of something: *I will weigh the apples.*

weak frail, lacking strength: *He was weak from hunger.*

week seven days: *We spent a week at the seashore.*

well a deep hole: *She carried a bucket of water from the well.*

well correctly: *You did well on the spelling test.*

wood part of a tree: *We cut the wood to make a treehouse.*

would past tense of *will: You said we would go today.*

your possessive form of *you: Your ice cream is going to melt.*

you're contraction of *you are: You're invited to my party.*

Diagramming Models

A **diagram** of a sentence shows how the words in the sentence relate to each other. You diagram a sentence beginning with the most important words, the simple subject and the simple predicate. A vertical line crosses the base line and separates the subject part from the predicate part of the sentence. (Sentences may contain words that you do not know how to diagram. You will learn how to diagram those words at a later time.)

The **simple subject** is the main word(s) in the complete subject. The simple subject may be a noun or a subject pronoun. The **simple predicate** is the main word(s) in the complete predicate. The simple predicate is the verb in the sentence.

The little frog jumped into the pond.

simple subject	simple predicate		frog	jumped

A **compound subject** has two or more simple subjects that share the same predicate. Joining words *and* or *or* connect the subjects.

Frogs and crickets jump.

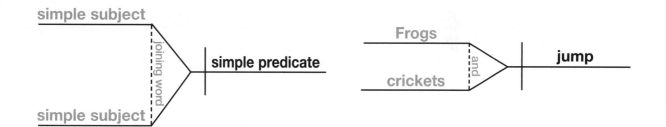

A **compound predicate** has two or more simple predicates (verbs) that share the same subject. Joining words *and* or *or* connect the predicates.

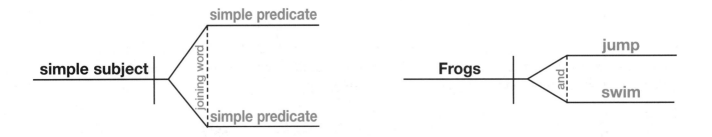

Frogs jump and swim in the pond.

simple subject | joining word | simple predicate | simple predicate

Frogs | and | jump | swim

A **compound sentence** contains two simple sentences connected by a comma and a joining word. A compound sentence gives two complete thoughts. **Joining words** are *and,* *but,* and *or.*

Frogs jump on land and they swim under water.

simple subject	simple predicate
	joining word
simple subject	simple predicate

Frogs	jump
	and
they	swim

Sentences can have different types of verbs. The type of verb will determine how the sentence is diagrammed. An **action verb** tells what the subject *does*. A **helping verb** helps the main (action) verb. Helping verbs always come before the main verb in a sentence. The complete verb includes the helping verb and the main verb but not any extra words between the verbs.

Frogs *have* **always** *jumped.*

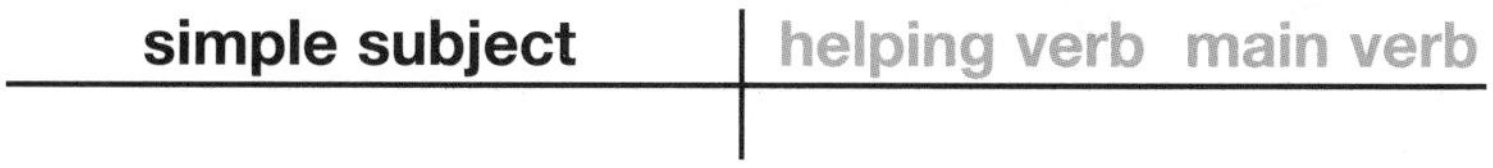

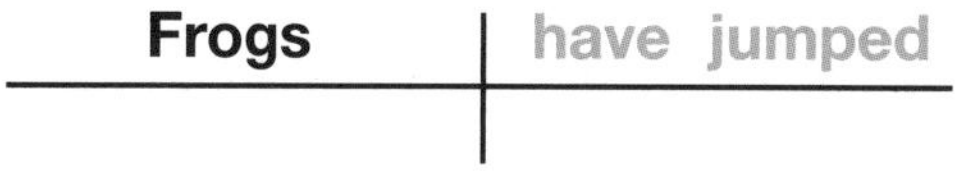

simple subject	helping verb main verb		**Frogs**	have jumped

A **linking verb** tells what the subject is by linking the subject to a *noun* or an *adjective* in the predicate part of the sentence. Notice how the slanted line points the predicate noun or predicate adjective back toward the subject.

A **predicate noun** renames the subject.

Frogs are amphibians.

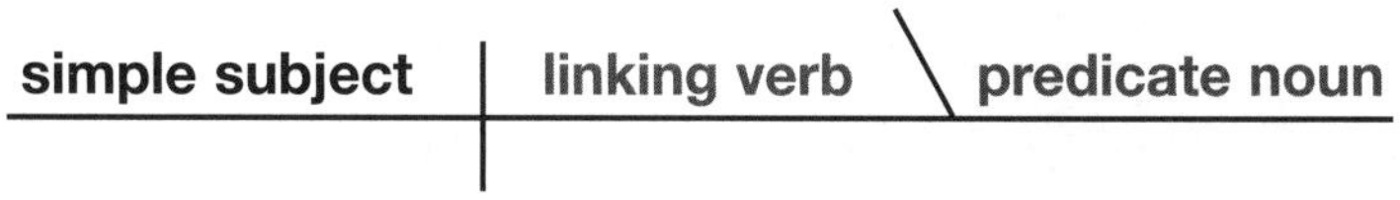

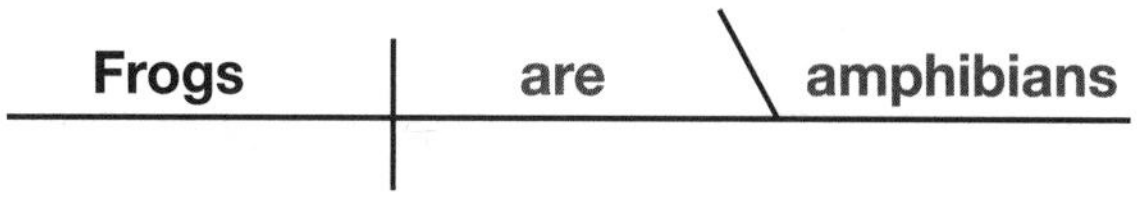

simple subject	linking verb	predicate noun	**Frogs**	are	amphibians

A predicate adjective describes the subject.

Frogs are slimy.

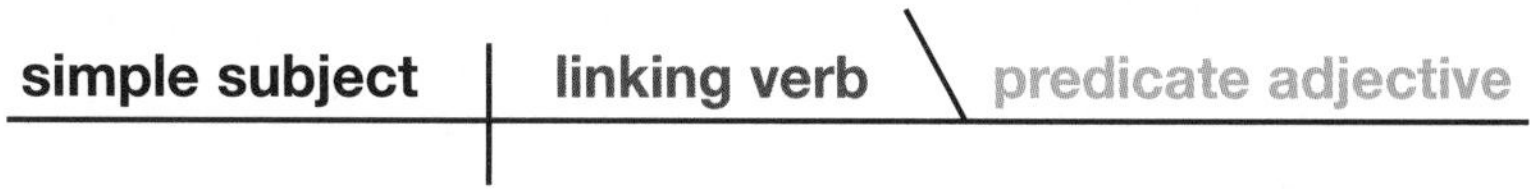

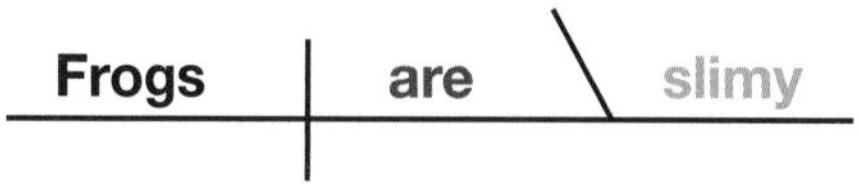

simple subject	linking verb	predicate adjective	**Frogs**	are	slimy

A **direct object** is a noun in the predicate part of the sentence that receives the action of the verb. It tells *what* or *whom*.

Since the direct object is in the predicate, the line between the action verb and the direct object comes to the base line but does not cross it. The line between the action verb and the direct object is straight. It is not slanted like the line on the linking verb diagram that points a predicate adjective or a predicate noun back to the subject.

The frog caught a fly.

| simple subject | action verb | direct object | frog | caught | fly |

An **adjective** is a word that describes a noun. Adjectives can tell *what kind* or *how many*. The words ***a, an***, and ***the*** are special adjectives called **articles**.

In a diagram, the adjective is on a slanted line under the **noun** it describes.

The fat frog sat beside a pond.

Adverbs describe verbs. They tell *how, when,* or *where* something happens. In a diagram, the adverb is on a slanted line under the **verb** it describes.

The fat frog sat quietly beside a pond.

Using a Glossary

A *glossary* is a list of special words and their meanings. A glossary is found at the end of some books. Unlike a dictionary, a glossary contains only words that are used in the book that the glossary is in. You can use this glossary to find the meanings of grammar and writing terms used in this book.

Entry words are arranged in alphabetical order. *Guide words* tell you the first and last entry word on each page. Each entry includes a definition (meaning or explanation) of the grammar or writing term. The entry may also give a *sample sentence* or an example to help you understand the term.

This guide word is the first word on the page.

This guide word is the last word on the page.

abbreviation

contraction

A

abbreviation Shortened form of a word, written with letters missing and often with a period at the end. *Dr. Johnson's office is on Main Street.*

acrostic poem Type of poem in which each line begins with a letter in a keyword, often someone's name.

> *My German shepherd*
> *Always gets in trouble for*
> *Jumping up*
> *On our sofa and barking—*
> *Ruff! Ruff!*

action verb Word that shows action; the word in a sentence that tells what someone or something does. *Jason kicked the ball to score.*

adjective Word that describes a noun and gives it a particular meaning by telling *what kind* or *how many. Jen's dad gave her a special gift.*

adverb Word that describes a verb and gives it particular meaning by telling *how, where,* or *when* the action happens. *The train chugged slowly to the station.*

alliteration Repetition of the same beginning sound in a group of words. *The balloon bobbed above Bobby's bike.*

antonym Word that has the opposite meaning of another word.

apostrophe Punctuation mark (') used to show that letters have been left out of a word, as in a contraction, or to show possession or ownership. *Mark's car can't go that fast.*

appositive Noun or a group of words that renames another noun. (Appositives are not necessary for the meaning of the sentence.) *Our teacher, Mrs. Sullivan, lives near the school.*

article 1. Special adjective: *a, an,* or *the. Should I tie a red bow or an orange bow on the gift?* 2. Part of a periodical.

atlas Book of maps.

author Person who writes articles, poems, or books to be published.

B

bibliography List of the sources used when writing a research report.

biography Factual report about a person's life and actions.

body (of letter) Main part of a letter, the message from the writer.

book report Description of a book a person has read which informs others about the book.

business letter Letter written to request information, to order a product, to give information, or to express an opinion. A business letter is usually written to someone the author does not know.

C

call number Number used to organize and find a library book.

character Person or animal that is in a book, story, or play.

clause *See* dependent clause and independent clause

closing Last part of a letter; says goodbye. *Your friend, Sincerely, Love,*

comma Punctuation mark (,) that separates words or numbers; used in a series, a date, a greeting, or a closing. *Marcy had a hamburger, French fries, and a drink for lunch.*

command Sentence telling a person or group of people to do something; also called an imperative sentence. *Take out the trash.*

common noun Word for a person, place, or thing that is not a proper name and needs no capitalization. *farmer, field, tractor*

compare To tell how things are alike or similar.

complete predicate All the words in the predicate part that tell what the subject does or is. *The busy farmer planted ten rows of tomatoes.*

complete subject All the words in the subject part that tell who or what the sentence is about. *The busy farmer planted ten rows of tomatoes.*

compound predicate Predicate with two or more simple predicates (verbs) that share the same subject. Joining words *and* or *or* connect the predicates. *The children whistled or sang.*

compound sentence Two sentences combined with a comma and a joining word such as *and, but,* or *or. The pie smells delicious, but it is too hot to taste.*

compound subject Subject with two or more simple subjects that share the same predicate. Joining words *and* or *or* connect the subjects. *Snakes and iguanas are reptiles.*

compound word Word made by joining two words. *baseball, doghouse*

conclusion Ending of a written work, often with a summary of the main points or the author's opinion.

contraction Shortened word formed when two words are made into one word with some letters left out. The missing letter or letters are indicated by an apostrophe. *didn't (did not); he's (he is)*

definition

sample sentence

Entry words are arranged in alphabetical order.

A

abbreviation Shortened form of a word, written with letters missing and often with a period at the end. *Dr. Johnson's office is on Main Street.*

acrostic poem Type of poem in which each line begins with a letter in a keyword, often someone's name.

> *My German shepherd*
> *Always gets in trouble for*
> *Jumping up*
> *On our sofa and barking—*
> *Ruff! Ruff!*
---

action verb Word that shows action; the word in a sentence that tells what someone or something does. *Jason kicked the ball to score.*

adjective Word that describes a noun and gives it a particular meaning by telling *what kind* or *how many.* *Jen's dad gave her a special gift.*

adverb Word that describes a verb and gives it particular meaning by telling *how, where,* or *when* the action happens. *The train chugged slowly to the station.*

alliteration Repetition of the same beginning sound in a group of words. *The balloon bobbed above Bobby's bike.*

antonym Word that has the opposite meaning of another word.

apostrophe Punctuation mark (') used to show that letters have been left out of a word, as in a contraction, or to show possession or ownership. *Mark's car can't go that fast.*

appositive Noun or a group of words that renames another noun. (Appositives are not necessary for the meaning of the sentence.) *Our teacher, Mrs. Sullivan, lives near the school.*

article 1. Special adjective: *a, an,* or *the. Should I tie a red bow or an orange bow on the gift?* 2. Part of a periodical.

atlas Book of maps.

author Person who writes articles, poems, or books to be published.

B

bibliography List of the sources used when writing a research report.

biography Factual report about a person's life and actions.

body (of letter) Main part of a letter, the message from the writer.

book report Description of a book a person has read which informs others about the book.

business letter Letter written to request information, to order a product, to give information, or to express an opinion. A business letter is usually written to someone the author does not know.

C

call number Number used to organize and find a library book.

character Person or animal that is in a book, story, or play.

clause *See* dependent clause and independent clause

closing Last part of a letter; says goodbye. *Your friend, Sincerely, Love,*

comma Punctuation mark (,) that separates words or numbers; used in a series, a date, a greeting, or a closing. *Marcy had a hamburger, French fries, and a drink for lunch.*

command Sentence telling a person or group of people to do something; also called an imperative sentence. *Take out the trash.*

common noun Word for a person, place, or thing that is not a proper name and needs no capitalization. *farmer, field, tractor*

compare To tell how things are alike or similar.

complete predicate All the words in the predicate part that tell what the subject does or is. *The busy farmer planted ten rows of tomatoes.*

complete subject All the words in the subject part that tell who or what the sentence is about. *The busy farmer planted ten rows of tomatoes.*

compound predicate Predicate with two or more simple predicates (verbs) that share the same subject. Joining words *and* or *or* connect the predicates. *The children whistled or sang.*

compound sentence Two sentences combined with a comma and a joining word such as *and, but,* or *or. The pie smells delicious, but it is too hot to taste.*

compound subject Subject with two or more simple subjects that share the same predicate. Joining words *and* or *or* connect the subjects. *Snakes and iguanas are reptiles.*

compound word Word made by joining two words. *baseball, doghouse*

conclusion Ending of a written work, often with a summary of the main points or the author's opinion.

contraction Shortened word formed when two words are made into one word with some letters left out. The missing letter or letters are indicated by an apostrophe. *didn't (did not); he's (he is)*

contrast To tell how things are different.

copyright page Page at the front of a book that tells the year the book was printed.

D

declarative sentence Sentence that tells the reader something or gives information. *This story is about the adventures of a dog and a bear.*

delete To erase or remove words; proofreading mark (◡) used during revising and proofreading to show which letters or words to remove.

dependent clause Group of words that has a subject and a predicate but cannot stand alone as a sentence because it does not express a complete thought. A dependent clause often begins with a joining word such as *although, after, because, before, until, when,* or *where. After I went to school*

diagram Drawing that shows how words in a sentence relate to each other. *Ryan ran.*

Ryan	ran

dialogue Conversation between characters in a story; shown with quotation marks.

dictionary Book that tells definitions, pronunciations, usage in sentences, and spelling of words.

direct object Noun in the predicate part of the sentence that receives the action of the verb. It tells *what* or *whom. The girl dribbled the basketball.*

double negative Two negative words used in a sentence. Use of a double negative should be avoided. *We do not have no carrots.*

drafting Writing your ideas and plans as sentences; the second stage of the Writing Process, in which you write the first version of a piece of writing.

E

electronic catalog Information in a library computer that allows you to search for books by the author's last name, the book's title, or the subject of the book.

encyclopedia Set of books that contains articles about many subjects including important people, places, inventions, animals, and events in history.

entry word Word you want to look up in a dictionary, glossary, or thesaurus. Entry words are listed in alphabetical order and are printed in boldface.

essay Piece of writing (composition) containing several paragraphs about one subject.

exclamation Sentence that shows strong feeling; also called an exclamatory sentence. *Your fish is huge!*

exclamation point Punctuation mark (!) that tells the reader that the sentence is saying something with strong feeling or is spoken suddenly and loudly, perhaps in surprise; used at the end of an exclamation. *Jerry won the race!*

exclamatory sentence Sentence that shows strong feeling. *That roller coaster goes fast!*

F

fact Something that is true; not an opinion.

fiction Story that is make-believe. The characters and events are made up from the author's imagination.

fragment Group of words that is not a complete thought because it is missing either a subject or a verb. A dependent clause is another type of fragment because it does not express a complete thought.

friendly letter Letter written to someone (often a friend or relative) to share news, to thank someone, to congratulate, to give advice, or to ask for information.

future-tense verb Verb that tells of a time in the future. *Mom will wash the dishes.*

G

greeting Part of a letter that says hello to the person receiving the letter. *Dear Katie,*

guide words Two words at the top of each dictionary, glossary, or thesaurus page to help locate an entry word. The left guide word tells the first entry word on the page. The right guide word tells the last entry word on the page.

H

haiku Poem based on a pattern of syllables that does not need to rhyme. The first line is five syllables, the second is seven syllables, and the third is five syllables.

heading First part of a letter; includes the writer's address and the date.

helping verb Word that comes before the main verb to show when the action takes place. *The piano tuner has come to check the piano.*

homophone Words that sound alike but differ in meaning and sometimes in spelling. *dear/deer; blue/blew*

I

illustrator Person who makes artwork for books.

imperative sentence Sentence that gives a command or request; tells a person or group of people to do something. (The subject is understood to be *you*.) *Give one page to each student.*

indent To start a line of print farther to the right (from the edge or margin) than the other lines. The first line of a paragraph is often indented.

independent clause Group of words that has a subject and a predicate. It expresses a complete thought and can stand alone as a sentence.

index List of topics and the page numbers on which they are found; located at the back of a book.

insert To add a word or words to a piece of writing; proofreading mark (∧∨) used during revising or proofreading to show where letters, words, or punctuation marks should be added.

inside address In a business letter, the address printed at the top of the page to show who should receive the letter.

interrogative sentence Sentence that asks a question. *Which flavor of ice cream would you like?*

introduction First sentence or paragraph of a written work; beginning.

irregular verb Verb that does not follow regular spelling rules when forming tenses. *go/went; bring/brought; do/did; come/came*

J

joining words Words such as *and, but, or, although, after, because, until, when,* and *where* that connect two clauses. These words can join independent or dependent clauses. *The boys ate lunch, and they rode bikes. After the boys ate lunch, they rode bikes.*

K

keyword Important word from a sentence or question that is used for finding information.

L

linking verb Verb that does not show action but links the main word in the subject to a noun or adjective in the predicate. *My dog is a poodle. Ryan was sleepy.*

M

mailing address Address of the person receiving a letter; written in the center of the envelope.

main idea Topic that a group of sentences tells about.

N

negative Word that means "no." *no, not, none, never*

nonfiction Book that is a true story or is about something real.

noun Word that names a person, place, or thing. *girl, desert, grapes*

O

object of the preposition Noun or pronoun that follows the preposition in a sentence. *The foghorn at the lighthouse alerts ships on foggy days.*

object pronoun Pronoun that replaces a noun used as an object, usually in the predicate of a sentence. *The pencil belongs to him.*

onomatopoeia Words that sound like what they mean. *The alarm clanged as the fire truck zoomed away.*

opinion What you think about something; a belief that has not been proved; part of a book report. *I think Major is the best dog in the world.*

outline Organization of information using main points and sub-points indicated by Roman numerals and letters.

P

paragraph Group of sentences about one subject or idea; a section of writing that begins on a new line. The first line of a paragraph is usually indented.

past-tense verb Verb that tells about what has already happened. *Mom washed the dishes.*

period Punctuation mark (.) which signals to the reader that he has come to the end of a telling sentence or command; also used in some abbreviations.

periodical Written work such as a newspaper or magazine that is published at regular times, or *periodically,* throughout the year.

personal narrative Story about something that happened to the author; a personal experience.

persuade To bring a person to agree with you or to do something you want him to do; to convince.

phrase Group of words that is not a complete sentence but has meaning.

planning First stage of the Writing Process, in which a topic is chosen, characters are developed, problem and solution are decided, or research is completed. Often a graphic organizer is used to plan ideas.

plot Sequence of events in a story.

plural noun Noun that names more than one person, place, or thing. *men, farms, trucks*

plural possessive noun Plural noun that shows ownership; may end with *'s* or *s'*. *The men's group sang on Sunday morning. The boys' chorus will sing next week.*

plural pronoun Word that takes the place of a plural noun or of more than one noun or pronoun. *we, they*

poem Type of writing arranged in an artful way. Some poems rhyme, some are serious, some are funny, and some make a shape.

possessive noun   Noun used to show ownership; this kind of noun has *'s* added to it. *The girl's coat is red.*

possessive pronoun   Pronoun that shows ownership and replaces a possessive noun. *Randy's dad gave him a skateboard for his birthday.*

predicate   Part of a sentence that tells what the subject does or is. The complete predicate contains all the words in the predicate. *The book is small. Emily ate chips.*

prefix   Group of letters added to the beginning of a base word to make a new word with a different meaning or use. *unzip, reread, dislike*

preposition   Word that shows the relationship between a noun or pronoun (object of the preposition) and other words in a sentence. *The cat jumped on the table.*

prepositional phrase   Part of the sentence that consists of the preposition, the object of the preposition, and all the words between them. *The U.S. Coast Guard manages the lighthouses around America's coastlines.*

present-tense verb   Verb that tells what occurs now or is continuing to occur. *Mom washes the dishes.*

problem   Question, trouble, or difficulty that must be solved in a fictional story.

pronoun   Word that takes the place of a noun. *he, she, it, they, we, him, her, them, us*

pronunciation key   Guide that shows symbols and sample words to help in the correct pronunciation of words.

ă pat	ĕ pet	î fierce	oi oil	ŭ cut	ə ago, item,
ā pay	ē be	ŏ pot	ŏŏ book	û fur	pencil, atom,
â care	ĭ pit	ō go	ŏŏ boot	*th* the	circus
ä father	ī pie	ô paw,	yŏŏ abuse	th thin	ər butter
		for	ou out	hw which	
				zh vision	

proofreading   Reading through a piece of writing to look for and correct mistakes in grammar, spelling, punctuation, and capitalization. This is the fourth stage in the Writing Process.

proofreading marks   Special marks used to show where corrections need to be made during the revising and proofreading stages.

Proofreading Marks

∧∨   Add

  Delete

≡   Capital letter

/   Lowercase

⌒→   Move

proper noun   Noun that names a specific person, place, or thing and must be capitalized. *Melanie visited her grandmother in New York.*

publisher   Person or company who edits and prints an article or book for others to read.

publishing   Last step of the Writing Process, in which the paper or book is written out or printed for others to read.

question   Sentence that is written expecting an answer; also called an interrogative sentence. *Who owns that shiny red car?*

question mark   Punctuation mark (**?**) that tells the reader that the sentence is asking a question. *Why does Mary collect butterflies?*

quotation marks   Punctuation marks (" ") that enclose a title of a story, a quote from another writer, or the words someone has spoken. They tell the reader that the words he is reading came from someone else first. *"Let's go home!" James said.*

reason   Why a person thinks or feels the way he does; cause.

reference materials   Materials that are used to find information quickly. A dictionary, an encyclopedia, a thesaurus, and an atlas are examples of reference materials.

regular verb   Verb that changes to the past tense by adding *ed. flick/flicked; rush/rushed*

research report   Report that gives facts about a topic, gained from researching the topic in nonfiction sources. It does not include opinions.

return address   Address of the sender of a letter; placed in the upper left corner on the envelope and in the heading of a letter.

revising   Changing words and sentences to improve the quality of writing. This is the third stage of the Writing Process.

rhyme   Two words having the same ending sound. *man/can; snow/blow; by/sigh*

rough draft   First version of a piece of writing, composed during the drafting stage of the Writing Process.

run-on sentence   Two sentences that are incorrectly written together as one; sentence that needs to be made into two sentences. *Churches long ago had pictures inside some pictures were mosaics.*

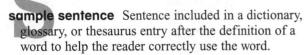

sample sentence   Sentence included in a dictionary, glossary, or thesaurus entry after the definition of a word to help the reader correctly use the word.

sensory word   Word that describes sight, sound, touch, taste, or smell.

sentence   Group of words expressing a complete thought and containing a subject and verb. *The little red hen baked the bread.*

series   Two or more words used consecutively in a sentence. *The flag is red, white, and blue.*

setting   Tells when and where the story takes place.

signature   Writer's name, written by hand, at the end of a letter.

simile   Phrase which compares two different things using the words *like* or *as*. *The doll's hair is soft as silk.*

simple predicate   Main word or words in the predicate; verb. *Marie threw the ball to the catcher.*

simple sentence   Sentence that tells one complete thought. *Mr. Alexander is my teacher.*

simple subject   Noun or pronoun that is the main word(s) in the subject. *The tiny yellow bird sang loudly.*

singular noun   Noun that names only one person, place, or thing. *man, field, horse*

singular possessive noun   Singular noun that shows ownership; may end with *'s. The kitten's fur is soft.*

singular pronoun   Word that takes the place of a singular noun. *he, she, I, it*

solution   Answer to the problem in a story.

sound poem   Poem that uses sound effects, or sound devices, such as *rhyme, alliteration,* or *onomatopoeia.*

story   Writing about something that happened or that has been made up.

subject part   Part of a sentence that names who or what the sentence is about. The complete subject contains all the words in the subject part. *The little dog is black.*

subject pronoun   Word that takes the place of a subject noun. *he, she, they, we*

subject/verb agreement   Agreement of the verb with the number of the subject in a sentence. A singular verb is used with a singular subject, and a plural verb is used with a plural subject or more than one subject. *The dog eats from a blue dish. The puppies eat from a red dish.*

suffix   Word part added to the end of a base word to make a new word with a different meaning or use. *preacher, singing, looked*

summary   Part of a book report that tells the main idea, characters, setting, and problem in a book.

synonym   Word that means the same thing, or almost the same thing, as another word. *big/huge*

table of contents   List located near the beginning of a book that gives the name and beginning page number of each chapter or other book division.

tall tale   Story that is so far-fetched that nobody would ever believe it. Elements include humor; colorful descriptions; and a hero who is bigger, stronger, or smarter than everyone else and does impossible acts.

telling sentence   Sentence that tells the reader about something; also called a declarative sentence. *The cows broke through the fence.*

tense   Form of a verb that shows the time of the action. *present, past, future*

thesaurus   Writing tool used to find words with similar meanings. Each entry includes the meaning of the word, a sample sentence, and a list of synonyms.

time-order words   Words used so that the reader knows the order of events or steps. *first, last, during, finally*

title page   Page at the front of a book that tells the title of the book, the author, the illustrator, and the publisher.

topic sentence   Sentence that tells the main idea of a paragraph or introduces the paragraph's topic.

verb   Main word in the predicate part of a sentence that tells what the subject does or is. *Michelle runs outside to play. Kelly is kind.*

writing conference   Time in which a student reads his writing aloud and receives positive comments and suggestions for improving his writing. The writing conference can be with a teacher, another student, or a group of students.

Writing Process   Stages or steps that a writer follows as he writes. The stages of the Writing Process include planning, drafting, revising, proofreading, and publishing. A writer can repeat the stages until he is satisfied with his writing.

INDEX

planning chart, 265–66
Proofreading Checklist, 270
purpose for, 259–66, 271
return address, 74, 76, 175, 269
Revising Checklist, 268
signature, 263

call numbers, 127–28

capital letters
    in greetings and closings of letters, 63–66, 69, 71–73, 118
    in proper nouns, 43–46, 57–58, 78, 117–18, 137
    in sentences, 3–6, 8, 17–18, 20
    in titles, 45–46, 57, 78, 153, 217
    proofreading symbol for (*see* proofreading, marks)
    rules for, 43, 45

Chapter Review
    adjectives and adverbs, 253–54
    book review, 153–54
    business letter, 271–72
    compare-contrast essay, 115–16
    instructions in a friendly letter, 75–76
    nouns, 57–58
    personal narrative, 37–38
    poetry, 307–8
    pronouns, 173–74
    research report, 233–34
    sentences, 19–20
    study and reference skills, 135–36
    tall tale, 195–96
    verbs, 95–96, 215–16

characters
    analyzing, 145, 183–84
    developing, 183–84
    dialogue, 26
    word web, 184

checklists
    proofreading (*see* proofreading)
    revising (*see* revising)

closing of a letter, 63–64

combining sentences, 17–18, 235
    combining predicates, 15–16
    combining subjects, 15–16

commands. *See* imperative sentences

commas
    between the city and the state, 63–64, 76, 289–90
    in compound sentences, 17–18, 20, 117, 289–90
    in a date, 75, 289–90

    after a dependent clause at the beginning of a sentence, 285, 287, 290
    in dialogue, 289–90, 292
    in a direct address, 289–90, 292
    in the greeting and closing of a letter, 63–64, 76
    after a long introductory phrase of five or more words, 289–90
    after introductory words (*yes, no, well*), 289–90, 292
    in a series, 289–90, 292

common nouns, 41–42, 47–54, 57, 77, 137, 235

commonly misspelled words, 342

compare-contrast essay
    comparing and contrasting words, 105–6, 110–12
    definition, 101
    model, 103, 337
    parts of, 103–4, 115
    Proofreading Checklist, 106
    Revising Checklist, 112
    T-chart, 102, 107–8, 115
    Venn diagram, 101–2, 107, 109, 115
    writing, 101–14

compass rose, 129–30

complete sentences. *See* sentences, complete

contractions, 91–92, 96, 138, 169–70, 346

copyright page, 119–20

cumulative reviews, 39–40, 59–60, 77–78, 97–98, 117–18, 137–38, 155–56, 175–76, 197–98, 217–18, 235–36, 255–56, 273–74, 293–94, 309–10

days of the week, 43–44

declarative sentences, 3–4, 7–8, 39, 97, 217

definitions. *See* dictionary, multiple definitions

delete. *See* proofreading, marks

dependent clauses, 285–88, 292

describing word. *See* adjectives

details
    in a book review, 149
    in a business letter, 67–68
    in a compare-contrast essay, 101–7, 110–12, 115
    in instructions in a friendly letter, 67–68
    on note cards, 131–32
    in outlines, 131–32, 136
    in a personal narrative, 26–28
    in a research report, 294
    in a tall tale, 184

diagramming models, 13, 15, 79, 83, 89, 237, 239, 351–54

diagramming sentences, 13–16, 20, 40, 77, 80, 83–84, 89–90, 95–96, 137, 155, 238–44, 273

dictionary
    alphabetical order, 121–22
    definition of parts, 121–22, 294
    entry words, 121–24
    guide words, 121–22
    multiple definitions, 121–24, 176
    part of speech, 121–24
    practice, 121–24
    pronunciation key, 121–24
    sample sentences, 121–24

direct objects, 87–90, 96, 159–60, 273

double negatives, 91–92, 96, 138, 255

drafting
    acrostic poem, 305
    book review, 148–50
    business letter, 267
    compare-contrast essay, 110
    instructions in a friendly letter, 65, 69
    personal narrative, 29–30
    research report, 227
    tall tale, 189–90

electronic catalog, 127–28

encyclopedia, 125–26, 135–36, 176, 197, 221, 223–24, 231–34, 273–74, 293

entry word
    dictionary, 121–24
    thesaurus, 23

envelopes, addressing, 74, 175

exclamation point, 5–8, 19, 39

exclamatory sentences, 5–8, 39, 97, 217

expanding sentences
    combining subjects and predicates, 15–16
    compound sentences, 17–18

facts, 153, 221, 260, 262–63, 266, 268, 272, 294

fiction, 127–28, 153

final draft
    model, 25, 63, 101, 103, 141, 143, 222, 259, 261, 299, 303
    publishing, 35–36, 74

fragment, 1, 19, 39, 117, 283–86, 292–93

friendly letters
    addressing envelopes, 74
    body of a letter, 63–64, 260
    Chapter Review, 75–76
    closing, 264
    details, 67–68
    greeting, 63–64
    heading, 63–64
    models, 63, 259, 334
    parts of
        body, 63–64, 260
        closing, 63–64
        greeting, 63–64
        heading, 63–64
        signature, 63–64
    Proofreading Checklist, 73
    reason for writing, 63
    Revising Checklist, 70
    signature, 63–64
    time-order words, 65, 67–68
    Tips for Making Instructions Clear and Simple, 65
    writing, 63–74

glossary, 355–60

Grammar Handbook
    abbreviations, 344–45
    contractions, 346
    diagramming models, 351–54
    homophones, 349–50
    prefixes, 347
    prepositions, 348
    suffixes, 347

graphic organizers for writing
    character web, 184
    events/details chart, 27–28, 265–66, 326
    opinion chart (persuasion), 144, 146, 329
    outline, 131–32, 332
    plot pyramid, 187–88, 331
    T-chart, 102, 107–8, 115, 328
    time-order chart, 67–68, 327
    Venn diagram, 101–2, 107, 109, 328
    word web, 301, 330

guide words, 121–22

writing

Photo Credits

The following agencies and individuals have furnished materials to meet the photographic needs of this textbook. We wish to express our gratitude to them for their important contribution.

Ricardo Azoury
Brazilian Tourist Board
William Britten
Cartesia Software
Paul Chauncey
Corbis
COREL Corporation
Digital Vision Ltd.
Getty Images
Hemera Technologies, Inc.
Kansas Cosmosphere
Gard Karlsen
KUAC Media Relations
Joyce Landis
Library of Congress
Lighthouse Digest Archives
Lisa Anne Miller
Michael W. Moore
The Museum of Printing History
Naismith Memorial Basketball Hall of Fame
NASA
National Oceanic and Atmospheric Administration
National Park Service
Saudi Aramco World
Bob & Sandra Shanklin
Six Flags Over Georgia
Carla Thomas
U.S. Air Force
U.S. Coast Guard
U.S. Department of Agriculture
U.S. Fish and Wildlife Service
United States Mint
U.S. Navy
Unusual Films
www.arttoday.com
www.freeimages.co.uk

Front Matter

Carla Thomas v (top); National Oceanic and Atmospheric Administration/Department of Commerce v (bottom); PhotoDisc/Getty Images vi, x; ©2004 www.arttoday.com ix

Chapter 1

PhotoDisc/Getty Images 3, 4, 11, 21 (top left, top right, middle right); United States Department of Agriculture 12, 13, 21 (bottom)

Chapter 2

PhotoDisc/Getty Images 24

Chapter 3

©2004 www.arttoday.com 41; U.S. Air Force photo by Cris L'Esperance 42; NASA 44, 47, 48, 61 (middle right); NASA courtesy of ©2004 www.arttoday.com 51; PhotoDisc/Getty Images 54, 55, 61 (top left, top right, bottom); Kansas Cosmosphere/Paul Chauncey 56; Corbis 58

Chapter 4

PhotoDisc/Getty Images 74

Chapter 5

Carla Thomas 79, 92; Unusual Films 82; PhotoDisc/Getty Images 83; courtesy of KUAC Media Relations 84; PhotoDisc/Getty Images 85, 89, 99 (top left, bottom); Corbis 99 (top right); Naismith Memorial Basketball Hall of Fame 99 (middle right)

Chapter 6

PhotoDisc/Getty Images 102 (both), 107 (both), 114, 115 (both); www.freeimages.co.uk 105; National Oceanic and Atmospheric Administration/Department of Commerce 116

Chapter 7

PhotoDisc/Getty Images 119 (both), 120, 123 (left), 125, 126, 133, 139 (top left, bottom right, bottom left); United States Mint Photo 123 (right); courtesy of Brazilian Tourist Board photo by Ricardo Azoury/Postais Digitais 127; ©2004 www.arttoday.com 128, 131, 139 (top right); Cartesia Software 129 (both), 130; Photo taken by Gard Karlsen, www.gard-karlsen.com 132; United States Department of Agriculture 139 (middle right)

Chapter 8

PhotoDisc/Getty Images 156 (both)

Chapter 9

PhotoDisc/Getty Images 157, 177 (top left); Gary M. Stotz/USFWS 160; National Oceanic and Atmospheric Administration/Department of Commerce 164; Joyce Landis 165, 166; Library of Congress 168; Unusual Films courtesy of Six Flags Over Georgia 169; U.S. Navy photo by Photographer's Mate 2nd class Alicia Tascz 171; Corbis 174; COREL Corporation (top right, middle right, bottom right); Corbis 177 (bottom left)

Chapter 10

PhotoDisc/Getty Images 197

Chapter 11

National Oceanic and Atmospheric Administration/Department of Commerce 200; PhotoDisc/Getty Images 202, 206, 216, 219 (middle right); National Park Service photo by Richard Frear 207; Brian Jonkers/USFWS 209; U.S. Navy 210; ©Digital Vision Ltd. 219 (top left, top right, bottom)

Chapter 12

PhotoDisc/Getty Images 220 (mountains), 228; Unusual Films 220 (children sledding); ©2004 www.arttoday.com 222; Joyce Landis 229

Chapter 13

PhotoDisc/Getty Images 237, 238, 239, 241, 248; ©2004 www.arttoday.com 240, 245, 246 (both); ©Digital Vision Ltd. 242; John Feeney/Saudi Aramco World/PADIA 247; ©2004 Hemera Technologies, Inc. All rights reserved. 257 (top left); COREL Corporation 257 (top right, bottom); National Park Service 257 (middle right)

Chapter 14

PhotoDisc/Getty Images 258, 261 (both), 269 (both), 272 (right); Michael W. Moore/Steel Ribbons & Iron Horses courtesy of Lionel Trains 260; The Museum of Printing History 263; COREL Corporation 272 (left)

Chapter 15

Lighthouse Digest Archives 276, 279, 281; U.S. Coast Guard photo by Gary Chalker 277; courtesy Bob & Sandra Shanklin 278; ©2004 www.arttoday.com 280, 287; National Oceanic and Atmospheric Administration/Department of Commerce 283, 288, 295 (middle right); Lisa Anne Miller 285; Corbis 292; PhotoDisc/Getty Images 293, 295 (top left, bottom); photo by William Britten www.lighthousegetaway.com 295 (top right)

Chapter 16

PhotoDisc/Getty Images 297, 300 (top right, middle left, middle right, bottom left, bottom right), 309; ©Digital Vision Ltd. 300 (top left)

Back Matter

PhotoDisc/Getty Images 335